To Mrs Cutter
From her friend
Mrs Jordan

Christmas 1914

# CALIFORNIA

Books by
# GERTRUDE ATHERTON
[PUBLISHED BY HARPER & BROTHERS]

THE STORY OF CALIFORNIA. Illustrated. Crown 8vo
RULERS OF KINGS. Post 8vo
THE BELL IN THE FOG. Frontispiece Portrait. Post 8vo
THE TRAVELLING THIRDS. Post 8vo
ANCESTORS. (Californian.) Post 8vo

[PUBLISHED ELSEWHERE]

## NOVELS AND STORIES OF CALIFORNIA

REZANOV (1806) } To be issued in one volume,
THE DOOMSWOMAN (1840) } "Before the Gringo Came"
THE SPLENDID IDLE FORTIES (1800–46)
THE VALIANT RUNAWAYS (1840)
A DAUGHTER OF THE VINE (The Sixties)
AMERICAN WIVES AND ENGLISH HUSBANDS (The Eighties)
THE CALIFORNIANS (The Eighties)
A WHIRL ASUNDER (The Nineties)

## OTHER NOVELS AND STORIES

PERCH OF THE DEVIL
PATIENCE SPARHAWK AND HER TIMES
SENATOR NORTH
HIS FORTUNATE GRACE
THE GORGEOUS ISLE
MRS. PENDLETON'S FOUR-IN-HAND
THE ARISTOCRATS
TOWER OF IVORY
JULIA FRANCE AND HER TIMES

## BIOGRAPHY

THE CONQUEROR
A FEW OF HAMILTON'S LETTERS

This monument was erected in San Francisco, September 9, 1897, to commemorate the admission of California to the Union, September 9, 1850, and dedicated to the Native Sons of the Golden West. The sculptor was Douglas Tilden, a native of California, and the monument was presented to the city by James D. Phelan.

THE NATIVE SONS' FOUNTAIN

# CALIFORNIA
## AN INTIMATE HISTORY

BY
GERTRUDE ATHERTON

ILLUSTRATED

HARPER & BROTHERS PUBLISHERS
NEW YORK AND LONDON
MCMXIV

COPYRIGHT, 1914, BY HARPER & BROTHERS
PRINTED IN THE UNITED STATES OF AMERICA
PUBLISHED OCTOBER, 1914

K-O

TO
## JAMES D. PHELAN
THIS STORY OF THE CALIFORNIA TO
WHOM HE HAS ALWAYS BEEN FAITHFUL

# CONTENTS

| CHAP. | | PAGE |
|---|---|---|
| I. | THE GEOLOGICAL DRAMA | 1 |
| II. | THE MISSION PADRES | 15 |
| III. | THE SPANISH GOVERNORS—I | 36 |
| IV. | THE SPANISH GOVERNORS—II | 47 |
| V. | THE MEXICAN GOVERNORS—I | 62 |
| VI. | THE MEXICAN GOVERNORS—II | 78 |
| VII. | FRÉMONT AND THE BEAR-FLAG REVOLUTION | 94 |
| VIII. | GOLD | 116 |
| IX. | SAN FRANCISCO | 130 |
| X. | CRIME AND FIRE | 144 |
| XI. | POLITICS | 162 |
| XII. | JAMES KING OF WM. | 174 |
| XIII. | THE VIGILANCE COMMITTEE OF 1856 | 190 |
| XIV. | THE VIGILANCE COMMITTEE AND DAVID S. TERRY | 201 |
| XV. | BRODERICK | 218 |
| XVI. | BRODERICK AND GWIN | 230 |
| XVII. | THE BRODERICK-TERRY DUEL | 249 |
| XVIII. | THE WAR | 263 |
| XIX. | THE TERRIBLE SEVENTIES | 272 |
| XX. | THE CHINESE IN CALIFORNIA | 282 |
| XXI. | "THE CHINESE MUST GO" | 290 |
| XXII. | LAST PHASES | 308 |

# ILLUSTRATIONS

| | | |
|---|---|---|
| THE NATIVE SONS' FOUNTAIN . . . . . . . . . . . | *Frontispiece* | |
| From a photograph by Charles Weidner. | | |
| KAWEAH MOUNTAINS, NEAR KERN RIVER CAÑON . . . | . *Facing p.* | 6 |
| THREE BROTHERS, SHOWING THE MERCED RIVER . . . . | " | 12 |
| From a photograph by Taber. | | |
| GLACIER POINT, 3,300 FEET, AND SOUTH DOME . . . . . | " | 12 |
| From a photograph by Taber. | | |
| STATUE OF PADRE JUNÍPERO SERRA . . . . . . . . | " | 18 |
| From a photograph by Charles Weidner. | | |
| SANTA BARBARA MISSION—FOUNDED 1786 . . . . . . | " | 28 |
| From a photograph by Graham & Morrill. | | |
| SAN GABRIEL MISSION (FIRST GOLD FOUND IN 1842) . . | " | 28 |
| From a photograph by Graham & Morrill. | | |
| DON JOSÉ DE LA GUERRA . . . . . . . . . . . . . | " | 80 |
| DON PABLO DE LA GUERRA . . . . . . . . . . . . | " | 80 |
| From a photograph in the Charles B. Turrill collection. | | |
| GEN. DON JOSÉ CASTRO . . . . . . . . . . . . . | " | 80 |
| From a photograph loaned by Delfina de la Guerra. | | |
| CASA GRANDE, THE HOME OF THE DE LA GUERRAS . . . | " | 90 |
| From a photograph loaned by Delfina de la Guerra. | | |
| JOHN A. SUTTER . . . . . . . . . . . . . . . . | " | 102 |
| From a photograph in the Charles B. Turrill collection. | | |
| JAMES W. MARSHALL . . . . . . . . . . . . . . | " | 102 |
| GEN. JOHN C. FRÉMONT . . . . . . . . . . . . | " | 102 |
| From *Harper's Weekly*, 1860. | | |
| GEN. M. G. VALLEJO . . . . . . . . . . . . . | " | 102 |
| From a photograph by Taber loaned by Delfina de la Guerra. | | |
| SONOMA MISSION . . . . . . . . . . . . . . . | " | 104 |
| MISSION SAN JUAN BAUTISTA . . . . . . . . . . | " | 104 |
| SUTTER'S FORT AS IT WAS IN 1848 . . . . . . . . | " | 116 |
| From *California Illustrated*, 1853. | | |
| MARCH OF THE CARAVAN . . . . . . . . . . . . | " | 118 |
| From *The Expedition of the Donner Party*. | | |
| FROM "LONDON PUNCH," 1860 . . . . . . . . . | " | 122 |
| THE "EL DORADO" GAMBLING SALOON . . . . . . | " | 122 |
| From *Annals of San Francisco*. | | |

# ILLUSTRATIONS

SACRAMENTO, CALIFORNIA, 1850 . . . . . . . . . . . *Facing p.* 136
    From *The United States Illustrated.* Published by H. J. Meyer.

SAN FRANCISCO . . . . . . . . . . . . . . . . " 136
    From an old print.

FIRST ADMISSION-DAY CELEBRATION, 1850, CALIFORNIA AND
    MONTGOMERY STREETS . . . . . . . . . . . . " 168
    From an old print.

JAMES KING OF WM. . . . . . . . . . . . . . . " 174
    From a photograph in the Charles B. Turrill collection.

BACK OF A TYPICAL LETTER-SHEET SUCH AS WAS USED FOR
    PERSONAL LETTERS TO CORRESPONDENTS "EAST" . . " 186
    From an old print in the Charles B. Turrill collection.

FORT VIGILANCE, OR FORT GUNNYBAGS. WILLIAM T. COLE-
    MAN, PRESIDENT OF THE COMMITTEE OF VIGILANCE. . " 210
    From a photograph in the Charles B. Turrill collection.

DAVID C. BRODERICK . . . . . . . . . . . . . " 252

COL. E. D. BAKER . . . . . . . . . . . . . . " 252

DAVID S. TERRY . . . . . . . . . . . . . . . " 252

WILLIAM M. GWIN . . . . . . . . . . . . . . " 252

WILLIAM C. RALSTON [INSERT], WHO FREQUENTLY TOOK HIS
    GUESTS TO YOSEMITE AND BIG TREES, WAS THE FIRST
    TO DRIVE A FOUR-IN-HAND THROUGH "WAWONA" . . " 274

JAMES D. PHELAN . . . . . . . . . . . . . . " 310
    From a photograph by Hartsook.

JUDGE LAWLOR . . . . . . . . . . . . . . . " 320
    From a photograph by Vaughan & Fraser.

RUDOLPH SPRECKELS . . . . . . . . . . . . . " 320
    From a photograph by Habenicht

FRANCIS J. HENEY . . . . . . . . . . . . . . " 320

FREMONT OLDER . . . . . . . . . . . . . . " 320
    From a photograph by Estey.

GOV. HIRAM JOHNSON . . . . . . . . . . . . " 324
    From a photograph by Pach Brothers.

PRUNE-ORCHARD . . . . . . . . . . . . . . " 328
    From a photograph in the Charles B. Turrill collection.

WHEAT-FIELD . . . . . . . . . . . . . . . " 328
    From a photograph in the Charles B. Turrill collection.

IN compressing the history of California, a state of unexampled variety and crowding interest, an uncommon number of personalities and dramatic incidents, into one volume it is only possible to select the main historic events for treatment, connecting them with a synopsis of the contributing causes and illustrating them with all the personalities and anecdotes available. The details necessarily sacrificed are so well worth reading, however, that I shall feel I more than doubly have achieved my purpose in telling this strange tale of California in rapid narrative if I have stimulated an interest that will send readers to Theodore A. Hittell's *History of California* (four volumes); Bancroft's many volumes on the Pacific coast; Josiah Royce's *California* (one volume and dealing mainly with Frémont); Jeremiah Lynch's *Senator of the Fifties* (Broderick); the memoirs of William M. Gwin and of Stephen J. Field; the various books relating to the Vigilance Committee of 1856, and to a possible reprint of that delightful and useful volume, *The Annals of San Francisco*, by Soulé, Gihon, and Nisbit, from which all historians of the period between 1849 and 1854 have drawn, with never an acknowledgment. For those interested in the later political history of the state, and particularly of San Francisco, there are the "Report on the Causes of Municipal Corruption in San Francisco," etc., made by a committee appointed by Mayor Taylor in 1908, of which Mr. William Denman, always keenly interested in the reform of the city, was chairman, and a forthcoming volume called *The System*, by Franklin Hichborn, who made a thorough investigation of the records of the San Francisco graft prosecution before they began to take wings.

To those interested in the geology of the state there are the works of Professor Whitney, chief of the first Pacific Coast Geodetic Survey sent out by the United States government in the early 60's; that impeccable classic by a member of his staff, Clarence King, *Mountaineering in the Sierra Nevada;* the works of John Muir, George Davidson, and of Professor Le Conte of the University of California.

I have striven to be as accurate as history—never accurate—will permit, while writing an interesting story —or a paradoxical drama—but I have enjoyed the reading of the many authorities as much as my own work, and therefore confidently recommend to Californians, at least, a thorough course in California history.

If I used the word "paradox" just now it was because I suddenly remembered how many good men we have produced in California and what bad history they have succeeded in making.

GERTRUDE ATHERTON.

NEW YORK, *August 11, 1914.*

# CALIFORNIA

# CALIFORNIA

## I

### THE GEOLOGICAL DRAMA

WHEN Gaspar de Portolá discovered the Bay of San Francisco in 1769 he found the surrounding country inhabited by Indians whose ancestors had dwelt on the peninsula and among the Marin hills ever since that uneasy coast had been hospitable to man. From them he heard the tradition that some two hundred years earlier the space covered by the great inland sheet of water had been a valley, fertile and beautiful, broken by hills and watered by two rivers that rose in the far north and found their outlet to the sea through Lake Merced. Then came a mighty earthquake, the valley sank, the hills of the coast were rent apart, the salt waters rushed in and covered not only the sunken valley floor, but all save the tips of its hills. A man on the peak of Mount Tamalpais might have seen the whole terrific drama, and then, later, marveled at the justice of Nature. Only the end of the fertile Central Valley was gone, and in its place the Pacific coast had been presented with one of the three great harbors of the world.

There are certain facts that give a strong color to the truth of this legend; and, although it makes a geologist

# CALIFORNIA

writhe even to intimate that any significant physical phenomena can have taken place within the historic era, the layman is sometimes reminded that the most conservative students of the rocks do not always maintain the theories they have inherited, or even advanced, long enough to permit them to grow quite hoary with age. The reader, therefore, is invited to take his choice.

It was on June 17, 1579, that Drake cast anchor in the little bay that bears his name. It is but fifteen miles north of the Golden Gate. He not only disembarked and lived with his officers in tents for thirty-six days, but took excursions over the Marin hills and valleys under the guidance of the friendly Indians who besought him to remain and be their king. Drake neither heard nor saw anything of this superb green jewel of ours; if he had, England, instead of being profoundly indifferent to the strip of land he dutifully took possession of in the name of the crown, would have grabbed it promptly. Even if he had sailed up the coast of California there would have been nothing remarkable in his oversight, provided he had not lingered in his little cove; for the long narrow cleft between the hills known as the Golden Gate is often obliterated by fog. But that after his long sojourn, during which he must have climbed Tamalpais and roamed the hills above Sausalito, he should have left the coast in ignorance of this inland tract of water, dotted with beautiful islands and large enough to harbor the combined navies of the world, is incredible save on the hypothesis that it did not exist. For all we know Drake and his party may have picnicked in the glades on the lower slope of Belvedere, now many fathoms beneath the green nervous waters of the bay.

# THE GEOLOGICAL DRAMA

The great valley of the Yosemite looks as if miles had been neatly sliced out of a high plateau and dropped like a plummet into the yawning earth; the walls are often perpendicular, rising to the height of several thousand feet. Professor Whitney admits that the bottom may have dropped out of the space covered by the present valley floor, although, being a wary geologist, he hastens to add that it was probably at a time when that section of the earth was semi-viscid.[1] Even conservative geologists admit that the subsidence which forms the Golden Gate and filled the end of the Central Valley with seawater occurred in later Pleistocene—that is to say, only about forty thousand years ago. But it is a mere idiosyncrasy of the scientific mind which persists in relegating any phenomenon of which it has not positive historical data to as remote a period geologically as the rocks will stand. An earthquake which metamorphosed some fifty miles of coast-land, however quick in action, was no more phenomenal than the performances of the Mississippi Valley in 1811–12, of Krakatoa in 1883, nor that titanic convulsion in India in 1762, when all but the higher parts of an area of sixty square miles of coast sank beneath the sea. For several days after the California earthquake of 1906, when San Francisco for a long minute seemed to fight with the very roots of the earth for release, government boats were to be seen daily in the bay taking soundings; much apprehension was felt lest the profound disturbance of its floor may have rendered it unnavigable, and closed the commercial history of the state.

James Perrin Smith, to quote but one of many authori-

[1] Glacial erosion is the popular belief to-day, but to one brought up in an earthquake country the old theory seems more natural.

tative writers on the disturbance of 1906, has this to say in *Science*, September 10, 1909: "The last phase of the physical history of the western coast is the recent subsidence that allowed the sea to encroach on the river-valleys forming the Bay of San Francisco and other bays along the coast. This has been going on in almost modern times, for Indian shell-mounds, apparently made by the same race that still exists in California, have been flooded by the continued subsidence of the Bay of San Francisco." It must be borne in mind that a geologist's modern time is not ours; but, as there is no evidence that Indians were living in California during any of the interglacial periods, nor, in all likelihood, for many years after the end of the Pleistocene—some twenty-five thousand years ago—we may believe, if we like, that the Bay of San Francisco is post-Drakian.

Far more sharply outlined and more independent of its Indian traditions is the history of the Salton Sea. There is no doubt that when Francisco de Ulloa explored the Gulf of California in 1539 that long arm of the sea differed little if any from its present channel and termination. Its lost two hundred miles, to be known by us as Salton Sink, had run their course from a dismembered part of the Great Pacific Ocean, down through long geological ages to a mere desert of salt.

The enemy here was the Colorado River, whose mouth was then some sixty miles east of its present location. It built, with true geological leisure, the delta that gradually separated the headwaters of the gulf from its main supply. This creature of a sovereign and cruel river was alternately toyed with and neglected; sometimes rejuvenated with an abundant stream of fresh-water,

# THE GEOLOGICAL DRAMA

when his majesty, the Colorado, tired of the less responsive gulf, abruptly swung aside and poured his offerings into the lake. But his long periods of neglect grew longer, the stranded sea contracted, its waters more and more alkaline; deserted, finally, it fell a victim to the dry winds of the desert, its aqueous history at an end for a thousand years. The Salton's chief title to fame other than spectacular is its depression below sea-level, 273.5 feet, a distinction it shares with but one other tract of land in the United States.

But although as recently as 1901 the Salton Sea looked as ancient and as dead as the moon, its history was not finished. During that year the Colorado River, via the Alamo and the New rivers, made one of its old capricious visits, overflowed the Salton Sink, threatened a section of the Southern Pacific Railroad with destruction, and obliterated a great corporation industry. It flooded the Sink, burying the productive salt-beds fifty feet deep. In the autumn of 1906 the Southern Pacific Company managed to shut it off, only to do battle once more in December, and again to conquer. Whether the science and determination of man will prevail against one of the most irresistible and wickedly resourceful forces of the Western Hemisphere remains to be seen. The river that made the Grand Cañon of Arizona, gnawing out mile after mile of solid rock, fighting Nature herself at every step, is likely to fume and fret under the harness of man and, finally, to take a swift revenge.

But both the San Francisco Bay and the Salton Sea, whatever their birth-dates, are the youngest of California's phenomena children, born in the last of her throes, picturesque hostages that her monstrous labors were over,

## CALIFORNIA

that, save for an occasional spasm along her earthquake rift, she would make geological history no more.

California, according to conservative geologists, reading the tale of the Archean rocks in the Sierra Nevada range, began her life some hundred and fifty million years ago. But it was not until the latter part of the Palæozoic era, some thirty million years ago, that an uplift began along the axis of the range, manifesting itself in outpourings of lavas and other volcanic ejecta. And it was not until several million years later, in Jurassic times, that these strange and formidable masses of rock, still insignificant in height, established themselves permanently above the epicontinental sea.

They are the oldest of California's children, sole survivors of the extrusive eon, during which life made its first negligible appearance on the globe. As the range rose higher and higher during vast succeeding reaches of geological time the Sierra witnessed the gradual unfolding of the California drama; destined itself to undergo many and terrific changes, it was the solitary spectator of the heroic and often thwarted struggle for existence of a younger range of mountains, born of the sea.

At first the Sierra looked west over an illimitable expanse of gray water that washed its very base. Whatever folding and crumpling might be going on under that stormy surface, it was many million years before a long low chain of rocks lifted its heads and tarried long enough to be so eroded that man—when, some forty million years later, he developed the scientific brain—should read the story as the old Sierra saw it. They were smothered for eons again, not only by the sea, but by sediments many thousands of feet deep, to be known later as the Franciscan

KAWEAH MOUNTAINS NEAR KERN RIVER CAÑON

# THE GEOLOGICAL DRAMA

or Golden Gate series. The boldest of the peninsula's headlands, Telegraph Hill, and the present islands in the bay are of sandstone interspersed with shales and rocks of peculiar interest to the geologist, not only for their age and record, but for their coats of many colors.

In late Jurassic or early Cretaceous times, some twenty million years after its first baffled attempt to live, the coast, including what are now its bay shores and islands, then but a part of the range, was born again. Folded and faulted on the sea's uneasy floor, the mass was pushed up into the light at last and permitted to grow and breathe, and harden and erode, and signal across a gray cold sea to the stately first-born of the west—for nearly a million years. Then down she went once more, and the Pacific stood on end and rushed with tidal ferocity at the invincible Sierra.

But the Coast Range, if her ambitions were curtailed, did not waste her time. During that long period of submergence she accumulated those deposits of fossiliferous, Cretaceous, Eocene, and Miocene treasures, so beloved of her students to-day. The sediments of the last period alone attained a thickness of eight thousand feet. This took time, and it was not until some twelve million years after her first appearance, and during the Miocene, that she got her hydra-headed masses out again. The faulting and crumpling and folding and deformation went on during that vast reach of time until, bombarded from below, the reluctant sea parted and there rose at last a real range of mountains, oscillating and bowing through the mists to the Sierra, who thought that her long and lonely watch was ended. But alas! Reckoning geologically, which was all the time she knew, her companionship was

# CALIFORNIA

brief. In late Pliocene the Coast Range subsided once more, and only a long low chain of hills held their heads obstinately above the sea and broke the ponderous attacks of the Sierra's old enemy.

It was during the Pliocene, late Tertiary, about six hundred thousand years ago, that the Coast Range achieved her wonderful series of deposits known as the Merced, which may be seen to-day along the edge of the ocean near San Francisco. The deposit is a mile in thickness, and at its base is what the sea has left of an old pine forest. During the last submergence it went down some five thousand feet, and so rapidly that the trees were buried under sediment before they could decay. In the upper beds are fossils of Recent Quartenary, which began (to be conservative) but twenty-five thousand years ago. Their elevation has been more gradual than their descent, and they are now tilted up at an almost perpendicular angle and dislocated by a fault.

It was not long before that doughty coast proved—what all geologists now admit—that her disposition, undaunted by cruel vicissitudes, is to grow, and not long after her subsidence she began once more to rise. At one time, indeed (early Quartenary), she stood some three thousand feet higher than now, if we read aright the tale of her submerged cañons, eroded by other elements than the sea. But although she was forced to accept a later subsidence—no doubt to fill a hole in ocean's floor—she kept her heads out, as we have seen, and she has been growing ever since.

It was at the beginning of the Miocene that certain faulting and folding developed the great earthquake rift of California. That was something over two million

# THE GEOLOGICAL DRAMA

years ago, and one shudders to think what it must have done in its heyday. For that old wound has never healed; every forty or fifty years the Coast Range has an acute attack of Miocene fever, accompanied by spasms and followed by many minor protests at this long chastisement of nature.

But these are merely the pangs of old age, which she endures with more equanimity than we do, ruminating as she must upon the visitations of her youth and maturity; and not only upon those painful births, deaths, burials, and reincarnations, but that terrific vulcanic period when she was forced to tear apart her smooth young flanks and the most lofty and aspiring of her brows to disgorge into the shrinking central sea the molten masses the earth could no longer contain.

That, of course, was the most spectacular era of our Western Hemisphere's history, but the great Sierra herself was too fully occupied letting the fiery blood of the swollen patient to observe and admire the new activities of her interesting neighbor. But to the men in the moon, whose atmosphere as it sank inward may have been converted, for aught we know (all things being so wonderful at that time), into a powerful lens, it must have been a stupendous drama: that red and roaring world, dulling the music of the spheres, ten hundred thousand thousand flames distorted into as many shapes, and seen fitfully through a smoky curtain rent with boiling rock magma.

The igneous activities began with the close of the Cretaceous period and reached its climax some seven million years later in the Miocene, although by no means its end. Of course, the Coast Range, being swallowed periodically, was unable to discharge her share of the

# CALIFORNIA

obligation during all of that time, but making due allowance for periods of rest—throughout long geologic ages—and these mean tens of thousands of years at best—torrents of flaming lava poured incessantly from the lofty craters and the mangled sides of both of California's mountain-chains. Before the waters retreated during the early Pliocene the central sea was a steaming hissing cauldron, hiding the throes of one range from the other, and after that the valley was dry and scorched, the thick Miocene deposits pelted with red-hot rocks and ash. Gradually, however, the valley floor was raised and built up by sediment, and during those intervals, now and then, when the plutonic energy of the mountains ceased, the ranges, scarred and battered but serene, smiled at each other across a magnificent valley, dotted with lakes and groves of trees, and, no doubt, ancient and fearsome monsters, now happily extinct save in museums.

And during all these measureless eons, while her neighbor was tossed aloft or recalled to stop a hole in the sea, the Sierra had many and varied trials of her own, holding her breath for centuries, wondering if she, too, were to be engulfed, if that persistent, ponderous, roaring ocean meant to devour her. There had been compression and faulting at the end of the Palæozoic, as well as some igneous activity and, later, erosion. The whole range, about eleven million years ago, at the close of the Jurassic, was once more compressed, folded, and then triumphantly uplifted. But the elements peneplained her until the close of the Miocene, and the sea tore at her roots unceasingly, although never again to dislodge them. Rivers wore away her surfaces, to lay the floor of the central sea until she was some four thousand feet lower than she is

# THE GEOLOGICAL DRAMA

to-day. It was during this period, when the vast Eocene sea threatened her existence, and she was torpid with fear and exhaustion, that her "aged rivers" rescued the gold from her battered veins and, crawling downward with their heavy burden, disgorged it into the lower cañons, or carried it out into the sea between the ranges, where it sank into the rising beds of future rivers.

In the late Miocene, or early Pliocene, the central waters receded for ever, and the Sierra, during a long and blessed interval between igneous violence, was elevated again, and her streams, like herself, rejuvenated. During these intervals of repose she no doubt was almost as beautiful as she is to-day; although the cañons and scenery of the highest portions of the range are post-Tertiary, the work of the ice-chisels, her vigorous streams carved deep cañons into her lower slopes, quite as fine as those cut into the lost pedestal of the Coast Range.

Then once more her great chimneys sent forth their pillars of flame and smoke and were answered by the watch-fires on the heights opposite, and the valley was pounded with rock and covered with lava and dust and the bones of monsters, for which there was no escape.

To this long age of alternate turmoil and the heavy fatigue of convalescence, or the brief periods of rejuvenation and beauty, succeeded an epoch of terrible repose. After the trial by fire the punishment of the ice. Although California was too far south to be included in the great ice-sheet that came down out of the north in the Pleistocene (glacial) era she had an ice age of her own which, with the interglacial periods, lasted some five hundred thousand years.

During the greater part of this time the Sierra was

# CALIFORNIA

covered with a continuous sheet of ice. The crystal masses were packed into every cañon and river and lake, covered every crag and table-land, rose in frozen waves from the dead craters of a thousand volcanoes. The ice laid its heavy weight on the harsh outlines of the mountains, mighty hands grasping a million little chisels to carve the high cañons, the pinnacles and domes and turrets, the arches and lacework and spires, that make the Sierra Nevada a thing of wonder to-day.

It was the turn of the Coast Range, less afflicted, to watch and admire and hold its breath in the face of that stupendous beauty which only death could create. For silent interminable centuries the crystal mountains flashed prismatically in the sunlight or lay white and cold under the gray mists that rose from the frozen earth. Then came the first long interglacial period, when the ice-sheets crept down the mountainsides, carrying great masses of decayed material to choke the Central Valley, whose lakes and rivers, released from the long and bitter winter, sparkled in a warmth and sunshine almost forgotten.

The rocks breathed again and called to the green hills of the coast, protected by the milder currents of the Pacific, from the assault of the ice, but only for a brief space of fifty to a hundred thousand years. Like the Coast Range, during her earlier trials, the Sierra was engulfed again, not by a vast and restless sea, but equally helpless under snow-fields and ice-sheets.

But all things come to an end, temporarily at least. The Coast Range witnessed the last of the interglacial periods, the last of the ice descents which is behind us; life struggled from below the soil; the mountainsides and

THREE BROTHERS, SHOWING THE MERCED RIVER

GLACIER POINT, 3,300 FEET, AND SOUTH DOME

# THE GEOLOGICAL DRAMA

the Central Valley turned green; acorns that had slept for centuries side by side with the nuggets torn from the veins of the high Sierra, stirred and swelled, and pushed their way out of the softened earth; trees burst from the mountainsides and lined her cañons. From the mountains of Asia wandered in due course what we call the Rocky Mountain goat, a beautiful spirited creature, as white as the polar bear. He is the surest proof that the Indians of our west came from the same region, following in his wake, or driving him before them. That was before a narrow neck of land between the hemispheres broke in two.

It is only twenty-five thousand years since the end of the ice age (or so we believe at this writing). Forests on the mountainsides, protected from the cold and blustering winds of the Pacific, rose and fell, were born and died, living for a longer period, perhaps, than man and the elements permit to-day. No one knows. The Merced book was old and closed long before Asia conceived the myth of Noah. The "Big Trees" (*sequoia gigantea*) are believed to have lived in Tertiary times, a few of their roots or seeds surviving the ice, to father those in existence to-day. It is estimated that there may have been a time when these trees, peculiar to a few hundred miles of the Pacific coast, flourished for five thousand years instead of a paltry fifteen hundred. Certainly the miserable degenerate Asiatics we call Indians—nowhere farther below the standards of the white races than in California—did not disturb them. The savages cut young trees for their wigwams or huts, as they lived on hares and goats and the rich products of the valley's soil which Nature planted and tended and watered.

# CALIFORNIA

But the great trees of the Sierra awaited the coming not merely of the white man, but of the genus *Americana* to fall before anything but storm and time. There is no historic proof, but it seems indubitable that the men of the early surveying parties, or the emigrants who followed in their footsteps, who were obliged to build cabins in the Sierra, were the first to lay an ax to the roots of the great sequoia. The missions were built of adobe and were far from the redwood forests. The ranch-houses were all built of adobe, and so was Sutter's Fort, although he was close to the oak-trees of the Sacramento Valley. The redwoods felled by Luis Argüello were in the Coast Range and of an inferior variety. As a nation we are prone to hitch our wagon to a star, and we therefore lay claim to be the direct connecting-link between a time, reckoned—as time goes and as typified by the Sierra—at a hundred and fifty million years, and the apologetic modern period which will follow this chapter.

## II

### THE MISSION PADRES

CALIFORNIA's historic period began very late. When New England was burning witches on the green, and the South was dancing the minuet, and New York was founding an aristocracy out of Dutch burghers, this vast and lovely tract, with a soil as rich as the minerals within her, was peopled by a few Indian tribes, so stupid that they rarely learned one another's language, so lethargic that they rarely fought. The squaws did what work was done; the bucks basked in the sun for eight months in the year, and during the brief winter sweated out their always negligible energies in the *temescals*.

Nevertheless, there were strange legends about California, and in the light of her actual inhabitants it would be interesting to trace their origin. When Ordonez de Montalvo wrote his astonishing yarn all the world (at that time principally a Spanish world) believed that the variously located California was a land of "romantic wonders and fabulous riches, splendid cities and vast magazines of wealth." There was a legendary "seven golden cities" which, Cortez failing to find during his visit to the southern peninsula in 1535, were later relegated to the western base of the great Sierra rampart. Montalvo begins his assurance to a credulous world in this wise:

Be it known unto you that at the right hand of the Indies [*sic*] there was an island formed of the largest rocks known and called California,

# CALIFORNIA

very near to the terrestrial Paradise. This island was inhabited by robust dark women of great strength and great warm hearts, who lived almost as Amazons, and no man lived among them. Their weapons and the trappings of the wild beasts which they rode after taming them were entirely of gold, and no other metal existed on the island. The people lived in well-hewn caves. They had many ships in which they made excursions to other countries, where they caught men whom they carried away and subsequently killed. During periods of peace with their neighbors they commingled with them without restraint. When children were born the females were preserved, but the males were killed at once, saving only those required to guard against depopulation, so that their domination over the land would be securely maintained.

There were many griffins on the island, and they were a great torment. There were also an infinite number of wild beasts which are found in no other part of the world. When these animals had young the women went to fetch them and carried them, covered with heavy skins, to their caves, and there bred them and fed them with the men and male children. The women brought up these animals with such skill that they knew them well and did them no harm, and they attacked and killed any man who entered the island and ate him; and when their appetite was sated they would take them up flying into the air and let them fall from great heights, killing them instantly.

This quotation, from a once famous book, is interesting, if only to reveal what a Spaniard of the sixteenth century believed to constitute a "great warm heart" in woman.

Certain romantic writers and even historians connected California with Asia via what we now call Newfoundland, and many expeditions were fitted out by Spain in the hope of discovering this golden land and claiming it in the name of God and the king.

But California might have taken one of her ancient dips beneath the sea, so elusive did she prove until 1542, when Cabrillo, convinced that the beautiful coast rising before his galleons was California (or might as well be), sailed into two of its bays and named them San Diego and Monterey. He took note of a country rich in scenery and

## THE MISSION PADRES

naked savages, but with no visible Amazons or gold. He died, and his captain, Farello, sailed as far north as Cape Mendocino, and so did Viscaino in the following century. Neither saw anything of the Golden Gate and the great inland sheet of water encircled by hills.

California, in spite of these formal acts of possession—the erection of cross and flag—seems to have lost her lure. Mexico (New Spain) already covered an immense area, in great part unexplored, much of it infested by savages, and but sparsely populated by the Spaniard. None of the explorers had learned aught of the fertile central valleys of California or of the golden skeleton within her. The Jesuits, against incredible odds, made repeated attempts to colonize that long strip of land that still belongs to Mexico, called Baja (Lower) California, and Christianize the Indians. But the country was so barren and arid that almost all material sustenance was brought from the other side of the gulf, and the Indians did not take kindly to the spiritual. Although the hardy priests managed to interest Spain to some extent in the pearl-fisheries, the beds could be ravaged without financing missions, and the poor padres were supported mainly by private funds. In 1768 Spain drove the Jesuits out of all her possessions, and those in Baja California were forced to abandon the Indians after seventy years of devoted but almost futile labors in a cause to which they had given not only their youth and strength, but their personal means. They left California, still believing it to be an island, and having made no attempt to penetrate Alta (Upper) California, which they also assumed to be an island and bounded on the north by the "Straits of Amien."

But California's first and greatest pioneer was born,

# CALIFORNIA

and her historic period was to begin in 1769, the year after the expulsion of the Jesuits.

Twenty years earlier a priest had left Spain for Mexico and spent the intervening time either in the College of San Fernando or the lonely perilous missions of the Sierra Gorda. His piety and exaltation were on every tongue, and by many he was hailed as the most remarkable man of his order since it was founded by his prototype, Francis of Assisi. His name was Junípero Serra. There is a monument erected in his honor in the Golden Gate Park of San Francisco, and another overlooks the harbor of Monterey. No name shines in the brief history of California with a brighter and more persistent luster. While he looked nine-tenths spirit, and no doubt was, and was endowed with a humility and simplicity of mind that permitted him to see a miracle in every meager bit of good luck that fell to his share, he was the born pioneer, resourceful, practical, indomitable. He knew no obstacle where the glory of the Church was concerned; neither weary leagues infested by hostile tribes, nor the racking ills of his own frail body.

Simultaneously with the expulsion of the Jesuits the Franciscans determined to succeed where the rival order had failed. They were encouraged by Charles III., King of Spain, one of the most enlightened princes of his time. He was quite willing to save the souls of the pestilential savages if it could be done, but his ardent missionaries were a cloak for his ultimate design; he purposed to occupy and settle that land of all possibilities, explored along eight hundred miles of its coast by Cabrillo, Farello, and Viscaino—to say nothing of the insolent foreigner, Drake, who had presumed to call the land New Albion—

STATUE OF PADRE JUNÍPERO SERRA

He was the founder of the California missions. He was hailed as the most remarkable man of his order since it was founded by his prototype, Francis of Assisi

## THE MISSION PADRES

thus linking it inseparably to the Spanish crown. The spiritual expedition was placed as a matter of course in charge of Junípero Serra, and he and his little band of priests went first to Loreto to re-establish the missions of Baja California. They arrived on Good Friday, April 1, 1768, with orders to separate to the different mission establishments left by the Jesuits and, while saving souls by baptism, await further orders from Don José de Galvez, who had been appointed Visitador - general and charged with the execution of the real purpose of the king.

Galvez arrived in Loreto two months later and held a long consultation with Father Fr. Junípero Serra, who, as president of the California missions, was almost his equal in authority. They mutually agreed that forces and missionaries should be sent early in the following year by land and sea to take formal possession of Alta California.

Serra at this time was fifty-five years old; his body was wasted by fasting and scourging and tireless missionary work, but animated by one of the most remarkable wills ever developed in the psychical anatomy. Although three ships had been placed at the disposal of the explorers, he elected to go with one of the land expeditions, which, of course, meant traversing hundreds of thorny miles either on foot or the back of a mule.

The ships sailed (one of them was lost). The first of the two land expeditions started under the leadership of Capt. Rivera y Moncada. The second was in charge of Capt. Gaspar de Portolá (also appointed governor of California), and left Loreto on March 9, 1769. Serra was to have ridden at the head of this party, but was forced to remain behind and in bed for several days. Since his arrival

## CALIFORNIA

in Mexico in 1749, when he had insisted upon walking from Vera Cruz to the City of Mexico for the glory of God, he had suffered from a painful ulcer in the leg, which was constantly irritated by his arduous and unremitting labors and received no attention from this devoted servant of the Church until he collapsed from weakness.

On March 25th, accompanied by two soldiers and a servant, he began his march over roads that might have been designed by Nature in her most vicious geological mood to test his unfaltering spirit. Baja California is little more than a rough mountain-chain, parched, stony, already blistering at this time of the year under a tropic sun. The only game was rattlesnake.

Serra's leg became so swollen that it threatened not only to become insupportably painful, but useless. But remonstrance availed not; resting but a day or two at the successive missions (where the beds were probably boards), he continued his march, losing himself in religious meditation or dreams of the beautiful land he was about to redeem. Mind triumphed over matter (aided by an opportune mule-doctor who poulticed him with herbs); he caught up with Portolá in May. On July 1st they arrived on the shores of the Bay of San Diego and found the party of explorers that had preceded them camped in the sandy valley, and two of the ships in the harbor. Serra went to work the day he arrived upon the latent religious sensibilities of a particularly suspicious and bloodthirsty tribe of Indians. First he celebrated mass, and then he made them presents.

Portolá gave them their first taste of beef. He and Capt. Rivera y Moncada had driven before them the ancestors of the herds and flocks the Americans found

# THE MISSION PADRES

in the California valleys three-quarters of a century later.

Portolá, having seen his missionaries and their guard safe, as he supposed, within a stockade, set out on the 14th of July to rediscover the Bay of Monterey. He was accompanied not only by his peons and a large bodyguard of *soldados de cuera* (leather-jacketed soldiers), but by Capt. Rivera y Moncada, Don Pedro Fages, Don Miguel Constanzo (engineer), Father Gomez, and Father Crespi—to whose diary the historian is so deeply indebted. A train of mules carried provisions for the journey. But Portolá could not find the Bay of Monterey. Indifferent to the Bay of San Francisco, which, pushing on north, he inadvertently discovered, and convinced that the bay most famous among California explorers had disappeared, he wended his weary and hungry way back to San Diego. There he was horrified to learn that Father Serra and his little colony barely had escaped massacre by the Indians; they had saved themselves less with their firearms than with their wits.

Portolá was thoroughly discouraged. He had been tramping for the greater part of six months over a dusty or muddy unbroken country, whose magnificent scenery was no compensation for the mule diet to which he finally had been reduced. The bay coveted by the King of Spain evidently had been obliterated by the elements; and, although he had found a superb bay farther north, he scorned it, convinced that it was the harbor discovered by Drake and the Spanish explorers, and held by Spain as of little account. As the Drake harbor was named San Francisco on the Spanish maps, he rechristened the inland sheet after the patron saint of the expedition;

## CALIFORNIA

to the unbounded delight of Father Serra, who looked upon Portolá's march north and discovery of the bay already named for St. Francis in the light of a miracle.

He was a handsome and gallant young officer, this Don Gaspar de Portolá, first governor of California, but there is no denying that he was stupid; and when he discovered later that he had camped for several days on the beach before the Bay of Monterey, perhaps he thought so himself. As none of the Spaniards ever appreciated the Bay of San Francisco, he lived and died in blissful ignorance of the greatest of his mistakes.

Only one of the ships remained in the Bay of San Diego, the *San Carlos*. The *San Antonio* had been sent back to San Blas in July, not only for provisions, but for sailors and soldiers, many having died on the voyage out from diseases caused by the abominable conditions. The *San Antonio* had not returned; Portolá doubted if it ever would. The provisions on hand were running low. He made up his mind to return to Mexico at once, and would have done so had it not been for the prayers and determination of Father Serra. There is no doubt that if the Spaniards had abandoned California at that time the government, upon receiving the discouraging reports of such seasoned officers as Portolá and Rivera y Moncada, would have lost interest once more. Without the picturesque if imperfect civilization of the late eighteenth and early nineteenth centuries men of a more energetic and adventurous breed never would have heard of California. Her "American" history would have been delayed for a century or more; and those enterprising citizens that have wrested fortunes from her vitals, her fertile surfaces, or their fellow-citizens, should render yearly thanks to that

# THE MISSION PADRES

old priest of racked body and unquenchable enthusiasm, and of a will too strong for Gaspar de Portolá. Otherwise they might be battling with the wilderness themselves instead of reaping the harvest of the argonauts and pioneers of '49.

Portolá unwillingly consented to wait till the 19th of March. On that date if the *San Antonio* had not arrived he should abandon California. She arrived on the 19th (another miracle), and only because she needed an anchor—she had been ordered to Monterey. Portolá, now convinced that God and the authorities were on the side of the heathen, and that if he valued his career he had better be also, immediately organized another expedition to search for the Bay of Monterey. But this time he went by sea, already half persuaded by Father Serra (who took care to accompany him) that the bay above which Viscaino had erected a cross—still remaining—could not have disappeared. Even when the ship steered straight for the cross, however, Portolá saw nothing that resembled a bay, but Serra recognized it at once and pronounced it a beautiful port. Portolá, who seems to have been able to see anything that was ticketed and labeled, agreed with him, and they took possession of Monterey with impressive ceremonies.

This was on June 3, 1770, a fateful day in the history of California. San Diego, sandy, barren, intensely hot, differing little from Baja California, would hardly have unloosed the purse-strings of the "pious fund" of Mexico had that second expedition north not been undertaken. But now even Portolá admitted that California was a vast orchard of plums, all worthy of the active appetite of Spain. He had eaten wild grapes and oranges himself

# CALIFORNIA

in the lovely valleys he had traversed, he now remembered, and seen pine forests of which seventy-times-seven cities might be built. These same forests had towered on the coast above them as the *San Antonio* crawled north; and along the cliffs was a narrow belt of ancient cypress trees, an advance-guard from the Holy Land to greet the cross.

Seals crowded the outlying rocks, over which the ponderous waves of the Pacific dashed on their way to assault the cliffs. They kept up an incessant and horrible racket, but the scene above was very cool and green and inviting to eyes weary of the glare of the desert.

On the ship had been packed not only the necessaries of camp life, but altars, vestments, all the paraphernalia of the Church, as well as the parade uniforms of the officers. On the morning of June 3d priests and officers arrayed themselves magnificently and assembled about an altar under the great oak named for Viscaino. The priests rang the silver bells they had hidden among the branches, summoning all that might hear to prayer. The Indians, who were hidden behind every rock, ignored the invitation, but felt sufficient awe of the impressive ceremonies to remain passive.

The little congregation was composed of Don Gaspar de Portolá and his officers, several priests, many soldiers, and the native muleteers, who had been Christianized in Baja California. They all knelt while Father Serra, in the white ceremonial robes of his order, blessed them and consecrated the ground and sands of the shore, sprinkled them with holy water, and planted an immense cross. The chanting was incessant, and, as there were no musical instruments, salvos of artillery and musketry were fired

## THE MISSION PADRES

during the mass. With the Te Deum the religious ceremonies finished and the military ceremonies began.

The royal standard was planted, and California (which extended to the north pole, for all they knew) taken possession of in the name of Charles III., King of Spain. The day finished with a great feast on the beach. The brave little band was tired and hungry, but happy. Not only had the Mission of San Carlos de Monterey been founded, but a royal presidio.

When the barracks were built the high stockade included not only the quarters of the governor and his officers and barracks for the soldiers and peons, but a parish chapel and rooms for the missionaries. Later a *castillo* (fort) was erected on an eminence above the harbor, and the presidio was rebuilt far from the shore and about a large plaza.

The natives proved docile and willing to be baptized. Father Serra soon made up his mind that Monterey was no place for a mission, owing to the absence of broad acres to till and waters to irrigate. Serra, like all the priests that came after him, was an excellent judge of soils; moreover, he was far-sighted, and did not mean that his missions should be encroached upon by future towns. Prowling up and down the coast, he soon discovered, about a league to the south, a beautiful and fertile valley on the shores of a river, which he named Carmel. The waves dashed over Point Pinos, and the mountains were black with pines, but there were hundreds of acres of rolling land which could be covered with grain and fruit, and there was a lake of fresh water besides the river.

He ordered certain of his Indians, old and new, to fell trees and erect a stout inclosure for a church, garrison, living-rooms, huts, and a corral. This he baptized with the name Mission de San Carlos del Rio Carmel, but then, as now, more briefly known as Carmel.

When this energetic little padre, propelling his tormented body by the living flame within, was not designing, projecting, overseeing, exhorting, or baptizing he was writing letters to the College of San Fernando in Mexico, dwelling with holy zeal and real descriptive ability upon the beauties of the new land, the richness of her soil, above all, of course, the precious souls to be saved. He asked for a hundred more missionaries, and he got thirty; not only did he communicate his enthusiasm to the Guardian of San Fernando, but to the more practical Viceroy of Mexico and the Visitador-general. The news of the solemn ceremonies on the shores of the Bay of Monterey had already been received, and the Marques de Croix, the viceroy, had published the news in the capital and ordered the cathedral and all the little churches to ring their bells.

Two years before when Portolá and his band were toiling over the Santa Lucia range Father Crespi had been deeply impressed by a valley seen from the summit and afterward crossed by the weary party. It was a valley of beautiful proportions, with waving fields of wild oats and grains, and fruits as wild. When word came from the College that the new missionaries with the necessary vestments, bells, and funds would start as soon as might be, Father Crespi recalled the beautiful fertile valley and infected Father Serra with his enthusiasm. That warrior soul mounted his mule, and, accompanied by two priests and a body-guard, set out for the spot, some twenty-five leagues south of Monterey. When he reached the wide valley, watered by a river, dotted with groves of stately

# THE MISSION PADRES

trees, the ripened oats looking like a waving sheet of gold, he lost the head that never had been as strong as his spirit, capered about in spite of his always swollen leg, and, as soon as the bells were hung in the trees, pulled the rope himself, shouting: "Come, oh ye Gentiles, come to the Holy Church! Come to the faith of Jesus Christ!"

Inasmuch as there was not a Gentile (Indian) in sight, and no church, and as his conduct was altogether unusual, his companions thought he had gone mad. But who knows what visions of the future flashed across his vision on that brilliant July morning? Given a starved and neglected body, a brain filled with the poisons of that body, an inner altar upon which the flame never burned low, surround these deviations from the normal by the blue and gold of a California morning, a thousand choirs of birds, the exquisite scents of the virgin earth, and visions follow as a matter of course.

Thus was founded the Mission of San Antonio de Padua. When I saw it more than a century later its ruins were crowded with evicted Mexican squatters, the women very fat, wearing a solitary calico garment, and the children, although the San Antonio Valley is bitter-cold in winter, quite naked. But it must have been a beautiful mission up to the days of secularization, long and low, red-tiled and painted white; the rancheria (Indian quarters) and factories close by, set in a magnificent valley, one of whose ranchos,[1] when I saw it, covered forty-five thousand acres.

[1] My father-in-law, Faxon D. Atherton, saw this ranch when a youth on his way to Chile in search of fortune. He vowed to himself that he would one day own it, and did obtain possession sometime in the 70's, after a lawsuit of several years; he had bought it as a Spanish grant, and the many squatters in possession claimed that it was government land. The Supreme Court decided in his favor, and the squatters (threatening my husband and the sheriffs with death, but doing nothing), were evicted,

# CALIFORNIA

During Father Serra's lifetime the neophytes numbered 1,084. Like all the missions, it was self-supporting; seeds and pits of fruits, cereals, grains, and vegetables, cattle and sheep were sent from Mexico, and the priests soon learned to cultivate the wild orange and grape.

San Gabriel was the next mission to be founded. It stands in another rich plain not far from the sea and walled in behind by a rampart of high mountains, white with snow when the oranges and olives are ripe in the valley. Near by to-day is the California Chicagito, still named for the little Spanish pueblo that once drowsed at its base, Los Angeles, City of the Angels! As few people know the meaning of the name they mispronounce, the incongruity is less painful than it might be.

San Luis Obispo, surrounded by bare chrome hills and beautiful valleys, arose next. Then, after passionate representations on the part of Father Serra as well as a trip to Mexico, during which he nearly expired of fever and exhaustion, funds and missionaries were sent, and the following missions built in quick succession: San Juan Capistrano, San Francisco de Assisi, Santa Clara, San Bueneventura, Santa Barbara, La Purissima, Santa Cruz, Soledad, San José, San Juan Bautista, San Miguel, San Fernando, San Luis Rey, and Santa Inez. These missions, with their barracks, factories, and rancherias for the neophytes, were about thirty miles, or one day's ride, apart. The spots chosen were as far as possible from the mountains on either side of the long valleys, and a constant lookout was maintained by sentries for hostile Indians. The churches were humble in the beginning, but were gradually replaced by large buildings of adobe, painted white, the roofs covered with bright-red tiles, and

SANTA BARBARA MISSION—FOUNDED 1786

SAN GABRIEL MISSION (FIRST GOLD FOUND IN 1842)

## THE MISSION PADRES

were, for the most part, of Moorish architecture. There was a long corridor before the living-rooms and facing the plaza, or courtyard, and under its sheltering roof a friar might tell his beads and meditate upon the hopeless Indian; few being as unremittingly enthusiastic as Father Serra.

The chain of missions beginning at San Diego on the south finished for many years at San Francisco, the bay being then an insurmountable obstacle to further progress. A road was gradually beaten out between the establishments, and the chance traveler was always sure of a welcome, a good bed, and a far better meal. Each was a hive of industry, for the Indians worked if the padres stood over them, and they had learned how to make cakes of chocolate and other delicacies, to till the soil, to turn the grape into wine and the wheat into fine bread. A sheep or a beef was always killed in honor of the guest; he was invited to remain as long as he pleased, and sent on his way with a fresh horse. No questions were asked, but he was expected to attend mass. For the visitors soon ceased to be merely priests. Many explorers cast anchor in the bays—La Perouse, Vancouver, Puget, Duflot de Mofras are the most celebrated—sailors deserted ships, and settlers had been encouraged to emigrate from Mexico at once. These came by every packet-boat—which, to be sure, was not often!—and they were given small farms near the presidios and furnished with two cows, two sheep, two goats, a mule, farming-implements, and a yoke of oxen. Those that settled at the pueblos (towns), founded in due course at San José and Los Angeles, were treated with even more paternalism, for the central government was anxious that these and other pueblos should grow and flourish.  Houses were built for each inhabitant, his farm and orchard staked off and his irrigation ditches dug.  In addition he was stocked as generously as the farmer.  Little can be said for these first settlers.  Some were convicts, and all were idle and dissipated.  The fine old Spanish-California families are descended, not from them, but from the officers that protected the missions.  Many of these sent for their families and in course of time —although bitterly opposed by the priests—obtained large grants of land and became the great ranchers of California's pastoral era; sometimes the younger officers, hastening eagerly to the City of Mexico, when their term of duty expired, returned by the next packet-boat, accompanied by their brides, and settled in a country which even then seems to have exercised a curious fascination.  There was little to do, an abundance of game and every other delicacy that cost nothing, sunshine for eight months of the year, a climate electric in the north and soporific in the south, and not too much discipline—save at the missions.

Padre Serra, in spite of his increasing ills and feebleness, spent much of his time visiting his long chain of missions.  He was granted the right to confirm by a special edict, there being no bishop in the country, and month after month, year after year, he traveled over those terrible roads, choked with dust in summer, knee-deep in mud in winter, making sure that his idle, thieving, stupid, but affectionate Indians would pass the portals of heaven.  A motorist skimming up and down El Camino Real to-day would stare hard at the vision of a shrunken figure in a brown habit, with a shining face above, plodding along on a mule, his body-guard of soldiers a few respectful paces

# THE MISSION PADRES

behind. There was not an inch of that long road between San Diego and Dolores, nor any trail that led from it, that was not as familiar to him as to the pleasure-seekers of to-day.

The missions, after an interval of warfare with the more aggressive and unfriendly tribes, in which they lost both priests and soldiers, settled down to a long period of simple peace and prosperity. Immense fields of grain were cultivated, vineyards were planted, and wine was made; the women were taught weaving and spinning, all fruits and vegetables seemed to flourish, and the horses and cattle and sheep multiplied in the land. That long chain of snow-white red-tiled missions, hedged with Castilian roses, surrounded by olive-orchards, whose leaves were silver in the sun, orange-groves heavy with golden fruit, the vast sweep of shimmering grain-fields broken by stately oaks, winding rivers set close with the tall pale cottonwoods, lakes with the long branches of willows trailing over the surface; bounded by forest and mountain and sea, and not a city to break the harmony, must have been the fairest sight in the modern world.

But there was another side to the picture. Father Serra and the other devoted priests who were willing to give their lives to the saving of heathen souls were terrific disciplinarians. It was not only their mission to convert and save at any price, but to use these instruments God had given them to insure the wealth and perfection of their establishments. Haussmann took no more pride in rebuilding Paris nor Ludvig I. in modern Munich than these clever priests, exiled to the wilderness, but educated in Madrid or the City of Mexico, in their beautiful adobe missions, some severely plain, others sculptured, but all

# CALIFORNIA

symmetrical and built by their brains with Indian hands. It is to be confessed that the hands had a sorry time of it. Father Serra had no cruelty in him, but many of the other priests in their pious zeal developed more than was good for either the soul or body of the neophyte. It was after Serra's death, and while Lausen was president of the missions, that La Perouse visited California. He wrote the story of his voyages, and as follows of Monterey:

> The Indian population of San Carlos consisted of seven hundred and forty persons of both sexes, including children. They lived in some fifty miserable huts near the church, composed of stakes stuck in the ground a few inches apart and bent over at the top so as to form oven-shaped structures, some six feet in diameter and the same in height, and illy thatched with straw. In such habitations as these, closely packed together at night, they preferred to live rather than in houses such as the Spanish built, alleging that they loved the open air which had free access to them, and that when the huts became uncomfortable on account of fleas and other vermin they could easily burn them down and in a few hours build new ones. The condition of the neophyte was that of abject slavery. The moment an Indian allowed himself to be baptized that moment he relinquished every particle of liberty and subjected himself, body and soul, to a tyranny from which there was no escape. The Church then claimed as its own himself, his labor, his creed, and his obedience, and enforced its claims with the strong hand of power. His going forth and his returning were prescribed; his hours of toil and his prayers fixed; the time of his meals and his sleep prearranged. If he ran away and attempted to regain his native independence he was hunted down by the soldiers, brought back, and lashed into submission. His spirit, if he ever had any, was entirely broken, so much so that in a short while after the establishment of a mission anything like resistance was almost unknown, and its three or four hundred or a thousand neophytes were driven to their labors by three or four soldiers like so many cattle. . . . They were roused with the sun and collected in the church for prayers and mass. These lasted an hour. During this time three large boilers were set on the fire for cooking a kind of porridge, called atole, consisting of a mixture of barley, which had first been roasted and then pounded or ground with great labor by the Indian women into a sort of meal, with water. . . . Three-quarters of an hour were allowed for

# THE MISSION PADRES

breakfast. Immediately after it was over all the neophytes, men and women, were obliged to go to work, either tilling the ground, laboring in the shops, gathering or preparing food, as might be ordered by the missionaries, under whose eyes, or the eyes of other taskmasters appointed by them, all the operations were performed. At noon the church-bells announced the time for dinner. . . . At about two o'clock the Indians were obliged to return to their labors and continue until about five, when they were again collected in the church for an hour of evening prayers. They lived on porridge, but on rare occasions meat was given them in small quantities. This was eaten raw. When a cow was slaughtered the poor wretches who were not at work would gather round like hungry ravens, devouring with their eyes what they dare not touch with their hands, and keeping up a croaking of desire as the parts for which they had the greatest avidity were exposed in the process of dressing. . . . In rainy weather they were kept as hard at work indoors, and on Sundays, although they were allowed an hour or two of games, they were driven for the most part into the church to pray.

Other travelers were horrified at the conversion, not so much of the heathen to Catholicism as of a race independent for centuries into unhappy machines; and there is no doubt that many of the instances of reported cruelty are true. But it must be remembered that this was in a day when more enlightened nations than Spain were buying and selling slaves, whipping them, and separating them from their families. Even the white underdog had not learned to raise his head, and schoolmasters and parents all over the world used the rod unsparingly. The Spanish priests had come to the wilderness not only to save souls, but to do their share in welding California to the crown of Spain. Moreover, no nation that brings its children up in the bull-ring can be otherwise than cruel, or callous at the best. These savages were the only instruments an all-wise Providence had deposited in California for the priests to use in the performance of their task, and they used them. If the instruments had to be remade, even by the process of fire, why not, if it were to the glory of God and the King of Spain?

There is no question of their pious zeal. And all for naught. Never were devoted services in the Garden of the Lord more futile. Brainless, little higher in the scale of life than the wild beasts of their plains and forests, these native Indians of California, so aptly renamed "Diggers" at a later date by the American, did not rise one step in the scale of civilization. Further enervated by diseases introduced by the Spanish soldiers, and reduced almost seventy-five per cent. by the ravages of smallpox, while still under the sway of the missions, they relapsed into savagery as soon as the priests were shorn of their power; meaner objects than before, for they had lost their ancient independence. It may be argued against the padres that the results of modern methods in California show that a certain amount of intelligence and character in the Indian can be developed by education and kindness. Even so he is far below any white standard, and there is no evidence of modern or any sort of civilization in his villages. He merely has the benefit of what he can assimilate from a more enlightened era, an era of which the priests of Spain had no vision; nor would have treated with aught but scorn and contempt had it been interpreted to them by an oracle. God made the poor to toil for the rich, the weak to be oppressed by the strong, and, as both were put upon the earth to glorify Him, why not?

Padre Serra loved them all, individually and collectively, being not a priest, but a saint. He saw nothing of their ugly squat bodies and stupid faces, only the soul within, which, of course, he never guessed was but a projection

# THE MISSION PADRES

from his own radiant and supernormal ego. He died at the Mission of Carmel, August 28, 1784, full of years and honors and bodily sores, and was buried under the floor of the church he loved best—the church in the Mission de San Carlos del Rio Carmel. It became in due course a magnificent ruin, with an owl-haunted belfry, and the weeds grew over his grave, and all the tombs were broken. But it is now restored and quite hideous.

Father Fr. Junípero Serra may have failed to reap the great harvest of Indian souls he had baptized with such gratitude and exultation, and that consoled him for all his afflictions, but he lifted California from the unread pages of geological history and placed it on the modern map. I wonder what he thinks of it.

# III

## THE SPANISH GOVERNORS—I

CHARLES III. had not a suspicion of the gold that lacquered the Sierra cañons and spangled the beds of the rivers, but it was the policy of Spain to add land and more land to her American dominions, and so recover, if possible, the power and prestige she had lost in Europe. There is no doubt that this far-sighted ruler purposed to encroach upon as much of the American continent as his soldiers could hold and his missionaries civilize. This, it must be remembered, was during the last third of the eighteenth century; the English and French were on the far eastern rim, curving north and south; Vancouver had not yet visited the northwest, nor is it likely that an echo of the rising storm of "American" discontent had reached the Spanish king. What we now call Texas, New Mexico, Arizona, Utah, Nevada already had been invaded by the Spaniards from their central stronghold, Mexico; no doubt, like the great Russian, Rezánov, after him, Charles dreamed of a new American empire that should extend as far as the Rocky Mountains, at least, and farther still, mayhap.

Portolá was succeeded as governor of the Californias by Felipe de Barri in 1771; and if he possessed even as much personality as Don Gaspar it has not come down to us through those early meager pages of California history.

# THE SPANISH GOVERNORS—I

His short administration was distinguished chiefly by rows with the missionaries over the vexed question of supremacy. Portolá, although a strict disciplinarian in the army, had too much respect for the president to interfere with the missions, but Barri aspired to be lord of all this vast domain, with the priests as his humble subjects. He was routed by Father Serra, although the friction continued. The chief weapon in the missionaries' moral armory, and one they never failed to flourish, was the avowed purpose of Spain to annex the Californias solely for the glory of God and the redemption of heathen souls. The military was sent along merely to protect the missions; and the civil administrations necessary to pueblos were even more incidental.

It was during the administration of the third governor, Filipe de Neve, although while he was still detained in Baja California, that the presidio of San Francisco and the neighboring mission were founded. During the previous year, 1775, Bucareli, the enlightened Viceroy of Mexico, had sent Juan de Ayala, Lieutenant of Frigate of the Royal Navy, to survey the Bay of San Francisco. This was done, not because even he realized its strategical importance, but to gratify Father Serra, who had long importuned him for means to establish a mission at a point hallowed by the name of the patron saint of California.

Ayala, the first white man, so far as is known, to sail through the Golden Gate, arrived in the Gulf of the Farallones on August 5th, and sent a launch ahead to navigate the straits. He followed on the same evening in his packet-boat, the *San Carlos*, and navigated the bay as thoroughly as one might in those days. He also named

# CALIFORNIA

the islands—Alcatraz and Nuestra Señora de los Angeles (Angel Island). In the following year, while men of English birth at the other end of the continent were filling the land with the clamor of liberty bells, the peninsula of San Francisco wrote her own first chapter in modern history. To the terrific cataclysms of the geological centuries had succeeded the camp-fires and dances and lazily gliding canoes of Indians; nothing more momentous enlivening the shores of the bay on any side than a wardance or a battle between rival tribes. But now there were to be forts on her heights and a fine presidio not far from the beach, officers strutting about in uniform, parades, love-making at grated windows, and cockfights. It was not a change that threatened the peace of the world, but it marked the end of the prehistoric era and the embarcation of San Francisco upon her changeful seas.

A league to the south the Mission of St. Francis d'Assisi was founded, to be known almost at once from the lake on which it stood, as the Mission Dolores. It had been the intention of Captain Anza, who had charge of the expedition, to found a pueblo close by, but the settlers whom he brought with him had just sufficient intelligence to see no prospect of farming sand-dunes. Governor Neve, when he arrived, sent Lieutenant Moraga to conduct them down to the Mission of Santa Clara, and the pueblo of San José was founded. The padres, however, appropriated many hundreds of acres to the south of Dolores, and this mission soon became almost as flourishing as the others.

Governor Neve also founded the pueblo of Los Angeles, and he composed a code of legislation (*Reglamento*) for

# THE SPANISH GOVERNORS—I

both presidios and pueblos, so minute and so far-seeing that it would serve them did they ever attain to the growth of large cities. But he was too big a man for a mere province, and was soon recalled to the City of Mexico with high honors. The missionaries saw him go with no regret. He disliked them intensely and did not hesitate to tell them that their policy of repression and cruelty was both unwarranted and short-sighted.

Pedro Fages succeeded him. He was one of the pioneers, and had accompanied Portolá on that first futile expedition in search of the Bay of Monterey. He was a man of enterprise and industry and high in favor with the Viceroy and the Visitador-general. He was also a favorite of Father Serra, but he disliked the missionaries in general and resented their power.

Fages had the ability to rule as well as the instinct, and if he could not force the missionaries to their knees he managed to make them feel the weight of his authority. He got a law passed that no one should leave the Californias without the consent of the governor. The priests had been in the habit of running over to Mexico to refresh their souls with civilization and the holy conversation of the College San Fernando. The new law emanated from the City of Mexico, and, although the priests gnashed their teeth and hated Fages, they were helpless. California in those days was pastoral, but not too pastoral.

He also curbed the immorality of the soldiers, and encouraged them to marry the neophyte girls, settle down, and become the real pioneers of the country. He seems to have been the first to punish horse-stealing and to interfere with the excessive sale and consumption of liquor. The eight years of his administration were spent either in reforms or in enforcing the original laws, and he took an equal interest in the domestic affairs of the colonists, settling their quarrels, prodding them to their work, berating and encouraging them.

But he had his match at home, and his own domestic affairs were the talk of California. His servants whispered the secrets of the gubernatorial household to the "wash-tub mail"—the women that washed in the stone tubs sunken in the ground near a convenient spring or creek—and they told other servants, who told their ladies, who wrote to other ladies at other presidios. Society was barely out of its shell in those days, and that first dish of gossip must have been a godsend.

The Señora Fages has the honor to be the first woman named in the history of California. If wives and daughters accompanied the previous governors and their officers they were too meek to win mention in the records, but the helpmate of Fages was an individual if not an angel. As it is not possible that she was with her husband during that first expedition into unknown territory, this lady of high degree, and consequence in the City of Mexico, must have had the courage to take the long and hazardous journey with a child and a retinue of ignorant peon servants, practically alone. But that same spirit made her too mettlesome for the hearthstone. And brave and hardy as she was, she abominated the rough presidio life that awaited her at Monterey. No doubt she had read Montalvo and dreamed her dreams.

To be sure, the missionaries and settlers were cultivating the fields, and her table was loaded with delicate fish and luscious fruits, venison, fowl, and bear-steak; there were pine woods on the hills where she and the officers' ladies

# THE SPANISH GOVERNORS—I

could roam and talk of the City of Mexico, and look at whales, spouting iridescent geysers in the bay, a bay as blue as the vice-reine's sapphires, and curving to silver sands; she could thrill at the whoops of unbaptized Indians prowling round the stockade at night; and on Sunday, after mass, she could attire herself in a flowered gown, drape her handsome head in a mantilla, and, coquettishly wielding a fan from Madrid, sit on the corridor surrounded by gallant officers and watch a bull fight a bear in the plaza; and there were festas aplenty at the missions. But, although everybody seems to have worked himself to the bone to please her, there was no peace in the governor's mansion—which she called an adobe hovel. She wanted the pleasures and excitements of the City of Mexico; and, as the governor could not import them and would not return, neither he nor all his minions could smooth her brow nor curb her tongue. The padres, called in by the unhappy governor, talked to her of the consolations of the Church, and were treated with high disdain.

Exhausting her resources in other directions, she pretended to be jealous of her husband, that stern dispenser of stocks and stripes to amorous soldiers. In her determination to amuse herself with a scandal she became a scandal herself, for she hurled her wrongs into the public ear, which expanded to twice its natural size.

Once more the distracted Fages appealed to the priests, and this time they entered her *sala* with the authority of the Church and threatened her with handcuffs and a sound whipping. Her silvery laughter could be heard all over the presidio. Well she knew that never would they dare to put such an indignity upon the Señora Gobernadora, even though she belonged to that sex held in such

# CALIFORNIA

casual regard by the men of her race. The padres gave her up, and Capt. Nicolas Soler, first in military command, was next called in. Soler was not only a disciplinarian of the first water, but diplomatic and resourceful. He began by upbraiding her furiously, telling her that she was a keg of gunpowder full of sparks which sooner or later would blow up California and lower the prestige of Spain in the eyes of the world. This flattered her, and she applied herself to calming the indignant officer, who in turn wheedled her. Perhaps her mood of revolt had worn itself out; in this more enlightened era it would seem that the poor exiled lady was merely suffering from nerves and idleness. She settled down finally into the leader of fashion, not only for Monterey, but for those growing pueblos, San José and Los Angeles, and for the other presidios. Her maiden name was Eulalia Challis, and she deserves fame as the first woman of California to assert her rights and stand upon them, albeit her methods were a bit old-fashioned. Peace was restored in the gubernatorial mansion by the unconditional surrender of the governor himself. Every packet-boat until the end of the Fages administration in 1790 brought her gowns and mantillas, guitars and fans, music and candelabra from the City of Mexico. But all breathed more freely when she left; and so, no doubt, did she.

Doña Josefa Romeau, whose husband succeeded Fages, had no chance to display what individuality she may have possessed, for she was fully occupied nursing a man who was a prey to insomnia and finally to tuberculosis. He died in 1792, and Don José de Arrillaga served as *Gobernador interino* for two years. Diego de Borica received the appointment of *Gobernador propietario* by a

# THE SPANISH GOVERNORS—I

royal order from Madrid in June, 1793, but did not arrive in Monterey until the following year.

It was not the fate that Diego de Borica would have chosen, exile to the wilderness of the Californias, a country comparatively uninhabited, believed to be too poor to progress far beyond its present condition and with no society worthy the name.

Borica was the first man of solid intellectual attainments to take up his residence in California. Mexico was already old enough to have its scholars and seats of learning, and with these Borica had been in close touch, delighting in literature and controversial hours. This was the more remarkable as he was an active soldier and made close companions of his wife and daughter. It is doubtful if there was even a book of old plays in California at that time. The priests had their hands full educating the Indians in religion, agriculture, and manufacturing. The comandantes of the four presidios—Monterey, San Diego, Santa Barbara, and San Francisco—found themselves as fully occupied with military duties, siestas, flirting, bull-fights, and cock-fights; they would have thought it a sin to waste time cultivating their minds. The settlers of the pueblos were men that had been failures at home, and degenerated instead of developing any pioneer traits. California was a veritable exile for an intellectual man.

But Borica, now a man of fifty, was also a soldier. He did as he was told. For a few weeks after his arrival in Monterey he had the consolation of the society of two explorers and men of the world, George Vancouver and Peter Puget, who were anchored in the harbor; but even before they sailed away he had set himself to work to

# CALIFORNIA

improve conditions in general with a zeal that never flagged throughout the five years and eight months of his administration. He determined to lay the corner-stone, at least, of a future civilization.

One of his first measures after strengthening the fortifications along the coast was to reform the pueblos. He scolded the alcaldes (the alcalde was an official who combined several administrative offices in one and finally wielded a power that led to great abuses) so vehemently and threatened them with punishments so dire that there was an immediate decrease in the amount of liquor sold and consumed; and the settlers, instead of spending their time gambling and drinking and fighting, cultivated their fields with an almost feverish ardor.

Knowing his sovereign's desire that many civil communities should flourish in the province, he next turned his attention to the founding of a "city" near the present site of Santa Cruz. It was laid out by the one engineer in the country, Alberto de Cordoba, a young man both able and thorough. The city he made on paper had a church, fine government buildings, houses of adobe for the colonists instead of huts thatched with tules like those of San José and Los Angeles. Nor was it huddled about a plaza; it covered four square leagues of land, with long streets and ample building-lots and grants beyond for farms. It was named the Villa de Branciforte in honor of the Viceroy of New Spain.

The most favorable terms were offered to colonists, but in spite of Borica's stipulation that they should include not only able-bodied men and women, but agriculturists, carpenters, blacksmiths, masons, tailors, shoemakers, tanners, and fishermen, only seventeen poverty-stricken,

# THE SPANISH GOVERNORS—I

diseased, half-naked emigrants arrived by the first ship, and the subsequent relays were no better. Lieutenant Moraga, however, made them work, and the first crops were good. But the Villa Branciforte barely survived Borica's administration nor traveled far beyond Cordoba's table. The enthusiasm and enterprise of one man cannot make a city, and the inhabitants of Branciforte were no better and little more intelligent than the native Indians. No doubt they were degenerated half-breeds, already degenerated at birth. In spite of its beautiful situation on the Bay of Santa Cruz it disappeared, while the little pueblos of San José and Los Angeles clung to the map and are cities to-day.

But Borica's chief and lasting work was the schools he founded. Not only was there until his time no teaching outside the missions for the white children, but the Indians themselves received no more than enabled them to understand the exhortations and orders of the padres. The priests opposed him violently, but he established secular schools and installed the best teachers he could find. He also controlled to a large extent the cruelties practised by the priests on the Indians, which, since Father Serra's death, had become a scandal in the land. As long as he remained in California the unfortunate natives were not hunted down like dogs if they ran away nor lashed in the missions until they bled. It was during Borica's administration also that the military post, Yerba Buena, the site of the future City of San Francisco, was founded.

If this enlightened man did not accomplish all he strove for he at least managed to fill his time during his long exile, and it is doubtful if he contemplated failure for a moment. And he accomplished a great deal. Not only did he compel parents to send their children to his schools, but, despairing of decent immigrants, he ordered the Spanish families — *gente de razon* — to have their boys taught the mechanical occupations. To this there was much opposition; the best families were all military in origin, or fact, and the blue in their veins kept family pride alive even in a colony. But Borica put his foot down, and the boys went to work. The province flourished as never before, for few dared to be idle. The fields and orchards yielded enormous harvests, and there were now hundreds of acres sown in hemp and flax. Blankets and cloth for even the *gente de razon* were woven; and cattle and sheep, horses and mules, roamed through every valley of the Coast Range; the great Central Valley at this time was almost unknown.

If severe and inexorable, Borica was a just man. He would not permit natives to be executed, no matter how grave their offense, holding that their contact with civilization was far too recent to have taught them the laws of right and wrong and the sacredness of human life. No doubt he reflected also that with the exception of the missionaries and the few officers of high character, the Indians had found little to admire and emulate in the ruling class. When they were sent on errands to the presidios and pueblos or ran away and hid in them, their associates were the soldiers and immigrants, whose only virtue was obedience.

In 1779 Borica felt himself worn out with his unremitting labors and asked to be relieved. His release came in January of the following year, and with his devoted family he returned at once to Mexico; but not to enjoy the society of scholars and books. He died six months later.

## IV

### THE SPANISH GOVERNORS—II

It was during the administration of Don José de Arrillaga, who succeeded Borica as *Gobernador propietario*, that California set the stage for her first romantic drama. To the principals it was real enough, but to us, looking down that long perspective to a vanished day, so different from our own, it would seem as if some great stage-manager had found a sad and beautiful play and then great actors to perform it.

Concha (christened Concepcion) Argüello grew up in the presidios of Santa Barbara and San Francisco, her father being alternately comandante of these posts. Don José Argüello was not only an able and energetic officer; he was so good that he was called *el santo*; and, although he had worked himself up from the ranks, he had married a Castilian, Doña Ignacia Moraga, and was the most eminent of his Majesty's subjects in the Californias. Although the republican ideas flourishing in the eastern part of the continent as well as in France horrified him, and he was an uncompromising monarchist, he was more liberal in other respects than most Spaniards of any rank, and permitted his daughter Concha, a remarkably bright girl, to take full advantage of the schools founded by Borica. She was only ten when the governor resigned, but she had heard much learned talk in his family; her mind had received a bent which impelled her to read all the books in the country that were not under the ban of the priests.

Although much of her time was spent in the lonely presidio of San Francisco, she visited at other presidios and at many ranch-houses. California was no longer a wilderness in the year 1806, although far from the climax of that arcadian life so famous in its history. The missions, but thirty miles apart, had been the first chain to link that long coast together; the ranchers were the next; and the young people, with their incessant desire to dance, picnic (*merienda*), and ride from one presidio and ranch to the next and then again to the next, took from the coast valleys at least all suggestion of a day, not forty years before, when the Indians ruled the land. Packet-boats brought mantillas and satins and embroidered shawls from Mexico, silks for rebozos (a simpler substitute for the mantilla) fans, laces for the ruffles of the men, fine linen, high combs, gold chains, and books for a few.

The population of Alta California in 1806 was about twenty-seven thousand, of which a little over two thousand were whites. The *gente de razon* consisted not only of the immediate military society and the official members of the pueblos, but of the rapidly increasing descendants of the first officers and a few soldiers and settlers, the most enterprising of whom had managed to obtain ranchos in spite of the opposition of the padres. The women of the upper class when not bearing children (which they did commendably) had little to do but oversee their numerous Indian servants, dance, and enjoy the climate. Some of the leading families had large adobe houses, white, with

## THE SPANISH GOVERNORS—II

red tiles, many of them on long irregular streets leading from the presidio; the Indians were now too broken in spirit to be dangerous—save sporadically at long intervals —or had fled to the mountains. They lived in such state as was possible with the accompaniment of whitewashed walls and horsehair furniture; and these estimable women (about whom there seems never to have been a scandal) and such of their lords as did not gamble away their grants and patrimonies laid the foundation of one of the few real aristocracies in the United States. Their names will be given later when they enter California history through the door of politics.

Concha, when her fate sailed through the Golden Gate on that April morning, 1806, was only sixteen, but she was a Spanish girl, with the early maturity of her race and a mind and personality all her own. She was *La favorita* of her day, and many men sang at her grating.

Even during Arrillaga's first administration he had avowed much anxiety over the long strip of exposed coast and the dilapidated condition of the presidios. He put them in repair and caused a fort to be built near the presidio and overlooking the Golden Gate. This spot is still fortified, and we call it Fort Point. Borica followed up this good work with his usual ardor, for Spain went to war with France and believed herself to be threatened by England. He also had heavy artillery sent over from Mexico and installed at all the presidios and at Yerba Buena. The war-cloud blew away, but the Californians remained alert and were under orders from the central government to do no trading with foreign vessels, nor give them encouragement to remain in port.

Arrillaga, when made *Gobernador propietario*, was the

## CALIFORNIA

eighth of the Spanish governors. He found about four hundred men in the military establishments of the two Californias, which cost the government nearly a hundred thousand dollars a year. There were thirty-eight men regularly on duty at San Francisco, sixty-five at Monterey, sixty-one in Santa Barbara and San Diego respectively, and seventy-one in Loreto, Baja California. Don José Argüello was chief of all the forces in Alta California, a great man in his little way, and enjoying the full confidence of the powers in Mexico, although for some reason they never made him *Gobernador propietario* of the Californias. Little he recked that he was to emerge from the dry pages of history as the father of his Concha.

This brilliant Spanish girl not only had the fine dense black hair and flashing black eyes of the handsomest of her race, but the white skin so prized by the blooded of Castile, and cheeks as pink as the Castilian roses that grew about her grating. All chroniclers and travelers unite in praises of her beauty and vivacity, and there is no doubt that she was high above the common, this first of California's many beauties, whose sad but exalted fate has given her a place in history. It is related by the descendants of Don José de la Guerra, of Santa Barbara, in whose house she lived for several years, that in her dark days she wished to cut off her eyelashes, which attracted too much attention by their extraordinary length and softness, but was ordered by a sensible priest to do nothing so foolish as to deprive her eyes of the protection the good God had given them.

At the time of Rezánov's arrival in California her father was in command at Monterey, and his son, Don Luis Argüello, at the San Francisco presidio. Luis was a man

## THE SPANISH GOVERNORS—II

of no little independence and individuality himself, as we shall see later. Concha, as well as her mother and the younger children, appear to have remained as his guests.

Baron Nicolaï Petrovich de Rezánov, first Russian Ambassador to Japan, and circumnavigator of the globe, a chamberlain at court and privy councilor, chief partner in the great Golikov-Shelikov fur company of Russian America (Alaska), author of a charter that when signed by the Tsar Paul made his company as formidable as a modern trust, a man of great gifts and ambitions and enterprise, who had tired early of court life and become one of the most active business men of his time, had spent the winter of 1805–06 in New Archangel (Sitka), and learned at first hand the privations and sufferings of his company during those long arctic months when the storms were incessant and there was little or nothing to eat.

But he heard also of a California rich in soil and climate, and he made up his mind to visit its capital and establish relations with the colony, which would enable him to obtain a yearly supply of cereals and other nourishing foodstuffs for his faithful subjects. He bought a barque, the *Juno*, from a Yankee skipper, and its cargo of merchandise; for he wanted immediate as well as future relief, and knew that it would be useless to go to California empty-handed. And then he set sail to play a part that never crossed even his ardent imagination. He was forty-two at this time. In his youth he had married a daughter of the merchant Shelikov, but she had died soon afterward. His mind was crowded with ambitions, duties, and business; his thoughts turned seldom these days to women.

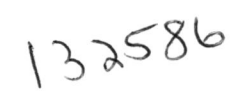

# CALIFORNIA

It was in the month of April, 1806, just one hundred years and six days before the earthquake and fire of 1906, which might have devoured a Russian city had this great practical dreamer lived a few years longer, that Rezánov sailed through the Golden Gate and into that romance which alone was to keep his name alive. He was a remarkably handsome man, both in stature and the bold outline of his rather cold and haughty face, towering above the Californians, and always wearing one or other of the superb uniforms of his rank and time. It is no wonder that there was a face at every grille on the day of his arrival, and a Castilian rose above every little ear at the ball that night.

He was received with anxious hospitality by Luis Argüello. Rezánov was a menacing figure, but his credentials were in order. That night a ball was given to him and to his officers and guests, and Rezánov devoted himself to the beautiful sister of the comandante. It was a long while since the Russian had seen female beauty of any sort; and, although he probably never had talked to so young a girl before, Concha was not as other girls, and attracted him as much by her dignity and vivacious intelligence as by her exceptional beauty. That she should lose her heart to this superb and distinguished stranger, the first man of the great world she had ever met, was inevitable.

Whether Rezánov would have permitted his heart to act independently of his cool and calculating brain, had he been able to accomplish his object and sail away in a few days, no man can tell. But he met with unexpected obstacles. It was against the law of the country to trade with foreign vessels, and it was not until after the

# THE SPANISH GOVERNORS—II

arrival of Governor Arrillaga (Rezánov was not permitted to go to Monterey) and Don José Argüello and long pow-wows with the subtle missionaries of Dolores (whose interest Rezánov had enlisted with diplomatic presents from his cargo) that they arrived at a compromise. There must be no trading, but Rezánov could sell his cargo, and with the California money immediately buy a hold-full of foodstuffs. So would the loyal governor's conscience (and possibly his official head) be saved.

Meanwhile six weeks passed. Rezánov saw Concha daily. He permitted himself to fall in love, having made up his ambitious mind that an alliance between Russian America and New Spain would be of the greatest possible advantage, not only to his starving company, but to the empire itself. He would take up his residence in California; little by little, and then more and more frequently, he would welcome colonists from his own frozen land. These, propagating rapidly in the hospitable climate of California, would soon outnumber the Spanish (he heard of the type of colonists induced to emigrate from Mexico); if necessary, sudden hordes would descend from the north at the propitious moment and snatch the province from New Spain, whose navy was contemptible and whose capital was too many arid leagues away to offer successful resistance by land. Nor was it California alone that Rezánov desired for Russia, but the entire Pacific coast north of San Diego and as far inland as he should find it worth while to penetrate.

There was a terrific excitement at the presidio when he asked Don José for the hand of his daughter. In spite of his personal popularity all her family, save Luis and Santiago, and even the priests, opposed the marriage;

being of the Greek Church, he was a heretic, and not for him was a Catholic maiden, particularly the daughter of *el santo*, loyal subject of king and Church.

But it was his personal quality, as well as his offer to go himself to Rome for a dispensation and to Madrid for the king's permission, that finally broke down their resistance. They even went so far as to permit a formal betrothal to take place; and late in May Rezánov reluctantly set sail to obtain not only the consent of the pope and king, but of his own sovereign to the marriage, which he now desired with heart as well as mind. Opposition, the fear that after all he might not win this girl, had completed the conquest of that imperious mind and ardent heart. And as bitterly as Concha did he resent the two years that must elapse until his return. Even communication might be impossible.

He sailed out of the Golden Gate filled with visions not only of a real happiness, despite his sadness and resentment, but of a magnificent gift to his country, a vast territory over which he as viceroy should rule with a power as absolute as the Tsar's in Russia. He saw the hills of San Francisco white with the marble of palaces and gay with bazars, flashing with the golden roofs and crosses that had made the fame of Moscow—cupolas, spires, lofty towers with bulbous domes! And about this wonderful bay, which he had had the wit to appreciate at a glance, a line of bristling forts, villas between, painted with the bright colors of Italy, and set in gardens sweet with Castilian roses. He was a great and practical dreamer, as the historians of his country testified after his untimely death; but the Fates were on the side of the Americans, as usual, and they had willed that

## THE SPANISH GOVERNORS—II

in the history of California his name was to shine not as a conqueror, but as a lover.

His health had been broken in Japan, where he had been a virtual prisoner on his ship for six months; and there had been no chance to recuperate during that terrible winter in New Archangel, where, like his employees, he had often gone hungry. Perhaps if he had set out upon his long overland journey immediately upon his arrival at New Archangel, while the weather was comparatively mild, he might have survived. But there he lingered to strike a blow at Japan, and it was October before he began that journey of four months and many thousands of all but impassable miles; with never a comfort and with the most hideous privations; drenched often to the skin; the infrequent boat alternating thousands of miles on horseback.

After lying several times in wayside inns with fever, he succumbed at Krasnoiarsk, in March, 1807, and all the fine fabric of his dreams, and the earthly happiness of Concha Argüello, lie under that altar-shaped stone in the cemetery of the little Siberian town.

Concha waited until definite news of his death came by the slow way of schooners from the north, and then left the world for ever and devoted her life to the care of the sick and the teaching of the poor; although at one time she had a school in Monterey for the daughters of the aristocracy. There was no convent to enter for many years, but she wore the gray habit of a "*Beata.*" When Bishop Alemany, of the Dominican order, came to California he saw at once to the building of a convent in Monterey, and Concha was not only its first nun, but Mother Superior. Another convent was built some years

# CALIFORNIA

later in Benicia, and she died there at the age of sixty. Practically all of the women of California's *gente de razon*, who have died of old age during the past twenty years, were educated by her, and, after the convent moved to Benicia, the daughters of several Americans.

Her life until she became a nun had some variety. She accompanied her father to Baja California, in 1814, when he was appointed *Gobernador propietario* of that territory, now dissevered from Alta California, and she was in Mexico when her mother died. After that she returned to the north and was a guest at "Casa Grande," the home of the De la Guerras in Santa Barbara, not mingling with the family, but doing her part unostentatiously among the poor until able to take orders.

Arrillaga was an active man of no particular ability, and far more friendly toward the missionaries than toward the Indians, who in spite of the worm-like state to which they had been reduced sometimes turned and bit like scorpions. Occasionally they murdered a priest more than commonly hated, and more than once they plotted uprisings. But there was no uprising during Arrillaga's times; and if severe. he authorized no executions of Indian delinquents.

He had none of Borica's antipathy to *aguardiente* and gambling, although a temperate man himself, and the pueblos of San José and Los Angeles, even while increasing in size, became a scandal for dissipation and idleness once more, while the pretentious Branciforte withered away. But several notable events occurred during Arrillaga's administration besides the romance of Rezánov and Concha Argüello. That great adventurer's colossal schemes died with him; but Baránhov, manager of his

## THE SPANISH GOVERNORS—II

company and governor of Russian America, a man of great ability, was fired by Rezánov's report of the fertility of California and the immense number of otters and seals the Russians had seen in the bay and along the coast. When news of Rezánov's death came he sent a copy of his report to St. Petersburg, and Russia at once entered into negotiations with Spain for permission to establish a colony on the northern coast of California "for the sole purpose of hunting the fur-bearing animals and curing their skins." These negotiations were brought to a satisfactory conclusion in 1811, and early in the following year Baránhov sent M. de Koskov with a hundred Russians and a hundred Kodiak Indians to Bodega, where they established themselves and began their hunting and curing. They brought with them sealskin canoes called *cayukas*, or *baidarkas*, with which they explored the coasts and islands of both arms of the Bay of San Francisco, and all its coves and creeks and sloughs and marshes. The Californians never did get used to them, and, although there were no conflicts, there were many uneasy reports from the successive governors to the Viceroy of New Spain.

There were weeks when they killed seven or eight hundred otters in the Bay of San Francisco alone. As the skins were worth from eighty to a hundred dollars apiece the profits were enormous. They also framed and succeeded in forcing trade relations with the Californians. Before long they built Fort Ross on the cliffs of Sonoma, a square inclosure with round bastions, ramparts, a Greek chapel, magnificently furnished, and a substantial log houses for the governor and his staff. It is a beautiful and lonely spot, and much romance is connected with

## CALIFORNIA

it. The hills rise abruptly behind to a dense forest of redwoods, and the gray Pacific rolls its big heavy waves to the foot of the cliffs, a viscid-looking mass which seems to drop with its own weight. In a little cemetery high on one of the hills and just below the forest are buried those that died during the Russian occupation; they are in copper coffins, it is said, for the Russians built ships here, among other things. One of the dead was a beautiful guest of the last governor, M. de Rotschev, and his wife Princess Hélène. One day she discovered that her lover, whom she believed to be in Siberia, was in the "town," the collection of huts beyond the fort and occupied by the laborers of the company. That night she met him in a mill, also without the inclosure, and they agreed to flee, and throw themselves on the mercy of the comandante of the presidio of San Francisco. The miller's son, whom she had never seen but who had stared often at her, followed her into the mill, overheard the conversation, and set the machinery revolving. It caught the girl's hair, and she was whirled upward and crushed to death. Her lover flung himself over the cliffs. Other convicts ran away now and again, carefully avoiding the Mission San Francisco Solano (Sonoma), where Vallejo reigned like a king and was friendly with the Russians (this, of course, is anticipating). When they were caught and brought back they were beheaded at the foot of the cliffs or put on a vessel, which stood out some distance, and then made to walk the plank. There is a tradition at Fort Ross that on windy nights you can hear the shrieks of the Russian girl in the mill, and moans of convicts in the process of decapitation; but, although I once spent three months in that

# THE SPANISH GOVERNORS—II

romantic spot, I am free to say that I heard nothing. The Russians remained until 1842, in spite of many alarms and protests, and then they went of their own accord. The fur-bearing animals were exhausted.

Meanwhile the missionaries indulged in much contraband trade of otter and seal skins with Boston skippers, and often under the very nose of Arrillaga, who was violently opposed not only to trade of any sort with foreigners, but to the mere visits of navigators or travelers. He had all the narrow suspicion of his time and race, and none of the brains and genuine ability that distinguished such men as Neve and Borica, to say nothing of the Argüellos. He was the more nervous as alarming reports came from Mexico, which was preparing to throw off the yoke of Spain.

It was during Arrillaga's administration that the first severe earthquake of the historic period occurred in California. The walls of the presidio of San Francisco, which were of adobe many feet thick and reinforced with the solid trunks of trees, were thrown down, and many of the buildings. The mission over in the valley suffered less, but great damage was done in the south.

Arrillaga died in 1814, and José Argüello was *Gobernador interino* until Don Vicente de Sola, the last of the Spanish governors, arrived in the following year. Mexico was then in arms against Spain; and, as the revolution was unpopular in California, Sola, as the representative of the crown, was received in Monterey with unusual ceremony and rejoicing. Priests, acolytes, distinguished subjects, and all officers that could obtain leave of absence came from the other presidios to take part in the ceremonies. The pillars of the "corridor" surrounding the plaza of the presidio were decorated with festoons of evergreens from the woods on the hill and hung with many lamps—little pots containing suet and a wick. At dark there was a social function in the presidio; and the guests, men and women, old and young, romped in the courtyard or along the corridor, strummed the guitar, danced and sang; it is not to be imagined that there was much conversation in those days. The capital held itself appreciably above the other settlements until American occupation, and it had already become the fashion among the women to wear only white at night, while the men wore dove color, silver buckles, white silk stockings, and much fine linen and lace. Let the cruder communities flaunt the cruder colors, but Monterey prided itself upon its elegant simplicity.

The next morning high mass was celebrated in the church of the presidio. The padres wore their sacerdotal vestments, and there was a choir of forty Indians, all dressed in gay colors and making music on viols, violins, flutes, and drums. They accompanied the chants of the priests in perfect tempo. The troops, both cavalry and artillery, were drawn up in front of the church, which was crowded with the *gente de razon* of the presidios and ranchos; those that could not find entrance knelt in the plaza and on the corridors. When the governor and his staff left the gubernatorial mansion and, crossing the plaza, marched into the church, the Te Deum Ladaumus was assisted by salvos of musketry and cannon.

The cavalry were drawn up immediately before the entrance. They wore their sleeveless bullet-proof *cueras*, or jackets of buckskin, trousers of dark cloth, low-crowned hats fastened with yellow straps under the chin,

# THE SPANISH GOVERNORS—II

rough shields on their left arms made from bull-hides, and lances in their right hands. They, too, knelt during the *gran funcion*, but sprang to their mettlesome steeds the moment it was over and stood at attention while the governor, followed by a gorgeous procession of padres, marched to the flagstaff in the center of the plaza and saluted the royal colors of Spain. The loyal demonstration from men and women and muskets and cannon that followed this simple act on the part of the governor could be heard at the ruins of Branciforte on the opposite side of the bay.

A magnificent banquet had been prepared by the ladies of the presidio of which all guests were invited to partake. A troop of young girls, three of whose names have come down to us—Magdalena Vallejo, Magdalena Estudillo, and Josefina Estrada, big names in the future history of Old California—led the governor to it. It was a day festa, and the young and slim wore skirts of fine muslin covered with gilt spangles, and colored jackets, and slippers with high wooden heels that clacked as they danced. Their hair was gathered in a net at the base of the head or held high with a tall comb, and all wore a string of Baja California pearls.

The ceremonies, religious, military, and social, lasted for days, both at mission and presidio, and then the governor settled down to work. He was the tenth and last Spanish governor of the Californias, and his rule was short. He came in 1815. In 1821 the revolution was successful, and Iturbide Augustin I. ascended the throne to reign briefly as emperor of the new and sovereign empire of Mexico.

# V

### THE MEXICAN GOVERNORS—I

Luis Argüello is known informally as the first Mexican governor of California, although he never was made *Gobernador propietario;* possibly because he had too much individuality and independence to suit either the Church or the powers in Mexico.

The reign of Iturbide was brief. He was compelled to abdicate in 1823, and, shortly afterward, the republic was proclaimed. Meanwhile, Sola had been elected a deputy to the Imperial Congress, and Luis Argüello became *Gobernador interino.* The Californians liked neither the empire nor the republic, but they were far from the seat of trouble; they were an indolent race, and their resentment soon expired in philosophy.

Luis Argüello was far more active and enterprising than most of his countrymen; he belongs to that small band of exceptions in the history of Old California that deserved to have been planted on one of the higher terraces of civilization. He thought for himself; was never dissipated until misfortune and bitterness overwhelmed him, and was devoted to the military service.

The presidio of San Francisco, of which he was co-mandante during the administration of Sola, was in one of its most acute stages of disrepair. Monterey was more than forty leagues away, and the governor much concerned over prowling ships and pirates in the south. Luis made up his mind to put his presidio in order without waiting for the slow permission that might or might not come from the capital. There happened to be an English carpenter in the country, and he ordered him to construct a launch. While it was building he sent soldiers by land to Corte Madeira, a point only twelve miles up the bay, but nearly two hundred by land, with orders to cut down a number of redwood-trees. When the launch was built he taught his peaceful soldiers how to sail it, and finally he set out with them across that bay so beautiful to the eye, but full of strong and treacherous currents, and subject to sudden squalls. The elements played him every trick, the boat was nearly swamped, the soldiers refused to do aught but pray. But Argüello kept his head, sailed the boat to safety, and towed back his timber. This feat he performed several times, until there were enough logs to repair the presidio. But his energies were abruptly checked by an infuriated governor. To this old disciplinarian, the most obedient of servants himself, it was unthinkable that any soldier should presume to act without the consent of his superior; while to build a launch in these times of trouble and revolt stank of high treason. He sent a guard to San Francisco to seize the launch and bring it to Monterey, and ordered the young comandante to the capital forthwith.

Luis was too good a disciplinarian himself not to obey orders without question, and he set out for Monterey on horseback, covering, with relays, fifteen miles an hour. A dashing soldier, a reckless rider, a gay and handsome caballero, haughty, amiable, independent, but always eager to serve his country, and withal an honest gentleman, Luis Argüello is by far the most interesting man in Old California history until Alvarado comes upon the scene many years later.

Barely stopping to rest, and injuring his leg from the stumbling of his horse, he arrived in Monterey, dusty, weary, and in much pain, but indomitable as ever. It was early morning; but, knowing the old man's impatient temper, he hurried to the gubernatorial mansion, discarded his stick at the door, and, supporting himself on his naked sword, entered the presence. The governor, who was drinking his morning chocolate, scowled at the uncourtly figure, and without asking him to sit down growled out a demand for an explanation of his abominable breach of discipline.

"It is plain to all," said Luis, "that I and my officers and our families are living in decaying hovels. Why should I waste time supplicating the royal treasury? I was quite capable of attending to the matter myself—as I have proved—without adding to your excellency's burdens."

The governor, who was always irascible in the morning, gave a roar of rage at this offhand reply, and seized the staff with which he so often administered chastisement, not only to peons and soldiers, but to the officers and quaking members of the gubernatorial family. But Luis, instead of bowing to the storm, lifted his haughty crest and put himself in an attitude of defense. It was then that the governor caught sight of the naked sword.

"What—what does that mean?" His excellency could hardly articulate. He paused in his onslaught, pointing to the sword.

"It means," replied Luis, coolly, "first, that I have in-

# THE MEXICAN GOVERNORS—I

jured my leg, and when I am tired of standing in one position I find it necessary to change to another; and second, that, being a soldier and a man of honor, I do not purpose that you or any other man shall beat me."

For the moment Sola was too stunned to reply. No one had ever thought of resisting him before, and seldom a day passed that he did not use his cane. He stared at Argüello but a moment, however, before he flung his stick across the room and advanced with outstretched hands.

"This," said he, "is the bearing of a soldier and a man of honor. I solicit your friendship. Blows are only for the pusillanimous scamps that deserve them."

Luis was quick to respond. The two shook hands, and, for aught we know, kissed each other on either cheek, then sat down to chocolate. Sola, paying a visit to San Francisco a few days later, admitted that Luis had been justified in making his repairs in his own way, but he liked the launch so well that he never returned it.

It was shortly after Rezánov's visit that Luis had been able to marry Rafaella Sal, a red-haired, gray-eyed girl, to whom he had been engaged for six interminable years. So important a subject as the son of José Argüello could not marry without royal consent, and that was long in coming. It is hard to realize in these days of steam and steel and speed that a hundred years ago California was almost as remote from the centers of civilization as had she been on the satellite, and communication as slow. But he married his Rafaella at last; only to lose her a year or two later. Time closed the wound, and in 1822 he wished to marry Doña Maria Soledad Ortega, of the Rancho del Refugia on the Santa Barbara channel.

# CALIFORNIA

That was during Iturbide's brief reign, and the City of Mexico was closer than Madrid. Sola, now his ardent friend, bestirred himself, and the permission arrived within a few months. There was a great wedding at the Rancho del Refugio. It faced a roadstead, and Luis came down by sea, as well as the guests from San Francisco and Monterey. Those from the ranchos came on horseback, the caballero often holding his doña before him; the older people in *carretas*, the wagon of the country—low, springless, made from solid sections of large trees, and drawn by bullocks.

For months before a hundred Indian girls had drawn the fine threads of *deshilados* for undergarments and bedspreads, fashioned silks and satins into gowns, while twelve of the girl friends of Doña Maria embroidered the flowers of the country on white, particularly the red-gold poppy, which had been named not long since for the good Dr. Eschscholz. This scientist had visited California in 1816 on the *Rurik*, when Otto von Kotzbue brought the first confirmation of Rezánov's death. How the girls, their needles flying, or sitting up half the night, serenaded and sleepless, talked with bated breath of that romantic tragedy and wondered what their own fates would be! There were Carillos and Oreñas, more Ortegas, De la Guerras, Estudillos, Vallejos, Alvarados, Castros, Picos, Estradas in that gay party, and those that could not be entertained even six in a bed in the great adobe ranchhouse met them at the Santa Barbara Mission, where the wedding was held; then rode over for the days and nights of festivity, when beds, so far as we can make out, were mere encumbrances.

Luis had sent to the City of Mexico for the *donas* of the

# THE MEXICAN GOVERNORS—I

bridegroom: mantillas black and white, silk stockings, fans, lace flounces, Roman sashes, pearls from Baja California, high combs bound with gold, a rosary of amethyst beads, a necklace of topaz, and, the fine flower of the wedding-gift which, if forgotten, would have cost the bridegroom his bride, six *camisas*, fine as cobweb, embroidered, *deshiladoed*, trimmed with precious lace. The bride's wedding-dress was made with a long pointed bodice and full flowing skirt, and a mantilla half hid her face and flowed almost to the hem of her gown. Luis wore his bravest uniform. It was the first great wedding that had taken place in California, and the priests of Santa Barbara celebrated it with all the pomp and ceremony of the Church. The older people vowed that it was worthy of a governor's wedding in the cathedral of the City of Mexico, but the younger were impressed only by the prospect of three days and nights of dancing.

When the festivities were over Luis and his bride set sail for San Francisco in the packet-boat that awaited them in the roadstead; and they were as glad and happy as they deserved to be, when at last they were in the quiet presidio, sheltered by its fogs and serenaded by the seals and the sea. Both are quieter to-day in the churchyard of Dolores, but for a while life seems to have smiled upon them. When they were tired of the gray peninsula they could go down to their ranch in the San Mateo Valley, El Pilar (sometimes known as Las Pulgas!), and bask in the sun or wander in the most beautiful woods in California; and while Luis was *Gobernador interino* they lived in Monterey.

Argüello had none of that petty jealousy of foreigners which closed the doors for so many years to legitimate trade with the outer world. William E. P. Hartnell, an English merchant from Lima, Peru, was the first foreigner to become a permanent resident of California and establish himself in business. This was in 1822, during Argüello's administration, and he found no difficulty in opening negotiations with the prefect of the missions for the purchase of hides and other native products. He married a daughter of Don José de la Guerra y Noriega in 1825 and became naturalized in 1830. It was during Argüello's administration also that another Englishman arrived who was to marry and settle in the country, William A. Richardson (some accounts say that he was a runaway sailor); and, shortly afterward, Capt. John Rogers Cooper, from Boston, who asked and received permission to trade, although the old law was still in force. But Argüello thought for himself, after his habit, remarking that "necessity was higher than law." Necessities, indeed, came more and more rarely from that hotbed, Mexico, and luxuries not at all. The priests as well as the ranchers were clamoring; and Hartnell and Cooper, who had a hold-full of merchandise, obtained their own terms as well as the hospitality of the country. This was the formal inauguration of trade in California.

Luis also purchased Captain Cooper's schooner and sent it under his command to China, laden with otter-skins. Cooper disposed of them for a large sum which enabled the governor to pay the arrears of his officers and soldiers (also overlooked by Mexico) and to repay half of twenty thousand dollars he had borrowed of the missionaries. For all of these transactions he made himself personally responsible.

But his liberal views were not confined to business.

# THE MEXICAN GOVERNORS—I

His foreign friends introduced the waltz, which promptly went to both head and feet of the entire department. The young folks danced every night at the presidios, pueblos, and ranchos. They discarded the dances of the country—*el son, el jota*, the *contradanza*—and whirled up and down corridor and *sala* like madcaps, while parents shuddered and priests thundered. Both might as fruitfully have ordered the sea to lie still. The waltz became faster and more furious. Finally the Bishop of Sonora was appealed to. He issued an edict threatening all with excommunication who waltzed either in private or public. The young people were thrown into a panic. They dreaded excommunication with all their pious souls, and with all their youth they resented being bereft of the most delicious excitement they had ever known in that isolated land.

Comandante José Maria Estudillo was giving a party in the presidio of Monterey on the night the edict was tacked to the door of the church. The governor and his young wife were present. No one could talk of anything but the edict; if they could not waltz they cared not to dance at all, these Californians that had danced out of their cradles. Finally some wide-awake spirit conceived the idea of asking the governor's advice.

Argüello shrugged his shoulders. "I am not a bishop nor an archbishop," he answered, "and have no jurisdiction over dancing. But if I knew how and felt like it I should waltz as much as I pleased."

The group about the governor cried "Brava!" The word flew round the room. In another moment the musicians were fiddling, and every young couple in the *sala* was whirling. The missionaries gave it up. Even

## CALIFORNIA

in those remote and unenlightened days public opinion and determined insubordination had their effect. They made no report to the Bishop of Sonora.

During his brief administration Luis did what he could to improve the lot of the mission Indians, who, as he wrote in his report to Mexico, were "poor and diseased, without medical attendance, and in a state of slavery." As Borica so often had done, he wrote warmly also on the subject of California's wasted fertilities, her vast valleys, her splendid forests, her "capacities of all kinds for becoming one of the richest and happiest countries in the world." But Mexico, although she finally sent money and supplies for the troops, took no heed of Argüello's prayer for commercial expansion and settlers.

Great Britain and the United States recognized the independence of Mexico. José Maria de Echeandia was appointed *Gobernador propietario* of the Californias (once more united), but did not arrive in San Diego until October, 1825, and meanwhile the Mazatlan troops, mainly composed of convicts and other bad characters, with which California had been inflicted during Mexico's period of unrest—to protect the coast—were withdrawn. These men had so misbehaved, taking night or day whatever they were sober enough to fancy, that Argüello had been driven to drastic measures. He had issued a proclamation to the effect that, owing to the leniency of his predecessors, crime had increased in the Department of California to a frightful extent, and that the usual punishments had no effect; he therefore ordered that every person guilty of stealing property of the value of two hundred reales or upward, or of burglary and housebreaking, should suffer death. Minor offenses would be

# THE MEXICAN GOVERNORS—I

punished with imprisonment and public flogging. Argüello was the kindest of men, but he was a strict disciplinarian and a keen student of his little world. This proclamation was conspicuously posted all over the department, and crime immediately lost its charms.

When Echeandia arrived Luis returned to the presidio of San Francisco as comandante. He died there March 27, 1830, aged forty-six. He lies under the tall pointed monument of the little church of the Mission Dolores, whose thousands of fertile acres have shrunken to a churchyard. After the earthquake of 1906 I went out to see what had happened to the "mission" and the monument of my friend Luis. Even the fire had spared Dolores, but the upper part of the monument had snapped off and the point flown into the wall. It was soon replaced, however, and the old cemetery, with its Spanish names, its periwinkles smothering the graves and crosses, and its Castilian roses, is once more a peaceful little oasis of the past. It looks singularly out of place.

Echeandia gave a cheerful attention to his duties; but, although the description has come down to us of a tall gaunt man constantly shivering with cold (for which reason he preferred San Diego to Monterey), and although he was the first to suggest that the missions be converted into pueblos and the Indians given ranchos of their own, and although he put down an Indian uprising with a firm hand, we see him as a man of little personality and no popularity.

Although secularization did not come in his time, his administration witnessed the curbing of clerical power; immense grants of land were made to distinguished subjects; Don José de la Guerra, of Santa Barbara, received grants from time to time until his acres numbered three hundred thousand. This really marked the downfall of the priests, who heretofore had claimed all the fertile valleys near the missions as their own, granting small ranchos to their favorites, and even these under protest. During this administration, also, foreigners received their first formal permission to marry and settle in the country provided they complied with the laws of the department. Other men of various nationalities, recognizing the possibilities of the country, were not long following Hartnell's example. California women seem to have married foreign men, and Americans in particular, whenever the opportunity was offered them; frugal, sensible, and virtuous, they no doubt recognized the inferiority of their own men as soon as they had a new standard of comparison.

With Echeandia had come from Mexico a young ensign of engineers, brave, handsome, and intelligent. His name was Romualdo Pacheco; and, although his life was brief, he was destined to found a family whose name lingered longest in the new California after the Americans had obliterated Arcadia. His son of the same name was prominent in the politics of the state, representing it in Congress, and successful in business; owing, no doubt, to the lady selected by his gallant young father.

Almost immediately upon his arrival in San Diego Pacheco met Doña Ramona Carillo, a woman of character and energy, although at that time little more than a handsome and clever girl, famous for a brilliant smile and uncommon vivacity. After her young husband's death she married a Scotchman, Capt. John Wilson, who brought up the little Romualdo without indulgence and gave his mind a practical instruction enjoyed by few

# THE MEXICAN GOVERNORS—I

Californians. For some years after the American occupation, however, he continued to practise the reckless hospitality of his race. A visitor brought a letter to the Wilsons and was invited to their great rancho, Cañada de los Osos, near San Luis Obispo. Romualdo took him to his room and, as he was about to leave the guest alone, wheeled and kicked aside a pile of saddle-bags in the corner, revealing a large sack. The neck was open; the sack was filled with "slugs" of gold, valued at about twenty dollars each. "Help yourself," said young Pacheco. "The house is yours. Burn it if you will." He had almost forgotten the sack was there.

But to return to 1825. Pacheco's comrade, Augustin Zamorano, became enamoured at the same time of Luisa, daughter of Santiago Argüello. Both the weddings took place simultaneously at San Diego, with all the gaiety and pomp of the time, and the two bridal trains, consisting of hundreds of relatives and friends of the brides, attired in their most brilliant plumage, mounted on splendid horses, accompanied the governor to Monterey. The long journey was enlivened with *meriendas* and dances and barbecues and feats of horsemanship, and every other festive antic which enabled the light-hearted Californians to forget that they were a stranded people on the edge of the world.

Don José de la Guerra had been commandante of Santa Barbara for many years, but he went, about this time, as a delegate to the Mexican congress, and Pacheco was appointed to fill the vacant post. He and his bride lived in the old military square of Santa Barbara (of which the adobe house built by Don José in 1826 is the only building of note remaining) until 1831. The superb valley is shut

# CALIFORNIA

in by a big and barren range of mountains which throw into bold relief the long white mission with its double towers and red tiles on the rising ground at its feet. There was also a white aqueduct in those days built by the padres, and the whole scene was full of color: the sky and sea, as always, of a deep hot blue, the green expanse between the mission and the presidio (also white, with red tiles on the low roofs) strewn with boulders, and here and there a tree; in the vicinity of the mission and presidio there were olive-groves shining like polished silver, and fruit of every color ripening under that golden relentless sun.

Echeandia was governor from 1825 until 1831. His successor, Manuel Victoria, remained in office ten months and nine days. No high official was ever more cordially hated or more quickly disposed of. Half Indian, cruel, ignorant, prejudiced, he was, altogether, a type of governor California never had been inflicted with during the authority of Spain. He gratified his hatred of aristocracy by exiling eminent citizens without reason, refused to call the territorial deputation which assisted the chief official in governing, and he gratified his lust of blood by enacting to the letter Luis Argüello's drastic law against criminals. In short, he threw the department into a ferment which quickly developed into a revolution. He was finally cornered with thirty soldiers under Pacheco, who believed it his duty to stand by his chief. Pacheco was shot through the heart. The soldiers, deprived of their captain, ran away. Victoria fled to the Mission of San Gabriel and delivered over the government to Echeandia, who had lingered in San Diego.

But Pio Pico, one of the most influential Californians

# THE MEXICAN GOVERNORS—I

of his day and the most eminent citizen of Los Angeles, high in politics and rich in acres, claimed the governorship *ad interim*, and Captain Zamorano started a counter revolution. In fact, from that time on the history of California until American occupation is concerned mainly with internal revolutions. As long as the kind but firm hand of Spain directed the destinies of its province it remained monarchical and submissive; but whether it was that the Californian had no respect for the governments set up in Mexico, or whether the spirit of revolution had entered his own blood, certain it was that pastoral lethargy was frequently enlivened by a restless desire to put almost any one in authority but the official who claimed the right. California also suddenly awakened to the fact that she had been oppressed by the missionaries, and began to demand secularization. This not only would be an act of poetic justice, but would divide tens of thousands of acres of the best lands for grazing and farming, between loyal subjects who would become rich and prosperous, and treat the miserable Indian with kindness.

Pio Pico, having wrested Alta California from the fuming Echeandia, expressed, as *Gobernador interino*, the public sentiment regarding the missionaries in a report to the City of Mexico:

> Such governors as have hitherto been sent to this country have been absolutely subject to the influence of the Spanish missionaries. These missionaries, unfortunately, owing to prepossessions in their favor and general fanaticism, acquired and enjoy a certain amount of acceptance among the larger portion of the population. This they have managed greatly to augment by means of the wealth of their territory, which they have administered to the prejudice of the wretched neophytes, who have been compelled to labor incessantly and without deriving any advantages whatever either to themselves or their children for their labor. Up to date, consequently, these un-

## CALIFORNIA

fortunates have remained in the same unhappy circumstances as at the beginning of the conquest, with the exception of a very few who have acquired some knowledge of their natural rights. But in general they have languished in oppression. They have been ground down with stripes inflicted with the purpose of suppressing in their minds the inborn tendency to seek relief from tyranny, in the liberty which manifests itself in republican ideas. During the entire history of the country the missionaries have never lost an opportunity of seducing the hearts of the governors and eradicating from their bosoms every sentiment of philanthropy in favor of the Indians.

The missionaries had obeyed that ancient instinct of the human heart to oppress the weak. Spain had invested them with great power, and it had gone to their heads. They had read history and seen something of the world: the strong ever waxed arrogant and ruthless, and the weak were born to submit. Now, alas, it was their turn!

From the moment the ball was set rolling toward secularization it never halted until the padres were first despoiled and then in many cases driven out. And never had the missions been so flourishing as when the ecclesiastics realized that their day was over. At the beginning of 1834 they reigned over thirty thousand neophytes, who tilled their fields (some of which yielded two crops a year), herded their flocks and cattle, and increased the value of those vast properties year by year. They owned, when the shadow of secularization rose, more than four hundred and twenty thousand cattle, sixty thousand horses, three hundred and twenty thousand sheep, goats, and hogs, and they realized annually thousands of bushels of maize, wheat, beans, and the like. In 1834 they slaughtered over a hundred thousand cattle for the sake of the hides, in such demand by the traders; and these, with the tallow, brought them for that year an income of over a million dollars. Every mission had its great orchard,

# THE MEXICAN GOVERNORS—I

vineyard, and beautiful gardens, although those of Dolores as well as San Francisco Solano (Sonoma) and San Rafael (two missions north of the bay which had been established in 1823 as barriers against the Russians) were less prolific than those farther south. Many were set in orange-groves, and few that were not shaded with the immense fig-trees that flourished in all the warmer valleys of California. It was not unlike the "terrestrial paradise" of Montalvo.

As soon as it became certain that secularization was inevitable the missionaries began a systematic work of destruction. Some sold what property they could dispose of favorably, and others uprooted their vineyards and ordered the slaughter of thousands of cattle, not only for the sake of the hides, but to leave as little to their despoilers as possible. At the Mission San Gabriel all were slaughtered. This mission was then the richest in the Department of California. It possessed over a hundred thousand cattle. They were struck down wherever they happened to be, the hides taken off, and the carcasses—strewn all over the beautiful valley and hillsides—left to rot. For years this region was white with skulls and skeletons; the new rancheros found them useful in the building of fences!

# VI

### THE MEXICAN GOVERNORS—II

An avowed object of secularization was to convert the missions into Indian pueblos surrounded by farms; in other words, to give the Indians the lands to which they were entitled by natural law. But it did not work. In the first place, the Indians had neither the intelligence nor the energy to cultivate even a small estate and make a living out of it; and in the second, they were still the weaker race. Numbers never have counted and never will count against superior brains and ruthless energies. The activities, mental and physical, of the Californians may have amused the Americans when they devoured them later, but they were infinitely superior to those of a race spawned by Nature while she was still an amateur in the game of life.

The conversion into pueblos proceeded slowly; these were ruled by white officials, and the Indian was tolerated according to the value of his services. San Juan Capistrano was the only exception; possibly as an experiment, or as a salve to the departmental conscience, the beautiful sculptured ruins of the mission—wrecked by the earthquake of 1812 and only partly rebuilt—was made into an Indian pueblo according to the original edict. Its career may be imagined.

Governor Figueroa, who arrived in California in time

to save it from another civil war, was half Aztec, and consequently in sympathy with the Indian; but his administration, owing to ill health, was brief. The impulse he gave to Yerba Buena will be described elsewhere. Barely had secularization been accomplished when he retired, and once more there was trouble.

He handed over the reins to José Castro, the first member of the territorial deputation, and a young officer of brilliant gifts, who was destined to play a part in California history. Castro, however, held the position of *Gobernador interino* for four months only. The central government ordered him to turn it over to Nicolas Gutierrez, who enjoyed the office for about the same length of time. In December, 1835, the Mexican government sent Col. Mariano Chico as *Gobernador propietario*, and the outsider proved himself to be as petty, tyrannical, and futile, as unjust and quarrelsome as Victoria had been. After three agitated months he was glad to escape fron the country with his life. The Californians had found themselves.

Gutierrez again assumed command, and a month later he also was taking passage for Mazatlan. A new sort of revolution had been accomplished under Juan Bautista Alvarado, the ablest man Old California produced. California pronounced itself a free and sovereign state. Alvarado was appointed governor, and he in turn appointed his uncle, Mariano Guadalupe Vallejo, that lord of the northern valleys whose home was in the mission pueblo, Sonoma, comandante of all the forces. The congressional deputation which heretofore had been called at the pleasure of the Mexican governor was turned into a constitutional congress, to meet at regular intervals; and, although the Roman Catholic religion was the only one recognized by the state, no man was to be molested on account of his religious opinions. This beneficent law was passed, no doubt, on behalf of the considerable number of foreigners now settled in the country, and who had become merchants or ranchers of importance.

Mexico, busy with irritations nearer home, ignored California; and the new state, barring the usual jealous explosion from Los Angeles (stronghold of the Picos, Carrillos, and Bandinis) went her way in peace and prosperity for several months.

The revolution had not been instigated by Alvarado, but, as the man whose abilities were now most conspicuous, he was pushed immediately to the front, forced to undertake its leadership, and upon its rapid and successful conclusion, as naturally made governor. But knowing that California was too weak to stand alone, he deftly wheeled it back to its old position under the Mexican flag, after having given the central government to understand that hereafter the department would choose its own governors and administer its own affairs. Meanwhile, he devoted himself assiduously to the reform of abuses and to bringing order out of the chaos caused by the rapid succession of governors. He rose with the dawn and worked far into the night with his secretary. His dream was to make California a model state; and if California had been wholly composed of Alvarados, Castros, Argüellos, De la Guerras, and Pachecos, and that pesthole, Los Angeles, had not existed, no doubt he would have succeeded.

But, although he had suppressed Los Angeles, which,

DON JOSÉ DE LA GUERRA

DON PABLO DE LA GUERRA

GEN. DON JOSÉ CASTRO

# THE MEXICAN GOVERNORS—II

since it emerged from pueblo swaddling-clothes, had longed to be the capital of California, it was for the moment only. He was suddenly dumfounded with the news that Carlos Antonio Carrillo had been appointed by the Mexican government to supplant him. Although he was the choice of all California, saving only Los Angeles, and the department now longed for peace and order, José Antonio Carrillo, late delegate to Mexico, had obtained the governmental ear, defamed Alvarado, exalted his brother, and claimed to speak for California.

Once more the north flew to arms. Alvarado, being above all things a patriot, high-minded and unselfish, would have yielded; but not so his compatriots. Not only were they determined that the wisest among them should rule, but no longer would they submit to the dictation of Mexico. Vallejo remained neutral until the issue should be plain. The army marched toward Los Angeles under José Castro. The south also flew to arms. Its general was Juan de Castañada.

Those internal "wars" were more to let off steam than anything else. Hot-headed as the Californians were, they were mortally afraid of hurting their opponents, possibly because they were all so closely knit by the marriage-tie. Generally it was the army that made the greatest display of force and noise that won, and so it was in this case. José Castro surprised Castañada at San Buenaventura and surrounded his army, demanding an unconditional surrender. When this was haughtily refused, Castro's men fired somewhere, certainly not into the enemy's ranks, whereupon the southern army ran away and Castro captured the leaders, including José Antonio Carrillo. When the northern general marched

# CALIFORNIA

proudly into Monterey with his quarry, Alvarado sent the prisoners to Sonoma. Vallejo had a reputation for extreme cruelty against the Indians, whom he had been sent out at various times to subdue. This may or may not be true, for General Vallejo had many enemies, like other rich men; but Alvarado is reported to have said, when he despatched the prisoners of war north to the stronghold at Sonoma, that if he sent these men to the devil they would not get their deserts, but they would if he sent them to Vallejo.

Vallejo was a man of many conflicting qualities; able, intellectual, the only man in the department besides Alvarado who in his youth had defied the priests and read extensively; reputed brave and cruel, but never backing Alvarado in his revolutions until convinced that success was assured; an admirable man of business until the gold-rush brought thousands of abler men to the country; haughty, arrogant, proud of his untainted Spanish blood, but withal a very fine gentleman and gallant soldier; if not one of the few great men of Old California, he was one of its pre-eminent figures. His treatment of the southern prisoners was all that Alvarado could wish, and that firm but amiable governor soon pardoned them and told them to go home and behave themselves.

Meanwhile, he sent an ambassador to the City of Mexico, Andres Castillero, the discoverer of the New Almaden quicksilver-mines near San José. This able man soon convinced the President of the Republic that it would be wiser to permit the ever-loyal Californians to choose their own governors. Simultaneously, Alta and Baja California, which had been separated once more,

## THE MEXICAN GOVERNORS—II

were reunited; and Alvarado became, without further opposition, *Gobernador propietario* of the Department of the Californias. Vallejo was *comandante militar*. Alvarado issued a proclamation ordering an electoral college to meet at Monterey in May, 1839, and returned to the work of governing wisely and peacefully and to the satisfaction of all concerned but Los Angeles. But, although his administration was comparatively serene, it was notable for many events of far more importance than bloodless revolutions.

When Alvarado became governor there were one hundred and forty-seven foreigners resident in Alta California, either naturalized or licensed, besides a number of vagabond hunters and trappers north of the Bay of San Francisco. The most distinguished of the new-comers were William E. P. Hartnell, merchant, trader, school-teacher, rancher, Visitador-general of Missions in 1839, linguist, translator, and interpreter; Thomas O. Larkin, United States Consul and resident of Monterey; Alfred Robinson, merchant, whose marriage to Doña Anita de la Guerra is so brilliantly described by Richard Henry Dana in *Two Years Before the Mast;* James Alexander Forbes, a Scotchman; Don Timeteo Murphy; David Spence; Capt. John Wilson, who married Doña Ramona Pacheco; Abel Sterns; Jacob P. Leese, a German-American, married to a sister of General Vallejo; and William A. Richardson, the first American resident of Yerba Buena.

During Alvarado's term of office there was a great influx of foreigners, the most notable of the Americans being W. D. M. Howard, who became a few years later one of the great merchants of San Francisco; and the most notable of all, John Augustus Sutter, born in the Grand Duchy of Baden (1803), a seeker of fortune in the United

## CALIFORNIA

States and the "Sandwich Islands" (H. I.) until 1839, when he made up his mind to try his luck in California. He arrived in the Bay of San Francisco in June, 1839, with a company of colonists, twelve men and two women. As he had no license, the authorities would not permit him to land; he therefore proceeded down the coast to Monterey and informed Alvarado that he wished to settle in California and found a colony.

Alvarado was fully alive to the dangers of too many foreigners in his isolated and ill-defended province, especially when they were of a low type. But he recognized in Sutter a man of uncommon ability and serious purpose, who intended to become a citizen of California and improve the conditions of that portion of the country where he should settle. Long conversations between the two men convinced Alvarado that Sutter was not only willing but able to keep the prowling vagabonds and restless Indians of the north in order; he gave him the license to enter and to settle on a fork of the Sacramento and American rivers, naturalization papers in the following year, a large grant of land, and appointed him a representative of the government on the "Sacramento River Frontier." This part of the country was infested with men of the lowest type, outlaws in their own country, that had wandered over the Sierras from the United States and Mexico, and by the more savage tribes of Indians; as there was now a considerable number of ranchers, both Californian and foreign, north of the Bay of San Francisco, it was necessary that these desperadoes should be turned back or reduced to submission by a strong hand in the north. Vallejo, it would seem, had not proved equal to this task.

# THE MEXICAN GOVERNORS—II

Sutter, who during the first year had built a fort and a house and outbuildings, all surrounded by a stockade, in that wild valley facing the Sierra, was authorized to arrest and punish thieves, robbers, and vagrants, and warn off hunters and trappers that were unlicensed; in short, while bearing in mind that the jurisdiction of the comandante at Sonoma extended even to the splendid domain, which Sutter called New Helvetia, and where he ruled like a feudal lord, he was to be the government's strong arm in the central north.

Sutter felt no hesitation in using the powers invested in him. As may be imagined, there was no love lost between him and Vallejo, who, although he may have lacked the personality and executive ability of Sutter, bedeviled him when he could, and let him understand at once that the troops of Sonoma would never be at his disposal to enforce the law. But Sutter was quite able to manage without his neighbor's assistance. He soon had a colony of three hundred Indians, whom he taught not only agriculture but the mechanical trades, and who became much attached to him. He established a primary school, built the natives comfortable huts, and altogether seems to have treated them with paternal kindness as long as they obeyed him blindly. When he was called upon by the ranchers to put down bands of horse-thieves he furnished his Indians with muskets, and they accomplished their purpose quite as effectively as the lazy Sonoma garrison would have done. In 1841 the Russians, having exhausted the fur-bearing animals, were ready to abandon Fort Ross and Bodega; and, although Vallejo claimed all their farms and other properties in the "sacred name of Mexico," Sutter quietly bought them out for thirty thousand dollars. Of course, he had no such sum in gold, but the property was turned over to him and the debt assumed by the government.

But, although Sutter was quite equal to the more disreputable of the adventurers, and, indeed, insured a certain degree of confidence among the residents of the north, the increasing stream of American immigrants, whose white prairie-wagons he could see from the roof of his fort through a spy-glass crawl down the long slopes of the Sierra, was quite another problem. These invaders were farmers and their families, some in search of productive soil, others merely itinerant and restless. The Americans in Texas had "unfurled the banner of rebellion" and won. The same danger might threaten California at any moment. Alvarado wrote to Mexico for a larger army; but, although the government was aware that the American newspapers were coveting California, it was unable to spare troops. The immigrants, who, in the course of a year or two, numbered several hundred, were advised of this and laughed at the proclamations of the governor and at Castro's display of military force. There was nothing to be done as long as the invaders obeyed the laws of the country. California was not strong enough to put them out, and persecution would have invited the wrath of the United States.

Alvarado fain would have kept California for Mexico, torn by civil wars, distracted by her losses, threatened on every side. He was too wise and clear-sighted not to have foreseen Mexico's ultimate fate, but he battled on, enforcing obedience to the laws of his department, and keeping the foreigners, save the few that enjoyed his confidence, out of politics. If his abilities had been recog-

# THE MEXICAN GOVERNORS—II

nized and he had been called to the City of Mexico, that turbulent nation might have told a different story for one generation at least.

Alvarado was a man of great dignity, coolness, resource, energy, and a born leader and administrator. Of fine commanding appearance, taller than the majority of his race, with black hair and eyes, regular features and the white skin of his Castilian ancestry, simple in his dress and reserved in manner, although courteous, he had been a notable figure in the province from boyhood, when he defied the priests and fed his ambitious mind on all the books he could find in the country or procure from Mexico. Beginning his public life at eighteen, he filled one office after another, indifferent to the dissipations of the young officers and rancheros, and winning more and more of the public confidence, until the time came to lead California both in war and peace. His ideal and model was Washington, and there is no question that if born to a wider sphere he would have achieved something more than a local fame. His most remarkable characteristic, considering his blood, was his self-restraint. His proclamations and state papers show nothing of the rhetorical bombast of his time and race; they are, indeed, models of style. He showed his independence at the age of fifteen by cutting off his flowing curls, and for many years was the only young Californian who did not wear his hair long and tied back with a ribbon. He was born in Monterey in 1809, and was therefore only twenty-seven when he became governor of the Californias. But even his enemies admitted that it would be impossible for a man of any age to make fewer mistakes than he did during the six years of his administration. In 1839 he married Doña Martina

# CALIFORNIA

Castro, of San Pablo. His mother was a Vallejo, which may have been the secret of his long patience with the unreliable general.

The other California families now active and prominent in the department were the De la Guerras, Carrillos, Peñas, Estradas, Osios, Gonzalez, Requenas, Jiménos (Ximénos), Del Valles, Martinez, Peraltas, Bandinis, Avilas, Picos, the Santiago Argüellos, and the Castros.

The greater number of these had immense ranchos, and did a yearly trading with the Boston skippers, exchanging hides and tallow for a hundred and one articles of merchandise—from fine silks and high-heeled slippers to carpenters' tools and pots and pans.

Don José Castro had a ranch at San Juan Bautista, but spent the greater part of his time in Monterey; his wife, Doña Modeste, a beautiful woman with black hair, white skin, and the green eyes so prized by the Spaniards, was California's leader of fashion until 1846. General Castro, who seems to have led all the California armies of his time into war, while Vallejo sneered in Sonoma and enjoyed the imposing title of *comandante militar*, was a gallant officer and a stern disciplinarian. He won his battles by superior tactics; and if a little given to grandiloquence in his proclamations, he was none the less quick, alert, and wary. Old California women who are now dead described him to me as a rather tall, dark, dignified man, very straight, with keen, flashing eyes, aquiline features, and beard worn *à la basca*, a narrow strip running from ear to upper lip. Vallejo wore his face hair in the same fashion for many years, but he had a large benevolent forehead and a fat chin. His expression was aloof and somewhat cynical, and his manner, while suave and courteous, did not inspire unbounded confidence. Sutter also had an immense forehead, caused by receding hair, a long fine nose, a mustache so heavy that his mouth is quite as well concealed in his pictures as a curtained window at night, and heavy eyebrows, under which twinkled large, deep-set, shrewd, but kindly eyes. He wore the sort of whiskers we now associate with stage butlers, and the underlip tuft with Napoleon III. In figure he was upright and authoritative, and his manners were as cultivated as his mind. He was an adventurer, no doubt, but an adventurer of the highest type. He did not come to California penniless, by any means; and if he induced Alvarado to give him a great domain he made good use of it, educated and drilled the Indians to better purpose than the missionaries had ever done, was a genuine and useful pioneer; and if he treated Alvarado with ingratitude, as we shall presently see, and made grave mistakes of judgment—for he fell short of being first-rate—he was on the whole loyal to the country he had adopted, not only under Mexican but American rule. The Americans, of course, gobbled him up, and the city of Sacramento now stands on the site of New Helvetia, although it has had the grace to preserve the fort.

Pio Pico, who is remembered chiefly because he was always agitating the question of moving the capital down to Los Angeles, and was the last Mexican governor of California, was short and very stout, with a snapping eye and a fat empurpled nose. He had brains and an extremely active mind, and lived to a great age; witnessing not only the passing of his own people, but of several generations of Americans. In his day Los Angeles was a beautiful little pueblo with a church of the mission period and a sleepy plaza. It was surrounded by ranchos that yielded abundantly wheat and fruits and hides, for it was on the edge of the rich San Gabriel Mission.

Don José de la Guerra y Noriega built his large adobe house (Casa Grande), which covers three sides of a court, in 1826, and moved into it from the presidio, where he so often had been comandante until politics claimed him. It was from this house that the great wedding took place described by Dana. Of his vast estate twenty-five thousand acres remain—the Rancho San Julian—the property of one of his granddaughters and her children. Casa Grande is in an almost perfect state of preservation, and occupied by two other daughters of his son, Don Pablo de la Guerra, who for several years after the American occupation played an important part in politics.

It was during Alvarado's administration that the establishment of Dolores, legally converted into the Pueblo San Francisco, was made the capital of the northern subdistrict, and the peninsula entered upon yet another phase of its history; although the site of modern San Francisco was still called Yerba Buena. The priests, shorn of their great estates, either returned to Mexico or clung to their mission churches and the crumbling rooms alongside; the *gente de razon* still attended mass. It was seldom that an Indian entered the doors of Dolores or any other mission, after secularization. They continued to live in their rancherias, unless they wandered off to the mountains or more interior valleys; but they relapsed into a deeper degradation, assisted by *aguardiente*, than had characterized them before they enjoyed the edifying example of the white man.

Alvarado's administration also was notable for the

CASA GRANDE, THE HOME OF THE DE LA GUERRAS

# THE MEXICAN GOVERNORS—II

first discovery of gold in California. In 1842 a ranchero named Francisco Lopez, living on Piru Creek about thirty-five miles west of Los Angeles, took his noonday siesta under a tree one day, and, as he awoke, absently played with a clump of wild onions. The roots were dislodged, and as the sleepy ranchero regarded his trophy his eyes opened wider and wider until he sat up quite straight. The roots were glittering with bright yellow particles, which, he made no doubt, were gold. He was not the man to keep a secret. There was a rudimentary gold-rush; and, although the news did not leave the state, about eight thousand dollars were panned out between the Santa Clara River and Mount San Bernardino. But its story was forgotten after 1848.

In 1842, Alvarado's health failing, he asked to be relieved; and Manuel Micheltorena was sent from Mexico as *Gobernador propietario*. Of course there was another war. This time, however, it was not only that several ambitious men wanted the position, but the entire department had just cause for complaint. Micheltorena arrived with an "army" three hundred and fifty strong (Mexico having decided that it was time to reinforce California), composed of the scourings of the prisons. Without a jacket or a pantaloon between them, and clad in tattered blankets, with manners and morals on a par with their appearance, this present from the Mexican stepmother was regarded by the proud Californians as a bitter insult.

To add fuel to the flame, Micheltorena halted at Los Angeles and announced that he should make it the capital of California during his administration. His reason was not inadequate. The United States, in the person of Commodore Thomas Ap Catesby Jones, had made a premature seizure of California, and occupied Monterey at that moment; being under the impression that Mexico and the United States were at war, and having, as he thought, raced a British squadron from Peru. Finding that the information upon which he had acted was in both cases false, or, at least, premature, he apologized on the day following his landing and elevation of the American flag on the custom-house (October 19th), and withdrew from Mexican waters. But California did not forgive a governor, particularly when commanding an "army" of his own, for not advancing at once upon the intruder. Micheltorena seems to have possessed a genius for doing the wrong thing. His next offense was an attempt to restore the mission lands to the Church, which, of course, would have meant the dislodgment of the now wealthy rancheros. He did restore twelve mission churches to the missionaries, and ordered the Indians to return to their old allegiance. But this was a mere farce and pleased no one. Then he turned his attention to reducing the salaries of high officials who had done little more than draw them, and the department reverberated. He attempted to accomplish something in the cause of education, but with little success, and he took certain active if futile measures to prepare California for the inevitable war with the United States. But he could win no favor from the Californians. His own offenses were supplemented by the abominations of the imported troops, who clothed themselves as they listed and fed from any larder that pleased them. No woman dared venture abroad, and if Los Angeles temporarily realized her ambition she payed dearly for the privilege, for she lost her popularity as a resort even in the south.

# THE MEXICAN GOVERNORS—II

Micheltorena arrived in 1842. The Californians stood him until November, 1844. Alvarado, although administrator of the custom-house at Monterey, spent the greater part of his time on his rancho, for he seems never to have recovered his health. However, he was called upon to head a revolution, and responded promptly. Vallejo being reluctant, as usual, the northern army marched south under the command of General Castro and of Alvarado himself. To their amazement, Sutter marched his forces to the support of Micheltorena; and, although he was bitterly repentant later on and tried to explain his conduct with the excuse that he had believed his allegiance to be due to his governor, he never regained his old prestige with the Californians.

Alvarado and Castro made short work of Micheltorena, his troops, and his allies. They ran him out in February, 1845.

Pio Pico succeeded him, becoming governor of the Californias in May, 1845. But during his administration events occurred too big with significance and results to be included in the account of any Mexican governor's administration. They marked the beginning of California's American era, and must be treated separately. Not even Alvarado's hand could have stayed them; and Pico, almost forgetting his morbid loyalty to Los Angeles, could only stalk about Monterey and fume, flee to Mexico, return and proclaim himself governor in a brave little attempt to defy the hated gringo, and finally subside. The superstitious may like to hear that he was not only the last Mexican governor of California, but the thirteenth.

## VII

### FRÉMONT AND THE BEAR-FLAG REVOLUTION

IN 1835 the United States offered to buy California from Mexico. The offer was rejected; Mexico knew that she had practically lost Texas, and had no desire to curtail her American possessions further.

The American colony in Texas was very large. In 1835, wearying of the tyrannies of Mexico, they declared their independence, and for nearly a year waged a sanguinary war with the Mexican troops sent to exterminate them. On April 21, 1836, the Texas-American forces under Sam Houston completely routed the enemy and took Santa Anna prisoner. The United States, in spite of its desire to expand westward, adroitly refused to annex Texas until its independence had been recognized by Mexico, having no excuse as yet to violate that elastic myth known as the faith of nations. Texas was told to go ahead and prove its power to stand alone and establish a government which the world would be compelled to recognize. Texas did the best she could; but, being constantly harassed by Mexico, she once more asked the boon of annexation in 1845. She had at least maintained her independence for eight years, and this time the United States was prepared to respond. No one could now accuse her of grabbing the greater part of another republic at the first excuse, but she had been impatiently awaiting

# THE BEAR-FLAG REVOLUTION

the right moment to become embroiled with Mexico and acquire California.

The United States cared little about Texas one way or another, and she might be working out her own destiny still had she not been useful as a cat's-paw. It was California that the government had its eye on, and underground wires had been humming for several years. The gold discovery of 1842 had attracted little attention, nor was the cupidity of the United States particularly excited by the letters of the American settlers—which frequently found their way into the newspapers—although the glowing accounts of soil and climate were responsible for many an emigrant train. It was the Bay of San Francisco that the government wanted and was determined to possess. At first, no doubt, the powers in Washington hoped that the American emigrants would solve the problem as they had done in Texas, and every means, subtle and open, was employed to encourage the farmers of states where nature had done little for soil and less for climate to take the long trip across plains and mountains to a land abundantly provided with milk and honey. Thousands rose to the bait, poured over the Sierras, and pitched their tents in the great Central Valley, to the dismay of Alvarado and Castro and the secret exultation of Vallejo and Sutter; who, if not so loyal, were the first to appreciate the advantage California would reap if delivered over to the enterprising American. That it would mean their own ruin never occurred to them. They believed that France had machinated, and that England hovered ready to pounce, and for reasons best known to themselves they preferred the neighbor next door. An Irish priest named McNamara dreamed of bringing two thousand Irish families to California, driving out the Spaniards and the Americans, and restoring the mission lands to the Church; although he talked of colonization only. Pio Pico favored this scheme, if only to spite the Americans. All knew that war between Mexico and the United States was inevitable.

Colonization is slow work. The policy of the United States has never been a bold aggressive one in regard to conquest. No country has ever been more certain of what she wants or more certain of getting it; but she refuses to grab, partly owing to an innate sense of justice, partly to a youthful taste for being patted on the back, and an equal distaste for criticism. In the beginning, no doubt, hers was the policy of a weak nation too wise to offend the great across the sea, but inherited Anglo-Saxon pharisaism may have had something to do with it. To-day it is a settled policy; and, although the United States has offered to buy and has bought, no one can deny that she can acquire more territory at less expenditure of blood and money than any nation in history. No one has ever been born as shrewd as a Yankee, nor as persistent, nor as fathomless, under his straightforward simple guile. If the United States ever falls into decay, after the fashion of certain European states, it will be because she has permitted the scourings of those states to swamp and exterminate the original Yankee.

And so it was in the early forties. Thomas O. Larkin, it is now known, drew, in addition to his pay as United States Consul to California, the sum of six dollars *per diem* for what in these crisp days would be termed "keeping on the job all the time." It was his duty to win the confidence of the leading Californians and inspire them with belief in the friendship of the United States

# THE BEAR-FLAG REVOLUTION

for this insulted and neglected department of Mexico; to animate them with a love of freedom, particularly under the protection of the United States flag; but if the idea of a change of flags alarmed them—for the Spaniards, too, have an adage combining the frying-pan and the fire—then he was to intrigue merely to separate them from Mexico and persuade them to cast themselves upon the protection and sympathy of a sister republic. Moreover, he was never to let them forget the wicked intentions of England and France, which had shown their hands so plainly by impertinent explorers, and squadrons at no great distance from Pacific shores.

The minds of the Californians being duly prepared, the United States, which also had a squadron in the Pacific, would, upon the outbreak of hostilities with Mexico, run up the flag in Monterey and San Francisco as a natural act of war, without opposition from the local authorities—it was hoped with their joyous consent. Larkin did his duty faithfully. He nursed along the leaders of thought and politics in the country he sincerely loved, planted American ideas in those bright but often empty brains, and even succeeded in quieting the apprehensions of all but a few regarding the long trains of emigrant wagons rolling like a thin cascade over the western flanks of the Sierras. All was going well, and the war-cloud was slowly rising on the horizon and taking such shape and form as would compel the United States to do the proper thing, when a young man upset Larkin's apple-cart as Jameson upset Cecil Rhodes's. His name was John Charles Frémont.

So completely forgotten is this remarkable man that it is difficult to realize that in the forties and fifties he

# CALIFORNIA

was the idol of the American boy, and was very close to being carried by a popular wave straight into the White House. "The Pathfinder" at the age of twenty-three had accompanied the French geographer Nicolett in his capacity of lieutenant of topographical engineers, to explore the northwestern prairies; and three years later was in sole command of an expedition to explore the South Pass of the Rocky Mountains, which opens the way to the Columbia River valley. Emigration was being encouraged not to California alone. The ostensible purpose of this and the two following expeditions was to mark out a suitable overland trail for emigrants and select the proper sites for forts; but Frémont seems to have received instructions from Benton, at least, never for a moment to lose sight of the principal object in spreading a net over the continent, which was to get the English out of Oregon and prevent them from getting into California. The immediate result of these expeditions was an enormous public interest in the West and desire for its ownership. Frémont's reports, published by the government and widely distributed, became the most popular literature of the day. Here were genuine hardships heroically endured, encounters with Indians in which real blood was spilled, harrowing adventures of every sort in which man's personal bravery and wit triumphed over Nature—and all told in a vivid and fascinating style. There can be little doubt that Frémont was selected for these expeditions as much for the manner in which he was able to portray the advantage of a region coveted by the United States, as for his talents as a pathfinder and his scientific attainments.

Everything was in Frémont's favor, not only to make

# THE BEAR-FLAG REVOLUTION

him a popular hero and current "best-seller," but to give him immortal fame. Born of a good family in Savannah, Georgia (January 21, 1813), at the time he first appeared upon the scene he was young, dashing, fearless, the born explorer and adventurer, and in appearance slender, admirably proportioned, and would have been handsome had he not cultivated a bushy beard and had not Nature presented him with a somewhat hard and staring eye. But youth and fame cover all defects, and for many years he was the most gallant and picturesque of America's heroes.

Upon his return to Washington after his expedition with Nicolett he made a friend of Senator Benton of Missouri, who had a bright and handsome daughter. With her he fell in love in his usual headlong fashion, and seems to have had little or no difficulty in rousing a like ardor in Miss Benton. The romantic young couple saw fit to elope, but were quickly forgiven, and then Benton and Frémont laid their heads together.

The government sent Frémont on the second expedition (1843), during which he reconnoitered Oregon and California. There was much uneasiness in Washington over England in Oregon. As a matter of fact, that astute nation when she lost California relinquished Oregon as not worth fighting about; but there was no doubt in the government's mind that she coveted the whole Pacific coast in the northern hemisphere. The time had come to strike, and the war-cloud was permitted to rise.

Polk became President of the United States in March, 1845, and he made no secret of his determination to acquire California. He would have purchased it, but this was recognized as impossible before Frémont started

# CALIFORNIA

upon his third expedition. Frémont claims that he had a secret understanding with the government to walk warily but to act at his own discretion. The Pacific squadron received orders to seize the ports of California as soon as war was declared; and, although no such definite instructions could be given to a young engineer in charge of a topographical expedition, there seems no reason to doubt that Frémont, encouraged by his father-in-law, with whom it was a ruling passion to acquire Oregon and California, and assisted also by his not inconsiderable faith in himself and his exalted destiny, believed in this silent commission from the government. He was not a model of discretion, but he was, all things considered, a necessary tool at the moment; and there is little doubt that the government fully intended to use him, and then applaud or repudiate him later, as circumstances might dictate.

In December, 1845, Frémont had crossed the Sierras and was for the second time a visitor at Sutter's Fort. Thence he rode down to Monterey to enlist the influence of the consul, Mr. Larkin, with the authorities, as he wished to bring his men to one of the settlements and replenish their ragged outfits, as well as to buy new saddles for the horses and lay in the necessary supplies for his "geographical expedition." Pico was away, but Larkin took him to call on General Castro, the prefect, the alcalde, and Alvarado. He informed these dignitaries that he was engaged in surveying the nearest route from the United States to the Pacific ocean, the object of the survey being geographical and in the interests of science and commerce. He made his usual good impression, and, the necessary permission being given, he sent for

# THE BEAR-FLAG REVOLUTION

both sections of his divided party and met them at a vacant rancho about thirteen miles south of San José. Here he remained until the 22d of February, purchasing horses and supplies and refitting his men.

Meanwhile Castro and Alvarado had been laying their heads together. They knew that Frémont was a son-in-law of the powerful Senator Benton, so deep in the confidence of the United States government; and he had a retinue of sixty men, a large number to the Californians, whose army rarely exceeded three or four hundred. Frémont had asserted that these men were, with the exception of the hunters and trappers, strictly scientific, and unarmed; but Castro had his doubts. Frémont also had had the imprudence to remark casually that ten thousand American colonists were prepared to emigrate to California and Oregon in the spring. What more likely than that this subtle gringo had come to consolidate the Americans already in the country and provoke an uprising? Better be rid of him at once.

It was no difficult matter to involve one of Frémont's men in a row with a Californian over a woman, and then protest that the California women were not safe when gringos were about. Castro wrote Frémont—who was now in the Salinas Valley—a peremptory order to leave the country immediately.

But Frémont had no intention of doing anything of the sort. It was too soon to give battle, for as yet there was no news of the outbreak of hostilities between Mexico and the United States; but he returned word by the messenger that he would not comply with an order that was an insult to his government. The next morning he moved his camp to the summit of Gavilan Peak; and his men,

# CALIFORNIA

who were jubilant at the idea of a possible fight, built a log fort and unfurled the American flag. From this eminence he could see the green Salinas Valley in all directions and San José in the distance. At his feet was the beautiful Mission San Juan Bautista, the residence of General Castro, and other buildings about the plaza. It may be imagined that the fort on Gavilan made a sensation. Every hour the rancheros rode into San Juan and tied their horses in the plaza and volubly discussed the audacity of a gringo of America, a nation incredibly young, insignificant, plebeian, but withal aggressive, to intrench himself and run up his ridiculous flag. Incidentally they hoped for battle.

But Frémont's designs were deep and well ordered. On the second day he saw a party of cavalry ascending Gavilan Peak and made ready to defend himself. Nothing would have pleased him better than an attack, for this would have been an act of aggression on the part of Mexico and directed against, not himself, but the American flag; and his men were all armed and experienced sharp-shooters. But the cavalry suddenly wheeled and rode down the mountain. Frémont waited another day and then reluctantly withdrew. It was evident that Castro also had no desire for the doubtful fame of precipitating war.

Frémont withdrew up the valley, and after a week at Sutter's Fort, where he bought more horses, he began to march toward Oregon, announcing publicly that he should return thence to the United States. He did not make any undue haste, however, and while he was camping on the shores of Klamath Lake he was overtaken by two men from Sutter's Fort and informed that Lieut. A. H.

JOHN A. SUTTER

JAMES W. MARSHALL

GEN. JOHN C. FRÉMONT

GEN. M. G. VALLEJO

# THE BEAR-FLAG REVOLUTION

Gillespie had arrived with despatches for him from the United States government and was under directions to find him, wherever he might be. He had trailed him for many weary leagues north of the fort, and was now in camp some forty-five miles south and surrounded by dangers from hostile Indians. "Then," says Frémont, "I knew that the hour had come!"

When Frémont was examined in 1847-48 before the Claims Committee in Washington he "protected" the United States with masterly evasions, but many years later, both in articles over his own name and in an interview with Josiah Royce, he asserted that the messages from headquarters—destroyed by Gillespie before entering Mexico—conveyed to him the authoritative information that the United States purposed to seize California, and that he was absolved from his duty as an explorer and left to perform his duty as an officer of the United States. As for Senator Benton's letters delivered by Gillespie, veiled as the language was, it was clear-cut to Frémont. "His letters," said he, "made me know distinctly that at last the time had come when England must not get a foothold; that we *must be first*. I was to *act*, discreetly but positively."

It must be borne in mind that Frémont was the only United States army officer in California at that time. Captain Montgomery, commanding the *Portsmouth*, was anchored off Yerba Buena, and Commodore Sloat had sent the *Cyane* and the *Levant* to Monterey. Sloat himself was hovering about Mazatlan awaiting definite news of war before sailing for California; but in all that vast and coveted territory Frémont alone represented the army of his country. If he felt a trifle important and disposed to act on his own initiative, who shall blame him? The trouble with Frémont was not so much that he thought too well of himself during this momentous chapter of his country's history, but that he was not so justified as certain other men have been in similar conditions.

The immediate result of that meeting in the northern wilderness, after the Indians had been disposed of, was that Frémont and his little company marched south and camped near the Marysville Buttes—a fine range of mountains rising abruptly out of the valley floor. Shortly afterward all the American ranchers north of the bay received an anonymous paper stating that two hundred and fifty Californians were on their way to the Sacramento Valley, destroying the crops, slaughtering the cattle, and burning the houses of the settlers. Men who valued their liberty were advised to go at once to the camp of Captain Frémont. A large number responded, and the captain informed them that, while he could not, as an officer of the United States army, commit any act that might be construed as a hostility by a nation which, so far as he knew, was still at peace with his own country, he could and would give them some friendly advice. The advice was as follows: They should elect ten or twelve of their number to harass the California troops; if possible they should secure the leaders and incarcerate them, thus possibly provoking the fiery Castro, already irritated almost beyond endurance with Frémont and Americans in general, to commit some overt act of hostility against the United States. It would also be advisable to have horses in readiness upon which to flee the country.

SONOMA MISSION

MISSION SAN JUAN BAUTISTA

# THE BEAR-FLAG REVOLUTION

The first act of the northern drama was the seizing of two hundred and fifty horses which Francisco d'Arce and fourteen vaqueros (the bugaboo army) were driving down to Castro's camp at Santa Clara. The American party, headed by one Ezekial Merritt, captured the horses, returned with the booty, and informed Frémont that he had told Arce to tell Castro that if he wanted his horses to come and get them. Then occured the Bear Flag episode, and whether Frémont suggested or encouraged it may never be known. Historians disagree; Ide—possibly out of personal vanity—says that it was his own idea, and Frémont himself indignantly repudiates it. However this may be, there is no doubt that it was he who despatched a force of settlers, again under Merritt, to Sonoma to take General Vallejo prisoner, although he remained himself in the background.

There were no soldiers in the Sonoma garrison at the time, as the troops were concentrated at Monterey and Los Angeles, Castro and Pio Pico being engaged in a furious controversy over the capital of the department, and both expecting to receive the news of war at any moment. Vallejo occupied a large house on one side of the square, and close by were the houses of Salvator Vallejo, Victor Prudon, and Jacob P. Leese. The barracks occupied another side of the plaza, and in the northeast corner was the mission church.

Just before sunrise of June 14th the Americans, having stolen into the pueblo at midnight, surrounded the house of General Vallejo; and Merritt, Dr. Semple, and William Knight rapped loudly on the front door. Vallejo, when invited to lead civil revolutions, may have declined through moral cowardice or cynicism, but there was

## CALIFORNIA

never any dispute over his physical bravery and his dignity as a soldier. He haughtily stuck his head out of a window and demanded to know who and what they were that they dared to disturb a personage of his importance at that hour of the night. While the trio were endeavoring to explain through Knight, who acted as interpreter, Salvator, Leese, and Prudon were escorted to Vallejo's "corridor" by an armed guard, and then Knight announced unequivocally that the Sonomans were prisoners. It was not necessary to mention Frémont's name. The Americans had real grievances and cause for uneasiness: General Castro had issued a proclamation ordering all Americans to become Mexicans at once or leave the country.

The dawn was breaking, and Vallejo saw that the plaza was filled with armed men. The California rancheros north of the bay were not within call, and they were far outnumbered by their American neighbors. He withdrew his head, dressed himself in his uniform, buckled on his sword, and then opened his doors and invited the three leaders to come in and have a glass of wine. The door closed and time passed.

It was very cold outside, as cold and gray as California dawns usually are. Those awaiting the return of the chiefs became first impatient and then alarmed. Could Messrs. Semple, Merritt, and Knight be poisoned? One of their number, John Grigsby, was elected to enter the house and return at once with a report. Grigsby entered without the formality of knocking; and he also did not return. More indignant, and still more alarmed, the victors laid their heads together and finally induced William Ide to venture within.

# THE BEAR-FLAG REVOLUTION

Ide knocked, but there was no response. He opened the door and found his way to the large dining-room. Merritt was lying half across the table among the empty glasses and bottles, asleep. Grigsby also slept. Knight's head was nodding on his chest. Semple, who seems to have carried his liquor better, was writing the formal articles of capitulation. Three of the prisoners were smoking and yawning. General Vallejo regarded his guests with some philosophy. They could take him prisoner, but he had made fools of them.

Ide went outside with the articles of capitulation and read them to the Americans. Over Spanish and American signatures was an agreement by the Californians to submit and to bear no arms, and an announcement that a government had been established on the principles of the Republic of the United States. Security of life and property was promised to the prisoners.

The next question was what to do with the illustrious quarry. Some were for marching them to Frémont's camp. Grigsby staggered out and demanded what were the orders of Frémont. Then it was that the Americans learned one from the other that the wily Frémont had given no orders, leaving all to the discretion of his wise and gallant countrymen. Grigsby fell into a drunken panic, vowed he had been deceived, and would run away. Semple ran him back into the house lest his panic be communicable; and there might, indeed, have been a general and ignominious stampede had not Ide, who, despite his absurdities, possessed some of the qualities of leadership, rallied them by crying out that rather than play the part of a coward he would remain alone. He sprang on a box and made a speech, reminded them of all the wrongs, real and imaginary, they had endured at the hands of the Californians, and darkly hinted of worse to come; then, having propped up those wilted spirits, he thundered that there was "nothing now but to see the thing through." "We must be revolutionists or suffer the fate of robbers and horse-thieves!" he cried; and this appealed to the true American spirit. They proclaimed Ide their leader, and the next step was to seize the fort. This act was committed against the will of Semple and the now comparatively sober Merritt and Grisgby, for seizing the fort meant the cannon and other ammunition in it as well as the treasury, and constituted an act of war. Their reasoning, in the light of their articles of capitulation, and seizure of the *comandante militar*, was somewhat obscure, but at all events they repudiated the new leader and rode off with their prisoners.

Ide was one of those vainglorious men who deceive themselves (and others for a time) with sounding phrases, refuse to recognize their itching desire for what they call fame, who are called idealists by their friends and asses by their critics, and who are quite certain of being animated by a mixture of patriotism, brotherly love, and Christianity. He had been a carpenter in Massachusetts, and was now a farmer, and father of a large brood in California; a long, lank, hairy person, who waved his arms and uttered many words.

His next speech was a ringing declaration of independence and a demand for a flag. Frémont had provided them with none, but there was an artist in the company, who claimed later to be a relative of Mrs. Abraham Lincoln. His name was Todd. He found a flour-sack, which he cut into the proper oblong shape. Then he

# THE BEAR-FLAG REVOLUTION

pressed into service a strip from the red-flannel shirt of another of that gallant band and sewed the red to the white. Then he found a pot of paint and in the northwest corner of the "flag" he painted a star, and not far away the counterfeit presentment of a bear (the Californians thought it was a pig) and the proud words "California Republic." The Mexican flag was hauled down and this

CALIFORNIA BEAR FLAG

work of art and patriotism given to the breeze. The Bear-flag Revolution entered history. The date was June 14, 1846.

Ide organized his forces, prohibited intoxicants, reassured the trembling native population (eighteen in all), promising them a liberty they never yet had enjoyed, but warning them to be his friends would they live to enjoy it. He frequently invoked the name of Washington while haranguing them. It was the only word of his dis-

# CALIFORNIA

course they understood, but they knew that the ablest man of their little world, Juan Bautista Alvarado, admired Washington; so they embraced the long ugly Yankee on both cheeks and promised to be his loyal subjects.

Frémont was growing restless. War had begun on May 13th; but, although he assumed that this must be the case, he had no information, and, full of military ardor as he was, had much difficulty to keep in the background. He moved his camp down to New Helvetia, and when the prisoners arrived consigned them to the fort. This act of hospitality must have enchanted both Sutter and Vallejo. Nor could Frémont hear of any act of reprisal on Castro's part. Finally on the 23d he received a letter from William Ford, of the Bear-flag party, begging him to come to Sonoma, as the Americans, who had now been reinforced and numbered one hundred and thirty, were despising Ide. He started at the head of seventy-two mounted riflemen, and when he reached Sonoma was informed that Capt. de la Torre, of the first division of Castro's army, was in command of the guerrilla forces north of the bay and harassing the American settlers. He ordered Ford to take command of sixty men and march on the enemy; he would go along with his seventy-two "to see the sport" and "explore the neighborhood of the bay." Ford, who seems to have made up in fervor what he lacked in practice, ran De la Torre so hard that the Californian, little used to real fighting, would have scampered back across the bay if Ford had not cornered him. So he resorted to strategy. Three prisoners were taken by the young American "general," and in their boots were letters betraying the fact that Castro was

# THE BEAR-FLAG REVOLUTION

marching on Sonoma. This ruse succeeded, and Frémont and Ford hastened back to Sonoma while De la Torre made good his retreat. The three unfortunate prisoners were shot as an act of vengeance for the death of two Americans; the famous scout, Kit Carson, who was in Frémont's train, boasting later that he was the executioner. Frémont turned about and pursued De la Torre as far as Sausalito, where he discovered that the Californian and his men had crossed the bay. He, too, borrowed a boat, and was rowed to Fort Point. The presidio was deserted. He spiked the fourteen guns and returned to Sonoma on July 1st.

But Castro had no intention of attacking Frémont. He realized that the Americans were too many and too determined for him, rumors of war were growing thicker every hour, and there were United States sloops of war in the San Francisco and Monterey harbors. He and Pico forgot their grievances and took counsel regarding armed resistance should the enemy appear in force. The Californians may have had quaint methods in battle, but there was never any question of their elaborate and warlike methods before the event.

Frémont was deeply mortified. He had fully expected that Castro would make an attempt to rescue Vallejo. He appeared to be side-tracked in Sonoma with these ridiculous Bear-flag warriors, for even Commodore Montgomery, who had furnished him with ammunition, while refusing Ide, had declined to follow and capture De la Torre. He could, however, publicly proclaim his lack of affiliation with the Bear-flag movement, dispose of the chief offenders, and prepare for another move. A number of naval officers had accompanied him back to

Sonoma, presumably to "see the fun." Frémont called a convention and stated explicitly before it that as an officer of the United States army he could not countenance such an act of aggression as the capture of Sonoma, nor could he interfere with politics or attack the government; but he did not consider it an act of war to pursue and capture Castro, who had insulted the government of the United States, and take him to Washington as a prisoner. He then invited the American settlers to enroll themselves under his banner, promising them protection and provisions from his commissariat, and pointing out that an undertaking of this sort, which, he hoped, would become a brilliant example to the oppressed throughout the world, must be led by capable and experienced officers. Ide protested, but was quickly overruled. These shrewd Americans, whatever may have been their secret opinion of Frémont's tactics, liked and admired him as much as they now despised Ide. With cheers they proclaimed him their chief and pronounced the Bear-flag revolution at an end. Frémont was to lead the American party in California to independence. Once more it looked as if Frémont would be able to provoke a battle and be the war's central figure in California; and if this had been the 5th of June, who knows what might have happened?

But it was the 5th of July. On the 2d Commodore Sloat, having heard that the Mexican troops had invaded Texas, entered the Bay of Monterey. On the 7th, although he had as yet received no confirmation of an engagement, he determined to land and run up the American flag on the custom-house. Not only was it imperative to get ahead of the British admiral, Sir George Seymour of the *Collingwood*, watching events at San Blas,

# THE BEAR-FLAG REVOLUTION

but he found the Californians in a state of war-like fury with Frémont, who for a time at least had the credit of forcing the war. Sloat believed that Frémont was acting under positive information and orders; in any case, he made up his mind that it was better to be sacrificed, if he had to be, "for doing too much than too little," landed his marines, hauled down the Mexican colors from the custom-house, and ran up the American flag. The *Collingwood* arrived on the 16th, and Sloat was prepared to give battle, if necessary. But Great Britain had no intention of going to war with the United States. She had lost the race and gracefully withdrew.

The next day the American flag was raised in Yerba Buena, and a day or two later at Sonoma and Sutter's Fort. Castro and Pio Pico were understood to be massing their forces in the south. Commodore Stockton arrived on the *Congress*, and on the 24th received full command, succeeding Sloat. Frémont by this time was in Monterey with his company, which consisted of about one hundred and sixty men. Stockton formed them into "The Battalion of California Volunteers," appointed Frémont major and Gillespie captain, and ordered them to San Diego by sea to engage the forces of Castro and Pico and complete the conquest of California; at last it was definitely known that the two countries were at war.

Gone was the dream of being received by California as a matter of course or with passionate gratitude. The Californians, although their army was not in sight, were known to be boiling with fury over the indignities in the north. To the possible war they had been indifferent, or to its outcome, but that bandaleros, horse-thieves, canaille, led by that arch-conspirator Frémont, should take

## CALIFORNIA

prisoner the *comandante militar* and other Californians, haul down the Mexican flag and elevate their own, and proclaim a republic, besides shooting three California soldiers in cold blood, and all unprovoked, seemed to them a wanton insult, and it aroused them to a deeper indignation than if Sloat had bombarded Monterey. With one accord they hated the Americanos; even the Montereños, who, under Larkin's subtle manipulation, had been on the verge of loving them.

Nevertheless, when Frémont arrived in San Diego he found no army, although horsemen were frequently seen on the horizon. It was rumored that Castro and Pio Pico had retreated to Sonora. Stockton, who had been routing various little California companies on his march south, took formal possession of Los Angeles and, leaving Gillespie in charge with a small force, returned with Frémont to Monterey. California might hate the invader, but it looked as if she was overawed and had concluded to submit.

The Americans congratulated themselves until August 28th, when a mounted courier dashed into Monterey crying that all the south was in arms and Gillespie fighting for his life in Los Angeles. This proved to be no false alarm, and it took the Americans under Frémont, Stockton, Talbot, and General Kearney, when he arrived overland from Mexico, until January 13th to subdue them. It is not necessary to give in detail those engagements in which the Americans were not always victorious; for the Californians, not being opposed to friends and relations, fought with valor and admirable tactics. But there was no question of the outcome, and on January 13th the entire force surrendered to Frémont, laid down

# THE BEAR-FLAG REVOLUTION

their arms and dispersed. Frémont by his clemency and generosity recaptured his lost prestige and was once more the popular hero. Stockton appointed him "governor," but by this time Stockton and Kearney were at sword's points over the supreme command in California. The upshot of many broils and the bitter enmity of Kearney was Frémont's trial in Washington for "mutiny" and numerous other charges. He was found guilty by the commission, and pardoned by the President; he resigned from the army, and returned to California to embark upon a political career.

And the Californians? Their day was over, their sun had set. Once more the strong devoured the weak.

# VIII

### GOLD

SUTTER felt very happy and secure with the American flag hanging limp above his fort in the windless valley summer. Although a European born, he had always despised the Spaniards as much as he admired the vigorous enterprising people of the Great Republic. To be sure, he reigned like a prince at New Helvetia, where his domain covered thirty-three square miles, with, just beyond, another vast grant of ninety-three thousand acres. He had thousands of head of cattle, horses, sheep, hundreds of Indians who were veritable subjects; his crops were magnificent in that warm Central Valley, and practically every trade was pursued at the Fort. It is not likely that he dreamed of greater wealth under the Americans so much as of security; for he distrusted Mexico. But he had known the cities and towns of the Eastern states, with their teeming industries, and he longed to see California roused from her lethargy, all her great resources developed. And in a sense he certainly forced the pace of California history.

For several years Sutter had watched the emigrant trains roll down the slopes of the Sierras; and what inspired a more or less vague mistrust in the minds of the Californians was a foregone conclusion to the clever Swiss. He dispensed hospitality to these weary adven-

SUTTER'S FORT AS IT WAS IN 1848

## GOLD

turers, selling them all the necessaries of life from his stores when they had the money to pay, and giving lavishly to the needy. He advised them where to pitch their tents and how to avoid encroaching on the ranchos, entertained the more presentable at his board, and sent many a relief party up into the high Sierras when emigrants had been overtaken by disaster.

Hundreds and hundreds of these covered wagons harnessed to oxen crawled down the mountain-trail during the years 1845-46, most of them from the Middle West, all of the immigrants in search of little farms in the land of climate and plenty. During the following two years, as if in obedience to the law of nature that sends the lull before the storm, the numbers fell off; but there was one party destined to live in the history of California at least, and its name was Donner.

This was a party of eighty-five people—men, women, children—that had started early enough to cross the Sierras before the snow fell, but lost time on a false trail and began the eastern ascent on the last day of October, with exhausted provisions. They encountered one blizzard after another. The snow buried their wagons and cattle; they built cabins of boughs covered with hides, fearing, in spite of those that pushed on ahead in search of relief, that they must spend the winter in these terrible fastnesses. Relief parties from Sutter's Fort were little more fortunate. They fell coming in, or going out with the few that were able to brave the storms and travel. The winter wore on, the blizzards increased in fury and duration. Men, women, and children died, exhausted or starved. The Sacramento Valley was covered with a brilliant carpet of the California wild flowers of spring before the last of the relief parties brought out the last of the ill-fated emigrants.

Donner, like a good captain, had refused to leave his foundering ship until those under his command had been saved. When the second relief party left Donner Lake they took all that were camped at this point except Donner, who was now too weak to travel, Mrs. Donner, who refused to leave her husband, and a man named Keysburg, who was ordered to remain and look after them. When the snows had melted somewhat a third relief party reached the lake to find Donner laid out in a winding-sheet, Keysburg looking like a gorilla and acting like a maniac, and no Mrs. Donner. They found her later in the camp kettle and a bucket, salted down. When Keysburg, assisted by a rope round his neck, recovered his mind, he confessed to having murdered and eaten portions not only of this brave woman, who had perhaps consciously dared worse than the Sierra storms to console her dying husband, but of others, before the second relief party had come. Nor did he deny the story that a child, perishing with cold, had crept one night into his blankets, and that he had devoured it before morning.

Such law as there was in the country seemed to break down before this monster. A year or two later the Americans would have lynched him; but Sutter, knowing the effect of the terrible stillnesses under falling snow, the monotonies of a long Sierra winter, and the hunger and privation that poison the brain with vitiated blood, let him go. He lived miserably in the mountains for the rest of his life, shunned as a pariah.

Sutter had had men engaged in looking for a site for a sawmill when Frémont arrived and set the country by its

MARCH OF THE CARAVAN
From "The Expedition of the Donner Party." Courtesy A. C. McClurg & Co.

# GOLD

ears. Yerba Buena, the immigrants, and various settlements springing to life along the Sacramento River demanded lumber, and the man who supplied them would make a fortune. Sutter, in spite of his baronial domain and his many enterprises, was always in debt, and he would have put this new idea for increasing his revenues into immediate execution had not Frémont carried off nearly all the able-bodied men in the north.

Sutter also wanted lumber for a projected flour-mill from which there would be another fine revenue, but the lumber must be brought from the Sierras. Finally an immigrant from New Jersey drifted in, a wheelwright by occupation, James W. Marshall by name, to whom Sutter gave work, and soon recognized as an honest and industrious man, if somewhat surly and erratic. He talked over his schemes for the two mills with him, and the upshot was that Marshall agreed to find a site and build and manage the sawmill if Sutter would take him into partnership. Those were frontier days when one did what one could, not what one would, and articles of partnership were drawn up: Sutter was to furnish money, men, tools, and teams, and Marshall would do the rest.

The point selected by Marshall was in a mountain valley about fifteen hundred feet in altitude; and in August of that year (1847) he started for the Sierras, accompanied by six Mormons, who after service in the Mexican War were on their way back to Salt Lake, but thankful for remunerative work; and ten or twelve Indians. The road across the valley, beaten out by emigrant trains, was about forty-five miles long, but the men rode or drove the wagons, and in the bracing Sierra air were soon at work.

# CALIFORNIA

They were four months felling trees, building the mill and dam, and digging the race. It was shortly after the gates had been put in place and the water had been turned into the race to carry off the loose dirt and rock that Marshall immortalized himself. The water had been turned off one afternoon, and he was walking in the tail-race when he saw something glittering on the bed. He picked up several of the yellow bits and examined them doubtfully. They looked like gold, but—he had also seen pyrites. However, certain tests convinced him that he had at least found an alloy in which gold might predominate. This was on Monday, the 24th[1] of January. Several days later he rode into New Helvetia and showed his little collection of golden peas to Sutter. He, too,

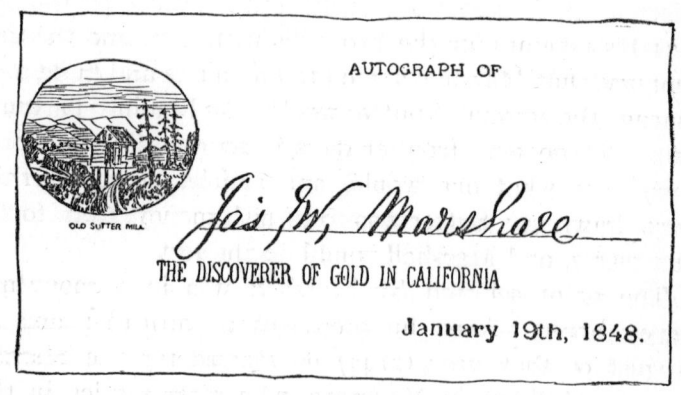

AUTOGRAPH OF

*Jas. W. Marshall*

OLD SUTTER MILL

THE DISCOVERER OF GOLD IN CALIFORNIA

January 19th, 1848.

AUTOGRAPH OF J. W. MARSHALL, FROM CALIFORNIA'S GOLDEN JUBILEE

was doubtful, but he possessed an encyclopedia. The two men read the article on gold carefully, and then applied the sulphuric-acid test; finally, with the further

[1] The mistakes in dates which prevailed for many years were due to the fact that Marshall was old and his memory feeble by the time historians asked him for statements.

# GOLD

assistance of scales, they convinced themselves that Marshall's trove was pure gold.

Neither of the men was unduly excited. The gold had been found in the mill-race only, and was probably isolated, a mere pocket. At all events, they made up their minds to say nothing until the flour-mill was completed. Sutter now had a number of intelligent men working for him, thanks to the Mormon wayfarers, and he had no desire to lose them.

But, although Nature may keep her golden secrets for several hundred thousand years, man is born of woman. One of Marshall's laborers was sent out every few days to shoot a deer. The gold discovery had interested this man Bigler mightily, and he invariably searched the edges of the streams he passed. He soon became convinced that gold was as thick in the Sierra cañons as the sands on the shores of the sea; in less than six weeks Sutter did not have an able-bodied man left at the Fort, and many of his Indians had joined the stampede.

Yerba Buena at this time was not a mere adjunct to the military post at the presidio, but a town of eight hundred and fifty inhabitants, the most important of whom were the American merchants and traders. Besides the large importing and exporting firms there were a number of small merchants that supplied the inhabitants with all the necessaries of life and did a quiet but remunerative business. The mechanics commanded about two dollars a day. The only excitement was the arrival of mail from the East, and an occasional fight or fandango, duly recorded in the two weekly newspapers, the *Californian* and the *California Star*. On March 15th the *Californian* announced casually that there was rumor of a gold-mine having been discovered at Sutter's sawmill; and shortly afterward the editor left to get what news there might be, at first hand. He visited the original "mine," escorted by Sutter himself, but returned to tell his public that it was all a sham, and advised them to stay at home and stick to business. A few weeks later he was forced to close his printing-office, as there was not a man left in Yerba Buena to set the type.

There was no telegraph wire in California, nor even a pony express, but it would seem that the word "GOLD" was carried on invisible waves and shouted into every ear. The large merchants closed their warehouses for want of laborers, and the small ones left their shops in charge of their wives, if they had any, or merely turned the key; mechanics threw down their tools, bought a pick, shovel, and pan and shouted that they'd work for other men no more; farmers left their crops to rot in the fields; the editors followed their printers. The great ranchos were deserted, for even the indolent Californians and their Indians were dazzled by the hope of sudden wealth, or by that subtle and deadly magnetism which emanates from the metal. By July the whole territory was at the mines or marching there, some in the family coach, many on horseback, more on foot, others by sloop to the *embarcadero* near Sutter's Fort. The ranch-houses looked like the castles of Europe in the Middle Ages, when all the men were at the wars and the women stayed at home to spin.

For a time the excitement was confined to California. There were rumors in the East; but, long before she took the discovery seriously, the ports of the Pacific, to which bags of gold-dust were sent to buy provisions for the

FROM "LONDON PUNCH," 1860

THE "EL DORADO" GAMBLING SALOON

## GOLD

camps, had recognized the significance of the placer-mines; and Mexicans, Peruvians, Chilians, as well as settlers in Oregon, had begun to pour into California. But Mr. Larkin wrote twice to the Secretary of State, Mr. Buchanan, giving a circumstantial account of the discovery. Before writing the second time he visited the mines and satisfied himself that they were of enormous richness and extent. It was already known that the placers extended for miles; and some men were taking out from one thousand to five thousand dollars' worth of gold a day. Mexicans told him that there was nothing so rich in Mexico. Governor Mason also paid a visit to the mines, and estimated that the gold yield was from twenty to thirty thousand dollars a day. The metal was so abundant that many men found their pickaxes, shovels, pans, and cradles superfluous, and pried it out from the crevices of the rocks with their jack-knives. These reports, when given to the public, banished any doubts that may have lingered in the minds of those who had received letters from their friends at the diggings, and in the spring of 1849 the great stampede began.

Once more Sutter watched the emigrant wagons roll down the slopes of the Sierra, this time looking not like thin cascades, but avalanches of dusty snow. Already he had rented buildings to enterprising storekeepers, who were paying him a hundred dollars a month for one room; but to the few mechanics he had induced to return he was paying ten dollars a day.

About twenty-five thousand of the gold-seekers crossed the Sierras that year. The government had made a contract with the Pacific Mail Steamship Company for a line of monthly steamers between New York and San Francisco by way of Panama, and thousands more took the journey by sea. There were few women in either wagon-trains or ships, and almost without exception, during that first exodus, the men were young, strong, and of good character. Many of them had recently been mustered out of the army that had reduced Mexico to terms; they were excellently disciplined and accustomed to hardships. Some were young men of good family whom necessity compelled to work, and—"good families" were not very democratic in those days—preferred to work with pick and shovel in distant California to clerking in aristocratic New York or Boston. California was truly democratic for several years, and some of these young men who were not strong enough for the hard work of the mines made a living as they could in San Francisco. One man who afterward, when fortune had smiled on him, became a brilliant member of San Francisco's young society and finally died of lockjaw as the result of being wounded in the aristocratic duel, peddled shoe-strings for several months until a family friend discovered him and set him up in business. But to return to the placers.

It is estimated that not less than seventy thousand immigrants arrived from the East during 1849 and went straight to the mines. Among them, of course, were many deserting sailors; and for months the Bay of San Francisco was crowded with craft marooned and waiting for the gold-fever to subside. Thousands more poured in from the Pacific ports; at the end of the year there were not less than a hundred thousand whites in California, most of them Americans. Every trade, every class, was represented, also every variety of human nature, as was soon discovered when the camps, so far from the towns, became a law unto themselves, although there was little trouble during that first year. The men worked hard by day, excited, silent, minding their own business strictly; in the evenings they spun yarns of home before rolling into their blankets to be lulled to sleep by the singing of the pines, rent now and again by the long yowls of the coyote or the snorting of the grizzly bear. The gold yield of that year was twenty-three million dollars.

But those rich and apparently inexhaustible placers soon became a magnet for the type of man that flocks where gold is after some one else has taken the trouble to make it or extract it from the earth. Gamblers and sharpers of all sorts began to take passage for California, many of them remaining in San Francisco, but others going to the mines and pitching their tents. Soon every camp had its faro-table and other varieties of gambling "hells"; dance-halls and the easy-money female followed as a matter of course; there were as many bars as there were gallons of bad whisky; and the work of demoralization began. Men who were tired of work or had worked as little as possible began to make a profession of gambling or mined only to have "dust" to stake. Fights were of daily occurrence, and if one of the antagonists fell no one bothered to try the victor. Thieves and disreputable characters were often run out of camp by the better class of miners, or left it at the end of a rope. Few men returned from that great orgie of gold precisely the men they were when they reached those beautiful silent cañons and began the work of tearing them to pieces; although many a man's character stood the test, and he returned to civilization with a fortune in his belt, no blood on his knife, and a character so hardened and toughened that he was quite equal to the task of founding the greatness of San Francisco. Others boasted to their dying day of how many times they had "killed their man"; and countless others, despite that auriferous abundance, failed to "make their pile," owing to physical weakness sometimes, but mental weakness generally; they slunk back to the towns or remained to haunt the camps, whine about their luck until they were kicked out or died of starvation, or blew out their brains "up the gulch." Darwin would have been delighted and socialists puzzled. Even Marshall died in poverty. His sawmill was soon overrun by the ruthless miner, and he seemed to have had little affinity for the metal he discovered. Either he was a poor miner or he could not get along with other men; like the rolling stone he had always been, he kept moving on, accomplishing nothing. During the seventies the legislature voted him a pension for a few years, then forgot him, and he died old and alone in a mountain cabin. A few years later California suddenly remembered him and spent several thousand dollars on a big bronze effigy, which now stands over his grave near the spot where he enriched the world and starved to death.

And Sutter? Wealth poured in on him for a time, for if he could not supply all the wants of that vast concourse of miners the men who did had to rent his land and buildings. His sawmill was destroyed, but his gristmills went day and night, and he could command any price for his cattle and horses. Moreover, his was the fame of the discovery, and he entertained constantly at his fort men who were his intellectual equals, or visited

# GOLD

them in San Francisco. His popularity was enormous, aside from his hospitality. He was now a man of forty-six, gray, but ruddy and erect, his blue eyes always full of good will, and he delighted in playing the *grand seigneur* either when entertaining his equals or giving largess to the unfortunate; his manners were more natural and simple than was to be expected of a man who had ruled so long. He seldom visited the mines himself, but often laughed at the names his droll new countrymen had given them: Whisky Bay, Brandy Gulch, Poker Flat, Seven-up Ravine, Loafer's Retreat, Git-Up-and-Git, Gospel Swamp, Gouge Eye, Ground Hog's Glory, Lousy Ravine, Puke Ravine, Blue Belly Ravine, Petticoat Slide, Swelled-Head Diggings, Nary Red, Hangtown, Shirt-tail Cañon, Red Dog, Coon Hollow, Skunk Gulch, Piety Hill, Hell's Delight. Whole chapters of mining history might be evoked from these names alone. No wonder that Bret Harte was inspired!

But although Sutter entertained many gentlemen, their dress differed little from that of the humblest of their associates: a blue or red woolen shirt, pantaloons finishing inside long heavy hobnailed boots and belted in at the waist, a slouch-hat over long hair and uncut beard. In the belt were the inevitable brace of pistols and bowie-knife. The typical miner of any class was as cool as he was reckless and hot-tempered; as time went on he became more and more laconic and more and more profane, and the best of them drank hard and gambled, little as it might affect them. They amused themselves at the gaming-tables for want of other entertainment and lost as lightly as they won. Some hated the thought of living in a house again, governed by the laws of civilization; others "made their pile" and returned to the city or "back

## CALIFORNIA

East," satisfied with their adventure and ready for the more serious matters of life.

The gold yield of 1850 was $50,000,000; of 1853, $65,000,000. Then the placers began to show signs of decline, and men left them in hordes. Sutter had laid out the town of Sacramento, a square mile about his fort, with two streets running through the marsh down to the *embarcadero*. This he had sold in lots, and as he witnessed the troubles and disgraceful riots caused by "squatters," the lawless element that had entered the country shouting that California belonged to the American and that no Mexican grant, despite the treaty, should be valid, he may have had some premonition of his own fate. If he did not, he was soon enlightened. These needy adventurers "squatted" wherever the land pleased them, swarming not only over the rich grants of Sutter, but of the rancheros. The only hope lay in the courts, and the result was years of litigation and either a complete loss in the end or the cession of the more valuable parts to lawyers to cover their fees.

And the lawyers that left their Eastern practices to come where prices were high and pickings abundant, were, with a few notable exceptions, men of as little decency and principle as the squatters. They had no desire to break their backs at the mines, but no aversion whatever from soiling their hands. They not only charged their clients exhorbitantly and were on sale to the other side, but, being real Americans, they despised foreigners and were solicitous of squatter votes.

The details of the despoiling of the Californians is one of the ugliest chapters not only of state, but American history; for Congress, by passing Senator Gwin's

# GOLD

bill, subtly worded but conceived entirely in the interests of the Americans in California, made despoliation of the original grant-holders practically certain.

Sutter's grants were worth millions, but in 1870 he had not a dollar. The California legislature of that year granted him a pension of two hundred and fifty dollars a month, but discontinued it when he went to Washington to ask for justice. He died in poverty, this great land baron, monarch of all he surveyed for so many years, and lies in Littiz, Lancaster County, Pennsylvania. The year of his death was 1880, and he was seventy-seven years old.

## IX

### SAN FRANCISCO

In April, 1806, Rezánov, anchored off the presidio of San Francisco, dreamed of a Russian navy in the bay, saw the gaunt hills and sandy amphitheater of the peninsula set with the palaces and churches and bazars, the lofty towers with their Tartar domes, the slender crosses of his native land; the gay California sun shedding a dazzling light on marble walls and golden roofs. In April, 1906, San Francisco, one of the ugliest cities in the world, but one of the most famous and prosperous, was destroyed by earthquake and fire. It has risen again, handsome, substantial, earthquake-proof and fireproof, its picturesqueness and "atmosphere" gone for ever, but on the eve of a larger population and commercial activities through the Panama Canal; climbing steadily over the hills toward the south, and threatening to embrace the towns around the bay; in the course of a few years bound to become one of the greater cities of the United States, as it has, almost from its beginnings, been one of the most notable.

Between the dreams of Rezánov, dust long since in Krasnoiarsk, and the triumph of American materialism over the desire of a few for the beautiful and artistic city Nature had in mind when she planned the site, San Francisco has passed through many changes intrinsic and fortuitous. It was these changes, in number out of all proportion to her brief existence, which made the "atmosphere" that went up in smoke in April, 1906.

The battery of Yerba Buena in Rezánov's day was situated between our Telegraph Hill and Rincon Point on a cove afterward filled and built upon, but then beginning at Montgomery Street. Coyotes and even bears roamed over the sand-dunes, and the sea-gulls were almost as numerous as on Alcatraz and Angel Island. It was in the month of May, 1835, that Governor Figueroa determined to lay out a settlement at Yerba Buena, and offered William A. Richardson, the Englishman who had arrived in California in 1822 and naturalized in 1829, the position of captain of the port if he would settle on the cove. Richardson, who was a business man, and who seems to have recognized the importance of Yerba Buena, consented, and with his family moved north at once from his home near the San Gabriel Mission.

The governor died shortly after Richardson reached the end of that long slow journey of many weary leagues with his train of bullock-carts packed with women, children, and household goods. He arrived at the cove in June, and literally pitched his tent, awaiting the next move of the government. After Figueroa's death José Castro, as primer vocal, confirmed Richardson's appointment and told him to select a site for the village. The alcalde of the Pueblo Dolores was the surveyor appointed, and in October he laid out the foundation street—La Calle de la Fundacion—running from a point near the present corner of Kearney and Pine streets northwest to the water. That seems to have exhausted him, and he retired to Dolores, while Richardson selected for himself a

## CALIFORNIA

lot one hundred *varas* square, embracing the present Dupont Street between Clay and Washington streets. There, with what assistance he could get from the Indians remaining at the Pueblo Dolores, he erected his rude dwelling. This is known in history as the first house built on the site of the future city of San Francisco; but it is to be supposed that the Mexican officers in charge of the battery for many years did not sleep in the sand.

The next settler was Jacob P. Leese, an American who had arrived in California the year before and engaged in the mercantile business in Monterey. He came to San Francisco to establish a branch house and do business of all sorts not only with the many ships that took shelter in Yerba Buena waters, but with the ranchers north and east of the bay. Governor Chico gave him permission to select a lot one hundred *varas* square, but not within two hundred yards of the *embarcadero*, that space being reserved by the government. Leese, who brought lumber and working-men with him, put up a frame building sixty by twenty-five, after choosing a lot near the present site of the Plaza or Portsmouth Square. Shortly before it was completed this astute merchant issued invitations for a great Fourth of July celebration, Captain Richardson, not being overwhelmed with work, riding north and east with the invitations. General Vallejo rode down to this entertainment with a retinue from Sonoma, himself a gallant figure on one of his superbly caparisoned horses. Sutter came by water in a large flat-bottomed boat manned by ten naked Indians. He sat alone in the stern, quite as imposing as General Vallejo.

The other rancheros and residents of the pueblos, Americans and Californians, men and women, came on horse and in *carreta*, and crossed the bay Heaven knows how. But they found, for that day, a grand entertainment awaiting them. Numerous tents had been erected for their comfort, and flying above them as well as at each corner of a great marquee and the new house were the American and Mexican flags. The officers of the presidio were there, visitors from Monterey, and the captains and supercargoes from the vessels in the harbor—which had furnished the bunting. They were entertained at a really magnificent banquet under the marquee at five o'clock on the 4th; a band composed of drum, clarinet, fife, and bugle discoursed airs national and sentimental, when the more important of the sixty guests were not on their feet complimenting one another and making toasts. Vallejo toasted Washington in flowery Spanish, and all cheered wildly when another speaker alluded feelingly to the union of the Mexican and American flags.

When the banquet finished the guests danced in the new house until the evening of the 5th, rested in their tents, and, again replete, dispersed regretfully to their homes, invoking blessings on the Fourth of July. A few days later Leese's store was packed with twelve thousand dollars' worth of merchandise, and his grateful guests were the first and most amenable of his purchasers. In the following year he married a sister of General Vallejo, and their daughter, Rosalia Leese, born April 15, 1838, was the first white child born in the future San Francisco.

Leese remained the most successful and energetic citizen of Yerba Buena until 1841, when he sold out to the Hudson's Bay Company and moved to Sonoma. Soon after Alvarado was firmly established in Monterey he asked that most enlightened and public-spirited of governors to give his attention to the languishing village on the cove. José Castro was prefect of the district, and immediately received orders from Alvarado to have a survey made of Yerba Buena and of such of the adjoining lands as were likely to become incorporated in a growing pueblo. Leese had in his household a young civil engineer named Jean J. Vioget, and Castro appointed him to survey the pueblo and give it streets.

Vioget's little city was laid out between the present Broadway, Montgomery, Powell, and California streets, obliterating the Calle de la Fundacion. This was in 1839, and soon afterward other merchants saw the advantages of living on that popular harbor. The more active business men were foreigners, Americans for the most part, although a few Mexicans had little shops, and one even had a grist-mill. William Thomes, who visited California as a sailor-boy in 1843, describes this fair sample of Mexican industry as follows:

We came to an old adobe building about a cable's length from Clark's Point and looked in. It seemed to be a mill for grinding wheat, for there was a poor disconsolate-looking mule connected with a pole, and it would make two revolutions of the ring and then stop and turn round to see what was going on at its rear. A cross between a poor Mexican and an Indian, who seemed to have charge of matters, would yell out in the shrillest of Spanish after each halt:

"*Caramba! Diablo! Amigo! Malo! Vamos!*"

Then the mule, after hearing such frightful expressions, quietly dropped its ears and went to sleep, and the Mexican would roll a cigarette, strike fire with flint and steel, and smoke contentedly for half an hour, then get up and hurl some more bad words at his companion. . . .

It may be imagined that this breed of Mexicans was of little more use for loading and unloading and working in the warehouses than the Indians; and, as a matter of

# SAN FRANCISCO

fact, the men employed, until the gold-rush brought thousands of American laborers into the country, were Kanakas—natives of the Hawaiian Islands. Even then there was an American saloon on the Plaza, but it seems to have done little business except when a ship was in harbor.

In 1846 there were about two hundred people living in Yerba Buena. The most notable of the California residents was Doña Juana Briones. She was a widow, handsome and vivacious, and, electing to live in what to her eyes no doubt was a gay and busy city, built an adobe house, raised chickens, and kept several cows in a corral, so wild that they had to be lassoed and their legs tied before they could be milked. She had a big whitewashed *sala* and gave many a fandango, to which all were invited, irrespective of nationality. But it must have been a very quiet life in the little gray, foggy, wind-swept village; and even the American business men, no doubt, took their daily siesta and closed their stores in the middle of the day. The first real excitement—for they paid little attention to the internal revolutions—was caused by Frémont and his escapades in the north, the arrival of Montgomery on the *Portsmouth*, and the news that the United States and Mexico might go to war at any moment.

On the morning of July 8, 1846, Captain Montgomery, accompanied by seventy sailors and marines, landed and marched to the Plaza. There, under a salute of twenty-one guns from the *Portsmouth*, he hauled down the Mexican flag and ran up the Stars and Stripes. The Plaza was rechristened Portsmouth Square by the delighted American residents, and shortly afterward the street along the *embarcadero* was named for Montgomery. The first American alcalde was Lieut. Washington A. Bartlett, of the

# CALIFORNIA

*Portsmouth*, and he appointed Jasper O'Farrell to resurvey the pueblo. The practical American crossed the streets at right angles and enlarged the blocks, but the achievement of which he and Bartlett were proudest was the naming of the streets, heretofore undesignated in that friendly village, after the men prominent in the history of the moment: Montgomery, Kearney, O'Farrell, Beale,[1] Mason, Powell, Stockton, and California.

It is to Bartlett also that we finally owe our San Francisco, between whose tonic atmosphere and uneasy surface we were thus permitted to grow up instead of in a remote and ill-weathered corner of a subsidiary bay. General Vallejo, Thomas O. Larkin, and Dr. Semple, landholders of the north, certain of the destiny of California, although ignorant of its great auriferous deposits, and desirous to be among the first to reap the benefit of a rapidly increasing population, conceived a subtle and farsighted scheme. They projected a town on the shores of San Pablo Bay, a continuation, in the north, of San Francisco Bay, to be called the City of Santa Francisca, nominally as a marital compliment on the part of the general, really because they knew that a city so identified with the famous Bay of San Francisco would be a natural bait both for settlers and sea-craft, becoming in the course of a few years the metropolis of the future state.

Fortunately, Bartlett's mind worked as quickly and astutely as theirs. Before they had time to record the title of their town he changed the name of his from Yerba Buena to San Francisco, publishing the ordinance in the

---

[1] Named for Lieutenant afterward General Beale, who distinguished himself during the final "war" with the Californians. He was the father of Truxtun Beale, a well-known citizen of San Francisco and mentioned in appendix.

SACRAMENTO, CALIFORNIA. 1850

SAN FRANCISCO
Authenticated picture of the city as it appeared in 1846-47

# SAN FRANCISCO

*California Star*, recently started by Sam Brannan. Vallejo, Larkin, and Semple protested in vain. Confusion must be avoided, and the fuming capitalists on the Straits of Carquinez were obliged to call their village Benicia, the second name of Señora Vallejo. There is to-day a town near by called Vallejo. But neither of these little northern communities has risen to the dignity of ten thousand inhabitants, although there is an arsenal at Benicia and the city named for the old general is close to the Mare Island Navy Yard.

Brannan had arrived on the 31st of July, 1846, on the *Brooklyn*, with a ship-load of Mormons. It was his purpose to found a colony on the bay and erect a great tabernacle. But he found the American flag flying in Portsmouth Square, and the United States government was not partial to Mormon colonies. However, they pitched a large number of tents on the sand-hills behind the little town and prepared to make the best of it. Some joined Frémont when he marched south to subdue the Californians, a few sought farms, and later many went on to Salt Lake; but for the moment they were a decided acquisition to Yerba Buena, as there were many excellent mechanics among them who had brought implements and tools. Their leader carried everything necessary for printing a newspaper, and on January 9, 1847, published the first number of the *Star*, having previously issued an extra containing General Taylor's official report of the battles of Palo Alto and Resaca de la Palma. Brannan's generous details in the issue of April 10th of the horrors of the Donner party pales to a mere modest primrose the yellowest efforts of to-day. So estimably has our taste for morbid, hideous, and exaggerated details decreased

# CALIFORNIA

since 1847 that it would be quite out of the question to transfer extracts on this absorbing topic from the *California Star* into a respectable history.

On May 28th there was a grand illumination in San Francisco in honor of General Taylor's victory over the Mexicans at Buena Vista. Every home, tent, warehouse, and shop flew the American flag and was as brilliant at night as a limited amount of oil and tallow would permit. Of course, there was a grand fandango. Fire-crackers cracked for twenty-four hours, and big bonfires flared on the sand-dunes and on the steep granite hills behind the settlement.

At this time there was every prospect that San Francisco would continue to be a peaceful and prosperous little town whose worst vice was gambling in moderation. It was well governed by the alcalde and the ayuntamiento, a town council of six members, initiated by Governor Figueroa; there was little strain on the spirit of law and order; a school flourished; the leaders and merchants were growing rich. There were two "hotels," several boarding-houses; private dwellings were slowly increasing in number, and there were one or two billiard-rooms, pool-rooms, and ten-pin-alleys. Lots on the water-front were selling, two wharves were in the process of construction. There were twelve mercantile and commission houses, agencies of large firms in the East, British America, South America, and the "Sandwich Islands" (H. I.). The little town was clustered just above Montgomery Street, that being the water-front, and if it had not the physical allurements of the southern towns, and only men seriously engaged in business were attracted to it, nevertheless it was the city preferred by the sea-captains, for it was full of bustle and

## SAN FRANCISCO

real business. The center of life by day was the Plaza; at night there were dances, and the men guided their womenkind to the scene of festivity with a dark-lantern; there was also much entertaining on the war-ships and commoner craft out at anchor. Men settled down to the business of getting rich slowly, enjoying life in a way, looking forward to retirement in some one of the civilized cities "at home." Only those that had married California women dreamed for a moment that they would spend their lives on this edge of the world where, the occasional news of the war over, the only excitement was when the ships sailed through the Golden Gate, bringing merchandise and mail.

And then, presto! all things changed.

For some weeks after the news of the gold discovery drifted into San Francisco that well-regulated community poo-poohed the idea. Then suddenly the stampede. When Governor Mason arrived in San Francisco from Monterey on June 20th he found not an able-bodied man in the place save the merchants (and not all of those), who were unloading the merchandise themselves, even the sailors having run off to the mines. He wrote to Commodore Jones, who was at Mazatlan, that, treaty or no treaty, the gold discovery had settled the destiny of California. But before this letter reached its destination definite news of the Treaty Guadalupe Hidalgo, which ceded Alta California (including what we now call Nevada, Utah, and Arizona), New Mexico, and Texas to the United States for the sum of fifteen million dollars, had arrived. Mexico cursed herself when she heard that one of her cheaply sold provinces had turned into a river of gold, but luck as ever was with the United States.

# CALIFORNIA

There was by this time another newspaper in San Francisco (removed from Monterey) called the *Californian*, and on the 29th of May, 1848, it published this indignant editorial:

> The whole country from San Francisco to Los Angeles, and from the sea to the base of the Sierra Nevada, resounds with the cry, "GOLD! GOLD!! GOLD!!!" while the field is left half planted, the house half built, and everything neglected but the manufacture of shovels and pickaxes, and the means of transportation to a spot where a man obtained one hundred and twenty-eight dollars' worth of the *real stuff* in one day's washing, and the average for all is twenty dollars *per diem*.

The following week there was no *Star*. Even the editor was on the highroad, a pick over one shoulder, a shovel over the other, and a pan under his arm.

In September certain leading citizens who had caught the gold-fever recovered and hastened back to the deserted city, and a number of American working-men, realizing the anxiety of those and other eminent citizens who had proved immune, to have their work done and erect new buildings, and that labor would command almost as much a day as an ordinary man could pan out while breaking his back, transferred themselves to San Francisco. Soon afterward, the first brick building erected in California was finished. It was on the corner of Montgomery and Clay streets and was the property of Mellis and Howard.

Still, those that remained in the town must have taken a gloomy view of the future. Shops were closed; it was difficult to obtain the commonest necessaries of life. The little city so serene and prosperous a few months before now looked like a deserted mining-camp itself. The windows of empty shops were broken by

# SAN FRANCISCO

the small boy, who never under any circumstance deserts the type; doors were barricaded; merchandise was rotting on the wharves; and prices threatened to wipe out tidy little fortunes. The streets of the town huddled on the bay looked like dreary cañons running up into the gray unfriendly hills. During the spring and autumn there was little change, although a number of unsuccessful miners returned to their old homes emaciated, feeble, and dispirited. Those that could work demanded ten and twenty dollars a day, and the price of all foodstuffs had risen four hundred per cent. The shopkeepers were among those that returned early, knowing the necessities at the mines. Within the first eight weeks after the territory was alive to the richness of the "diggings" two hundred and fifty thousand dollars in gold-dust had reached San Francisco, and within the next eight weeks six hundred thousand dollars more; all to purchase supplies at any price for the miners.

But early in 1849 San Francisco, predestined city of many changes, entered upon a new phase of her checquered career. Ship-load after ship-load of immigrants arrived from the East, and of necessity passed through San Francisco and were fitted out for the mines. They paid what was demanded for picks, shovels, pans, and camping-outfits: about fifteen dollars apiece for the implements of mining, and from fifty to eighty dollars for a rocker. These, with the overland immigrants, were the men who were to go down to history as the "pioneers of '49," and there were some thirty-five thousand of them.

Before the year was well advanced San Francisco could no longer complain of dullness. Not only had many more ships arrived in the harbor—where they remained

## CALIFORNIA

helpless for months—but the later ones brought as many scalawags as honest miners. In a short time San Francisco had more saloons and gambling-houses than she had dwellings, and they were open twenty-four hours of the day. By this time many of the miners were returning, some with mere sacks of gold-dust, others with fortunes, but all longing for at least a semblance of civilization once more after the incredible barbarisms of mining life. Many intended to return to the East as soon as a ship could be manned, and it has been stated that not one of those that really enriched themselves remained to build up San Francisco; all found amusement meanwhile at the gambling-houses.

These were scattered all over the town, but the largest and most dazzling were clustered about the Plaza. No matter how rough the structures, they invariably had large plate-glass windows, music, a handsome bar, a handsomer cashier, and dozens of little tables. Day and night these tables were surrounded by men in flannel shirts, top-boots, and sombrero or silk hat. On the tables beside the cards were little bags of gold-dust and piles of "slugs" worth ten or twenty dollars each. In the aisles hundreds of people passed continually, watching the gambling or awaiting their turn at a table, while hundreds more pressed eagerly against the plate-glass windows. And every grade of life was represented, as at the mines: scions of good families, young soldiers, small merchants, mechanics, parsons, school-teachers, editors and their former printers, sailors, firemen, farmers, tramps, and professional gamblers. Of all these gambling-houses "El Dorado" became the most famous. Fortunes were lost and won.

New "hotels" were erected in an incredibly short time,

## SAN FRANCISCO

but could not catch up with the demand, and hundreds slept in bunk-houses that looked like the worst of accommodations on a river steamboat. Tents also were pitched in the city streets, and the abandoned hulks of two beached vessels served as quarters for the night. But all were gay and philosophical, unless they ruined themselves at the tables, when they either remained philosophical or shot themselves out in the sand-hills.

The merchants soon adapted themselves to the high prices and wages, as employers ever do, and gouged somebody else. At the end of July, 1849, the population numbered five thousand, and in September twenty thousand. Real estate was booming, the city was spreading over the hills, the new houses being mainly "canvas, blanket, and bough-covered tents." But building-lots had been surveyed, and a large number of warehouses and stores were building, while the bay was a forest of masts. The streets were almost impassable with shifting sand-banks in summer and mud after the first rains. The plank sidewalks were seldom repaired. Rats played in the ooze, and there were enormous heaps of rubbish everywhere. But no one minded these trifling drawbacks. All were rich, or expected to be. The shopkeepers cried aloud their wares in front of their doors, "sized up" a new arrival's qualifications for being "done," and made their charges accordingly. As for the mechanic, he made thirty dollars by day and lost it at night in one of the gambling-saloons "glittering like fairy palaces, where all was mad, feverish mirth, the heated brain never allowed to get cool while a bit of coin or dust was left." Such was San Francisco in 1849.

# X

## CRIME AND FIRE

DURING San Francisco's short existence as a growing pueblo everybody made a good living without extortion, and the more energetic of the merchants looked forward to independence in the course of a few years. Leese and Richardson had already retired to the country, and the little town, despite fogs and winds and rats and fleas and isolation, must have been as light of heart and free of care as is possible to any community of human beings on this imperfect planet. There is no record of bitter enmities, murder, or even the lighter crimes. There was not a policeman in the city, and if they had no church neither had they found it necessary to build a jail. It is true there was some gambling and the inevitable saloon, but neither led to excess nor crime. Moderation, temperance in the real meaning of the word, seems to have been the keynote between 1835 and 1848.

But that was the last tranquillity San Francisco was to know. Her history has been singularly unhappy. Both nature and man have done their utmost to destroy her; and even now it remains to be seen whether she has survived grafting politicians only to be throttled by labor-unionism, too ignorant to realize that dead geese no longer lay golden eggs.

The exodus to the gold-mines was the first convulsion

## CRIME AND FIRE

to shake San Francisco fairly out of her true Californian serenity; but as the greater number of the sober-minded citizens returned within a few months, little harm would have been done as far as law and order were concerned had all emigrants elected to cross the Sierra Nevadas. But the thousands that passed through San Francisco left their refuse behind them, men who since the beginning of history have preyed upon their fellows, sometimes frankly as thieves and highwaymen, as often endeavoring to deceive the public, and possibly themselves, under sounding titles and protestations of brotherly love.

It was in the spring of 1849 that a gang of young desperados calling themselves "The Regulators," but soon rechristened "The Hounds," loudly proclaimed that they were an association formed to protect the weak against the strong, to succor those that were too "green" to bear the new burden of wealth alone—there being so little law in San Francisco—to be as a reliable squadron in times of danger. On Sundays they paraded the streets with flags flying and band playing. But busy and absorbed as San Francisco was during those exciting months, it did not take her long to define the status of the Regulators. They were, in truth, an admirably organized band of cutthroats, thieves, cowards, and bullies. Wise enough to avoid the muscular American, unless he was quite alone, they confined their attention to the Chilenos and other foreigners who lived in tents beyond the city limits. Their own headquarters were a large tent near the Plaza, which, in fond memory, no doubt, of the great city of the East, they called Tammany Hall. It is to be presumed that they slept by day, for every night, armed with clubs and bludgeons, they sneaked from their lairs on Tele-

## CALIFORNIA

graph Hill to the isolated tents, taking the gold-dust of those more recently returned from the mines, and anything else they fancied, and beating all that presumed to resist. These foreigners, being far less robust than the Americans, remained at the mines only long enough to accumulate a bag of dust or nuggets; and, owing to the enterprise of the Hounds, seldom enjoyed the excitement of losing either at the gaming-tables. It was useless to appeal to the alcalde, for no alcalde could enforce laws without police. In those early days no wrongs were redressed until they became so abominable as to call for a mass-meeting of the citizens.

The citizens stood this infliction for several months with the notorious patience of Americans. They no longer ventured into the street at night, and barricaded their doors and windows; but their gorge rose slowly.

It was these very people scattered in tents over the hillsides that the Hounds claimed to be waging war against for the benefit of the good American citizen; many of the men and all of the women of the tent colony were wayfarers of little character, and as they were Chileans, Peruvians, or Mexicans, no doubt it was that contempt of foreigners so ingrained in the American mind that permitted the outrages to last as long as they did.

The Hounds naturally grew bolder and bolder. On the afternoon of Sunday, the 15th of July, they returned from a piratical adventure among the ranchos across the bay; triumphant and very drunk, they suddenly determined to outdo themselves. Flourishing firearms and bludgeons, and led by their "lieutenant," who wore a uniform of sorts, they paraded the streets shouting and screaming and occasionally discharging a gun into the

## CRIME AND FIRE

air. At sundown they made a violent descent upon the foreign quarter, tore down the tents, plundered the terrified dwellers of their last dollar and everything portable, then beat them until the hills resounded with groans and screams, pelted them with stones, and yelled like Indians as they saw the blood flow; finally, they let off their firearms, killing a number of those that were unable to hide in the brush or find refuge in the town. They kept this up all night.

On the following day San Francisco rose to a man. Alcalde Leavenworth, urged by Sam Brannan, a better citizen than Mormon, issued a proclamation calling a mass-meeting at three o'clock in the Plaza. At that hour all work was suspended, all shops and places of business closed. Every resident of San Francisco except the Hounds and their victims packed Portsmouth Square. Mr. W. D. M. Howard, one of the many Eastern men of education and ability who had settled in the country, was called upon to preside, and Dr. V. J. Fourgeaud was named secretary. Brannan addressed the meeting, expressing the alarm and disgust of all at the criminal horde which they had permitted to attain full growth in their midst, and giving a terse but eloquent recital of the Hounds' many outrages. A subscription was taken up for the wounded and plundered foreigners, and then a volunteer force of twenty-three grim and determined citizens were organized as constables to dispose of the Hounds. They were armed to the teeth, and that same afternoon arrested twenty of the outlaws and imprisoned them on the United States ship *Warren*.

Another meeting meanwhile was held in the Plaza, and Dr. William J. Gwin and James C. Ward were elected

## CALIFORNIA

associate judges to assist Alcalde Leavenworth, who has not left a very high record for efficiency; Horace Hawes was appointed district attorney, and Hall McAllister his associate counsel. Mr. McAllister, who soon afterward rose to the leadership of the California bar and maintained it until his death, won his spurs in this the first sensational lawsuit of his adopted city.

There was little difficulty, however, in proving these wretches guilty. They were condemned to various periods of imprisonment; but as there was no prison in the city, the authorities were forced to set them at liberty. Their backbone was broken, however, and they feared lynching. Many of them left the country, others returned to the mines, where for the most part they were disposed of by buzzards while dangling from trees "up the gulch."

As the treasury was empty and there was a crying need for policemen, watchmen, and street-lighting, there was another mass-meeting; and after a furious debate a law was passed licensing the gambling-houses and imposing a heavy tax upon them as the likeliest source of revenue. Hundreds of gambling-houses were now flourishing, and every hotel had its tables: faro, monte, roulette, rouge-et-noir, vingt-et-un. Heavy taxes were also levied upon real estate, auction sales, and licenses of all kinds. The hulk of the brig *Euphemia*, then anchored at what is now the corner of Jackson and Battery streets, was bought and converted into a city prison. On August 31st a Baptist church was dedicated; and other denominations, which already had Sunday-schools, bestirred themselves to build stable places of worship, if only to counteract the licensed vice of the town. A little steamboat was sent out from Boston, and new town lots were surveyed. The streets

## CRIME AND FIRE

and Plaza were now almost constantly filled with a changing throng, representing practically all the races of the world, many in their native costumes: Chinamen, Malays, Negroes, Abyssinians, Kanakas, Fiji-Islanders, Japanese, Russians, Turks, Jews, Spaniards, Mexicans, Peruvians, Chilenos, Englishmen, Italians, Frenchmen, and Americans.

> Among this vast motley crowd [says Soulé] scarcely two men from any state in the Union could be found dressed alike. . . . The long-legged boot with every variety of colored top, the buckled-up trousers, serapes, cloaks, pea-jackets, broad-brimmed slouch-hats and glazed hats. . . . On one if not three sides of the Plaza were the open doors of the "hells" of San Francisco. On other portions stood hotels, stores, and offices, the custom-house and courts of law. . . . The little open space which was left to the crowds was occupied by a multitude of nondescript objects, by horses, mules, and oxen dragging burdens along, boys at play, stalls with sweetmeats, newspapers, prints, toys, . . . occasionally even at this early period the crowd would make way for the passage of a richly dressed woman, sweeping along, apparently proud of being recognized as one of frail character, or several together of the same class mounted on spirited horses dashing furiously by, dressed in long riding-skirts or, what was quite common, male attire.

The average age of the men was twenty-five, and there were few, if any, over thirty. These men when they came in from the mines wore the usual red or blue flannel shirt, top-boots almost concealing the trouser-leg, a heavy leather belt in which two pistols and a knife were conspicuously displayed, and on their heads a silk hat. This last, worn at all hours, was a sort of advertisement of its proud possessor's good luck at the mines.

In that year of '49 there were few decent women in the city, and no homes save those that had existed before the discovery of gold. The women of commerce had followed the invading army as ever, and those that did not go to the mining-camps to share the golden harvest without toil

# CALIFORNIA

presided over the gambling-rooms or were employed as decoys for the restaurants and saloons. The young men returning from the mines heavy laden, eager for new excitements and any kind of civilization, sought the company of these women, there being none other to seek. They paraded the streets with them by day, to the scandal of the few but increasing number of decent and permanent citizens, and crowded the gambling-rooms at night. San Francisco at that time was a sort of crucible in which human character became fluid, only the wildest and most lawless impulses crystallizing on the surface. Perhaps the human character never has been put to so severe a test. Most of these young men had been well brought up, many would return, if they did return, to a social position in their native town. But they were in a country almost without law, with none of the restraining influences of organized society, their brains reeling with sudden wealth taken from the earth in the most romantic surroundings, and further exhilarated by the electric air; all that was primitive in them became rampant.

To characters naturally strong came the inevitable reaction before harm had been done, and many of these wild young men lived to become "leading citizens" in San Francisco and elsewhere. But others formed habits never to be broken, squandered all they had on worthless women and in the gambling-halls, and either drifted whence they came or hid themselves under the brush of the sand-hills and blew out their brains. The mines themselves were a relentless clearing-house. It required not only physical strength but moral endurance to succeed greatly; and hundreds of miners, weakened by hardships and the unsanitary conditions, and despairing of ever "striking it

## CRIME AND FIRE

rich," crept back to the city to die of pneumonia, dysentery, or by their own hand; unless they had saved the price of the return voyage or could borrow it.

Only the clean tonic air of San Francisco saved it from hideous epidemics, for its population grew daily, and most of it was herded in bunk-houses made of lath and cotton, or was camping in tents. The refuse was left in the streets; there was a garbage-heap at every door. As it was, there were several light epidemics of cholera, and it is possible that even the keen Pacific winds would not have saved the city from sudden depopulation had not another element come to the rescue. Within eighteen months San Francisco was almost burned to the ground six times. The first of these fires occurred on December 4, 1849, and a million dollars went up in flames, but with them a vast amount of germ-breeding filth. On the 4th of May, 1850, property was destroyed to the amount of four million dollars. The greatest of these fires was on the 14th of May, 1851, in which twelve million dollars' worth of business blocks and merchandise were consumed.

After each of these fires, almost before they were extinguished, the citizens began to rebuild with dauntless courage and energy, and in spite of the cumulative effects of disasters seeming to hint that Nature had not lost her old spite against that coast of so many geological vicissitudes. But the final result was, that after the most leveling fire in her history, not to be surpassed until April, 1906, she erected the greater number of her hotels and business houses of substantial materials and organized a proper water system; an improvement entirely overlooked before. The indomitable spirit and enterprise of that day can be laid to the survival of the fittest.

# CALIFORNIA

The times needed strong men, strong of body and brain, and only the strong could survive in the face of unparalleled hardships, trials, temptations, and disasters. These men, not all saints by any means, formed a nucleus which enabled San Francisco itself to survive and become the great city of the Western world.

It is to be remembered that although a year and a half is a negligible period in an old community, every month is a crowded year in such conditions as existed in San Francisco during and immediately after the gold-rush. Scarcely a day that men did not have their faculties and characters tried to the limit of human endurance. The strong men saw the weak falling on every side, dying like flies, creeping back from the mines unrecognizable wrecks of the men that had struck the trail a few months before with the insolent boast that they would sail for "the States" with a million in their pockets before the year was out. The men born to survive spent their days in keen business competition, money crises, and in a feverish atmosphere whose temperature never seemed to drop; their nights with one ear open for the horrid cry of fire and the sharp clang of alarm-bells. At the first signal they were out of bed, doctors, lawyers, merchants, politicians, mechanics rushing to the engine-houses, of which the greater number were enrolled members, thence to the hills to watch a sea of flame roll over all they possessed. They had their moments of despair, of wild excitement, but out of each succeeding conflagration they emerged more finely tempered, more grimly determined that this city of San Francisco should become as great a city as any they had left behind, and their own fortunes rise from the ashes seventy times seven if the Fates pursued them.

# CRIME AND FIRE

When one remembers the character of these men and the spirit with which they animated the city and stamped it, one can the more easily understand the courage and energies which astonished the world after the great disaster of 1906.

But the sturdy citizens of San Francisco were not tested by fire alone and the demoralizing atmosphere of the times. No sooner had they disposed of the Hounds than they became aware of a new menace to their security, although these fresh additions to the young city's underworld were difficult to locate. Taking warning from the fate of the noisy and defiant Hounds, these scoundrels did not advertise themselves by a headquarters, nor did they parade. A few of this new band of criminals were Mexicans, but the greater number and by far the bolder were released criminals and ticket-of-leave men from Australia. At the end of 1849 a hundred thousand immigrants had poured into the territory. A similar number arrived in 1850, advancing the population of San Francisco alone from five thousand to nearly thirty thousand. Naturally, it was easy for criminals to slip in singly or in hordes, for all claimed to be bound for the mines, which were turning millions a month into the pockets of the industrious, the persistent, and the lucky. The "Sidney Coves," however, had no intention of working with pick and shovel at the mines; San Francisco was a gold-mine itself.

The citizens, after their exercise of summary justice by popular tribunal, had elected officers to keep the city in order, and returned to their personal avocations. But while the merchants, bankers, and other business men snatched the city again and again from ruin by fire, financial shipwreck, and the still greater menace of moral evil, the judges, lawyers, and public officials in general were no credit to the community. The Hall McAllisters were rare, and lawyers of the order of shyster and shark had come to the new territory in droves, knowing that they could establish themselves unnoticed and make as much money with their dishonest wits as all but the luckiest at the mines. These men could be bought by the enterprising members of the underworld with gold-dust and promise of votes, and the human vultures that now infested the city were able to conceal their individualities and their dwelling-places from the citizens as long as they chose, looting the town with such frequency and thoroughness that every man went to business with a pistol in his belt and slept with it under his pillow. Once more nobody stirred abroad at night; and those that patronized the gambling-rooms entered before dusk and remained until daylight.

Where the Hounds had dared to kill upon one occasion only, these desperados murdered nightly and often by day, partly because it amused them, partly to cover their tracks. The few police were terrorized and rarely interfered with their adventures. They were more than suspected of starting the fires that they might loot by wholesale, and they even raided the gambling-houses in broad daylight, filling their hats with the gold on the tables and leaving a trail of blood behind them.

It is true that some were arrested, but their lawyers were well paid and specious, and it was seldom that a judge could be found to convict them. Theft, robbery, burglary, murder were all in the day's work, and as their contempt for law increased, a community of un-

## CRIME AND FIRE

speakable wickedness and degradation called Sidney Town flourished openly on the outskirts of the city at Clark's Point. Its denizens seemed to increase with the malignant velocity of locusts. The busy harried citizens of the little community endured their outrages from the end of '49 to the beginning of '51, hoping against hope that the law would prove equal to its obligations and leave the good men free to build and rebuild and attend to their ever-increasing problems. But although the San Franciscan is noted for his philosophy and his patience, he is equally distinguished for the sudden cessation of those virtues and for his grim and immovable attitude when he has made up his mind to exterminate and reconstruct.

The citizens of San Francisco suddenly and without warning "sat up" in June, 1851, and formed the first of the two famous Committees of Vigilance.

One hundred and eighty-four of the wealthiest, most prominent, and, what was more to the point, as it meant neglect of business, the most industrious and enterprising of San Francisco's men formed themselves into a secret Committee of Vigilance for the purpose of cleaning up the city morally and restoring it to order. Although it had been mooted for some time, it was not organized until June, and then not until a desperate attempt had been made to induce the proper authorities to enforce the law. The patience of the general public being exhausted, there had been daily mass-meetings, and indignation reached its climax when two alleged murderers, an Englishman named James Stuart and a confederate, Joseph Windred, were taken to the City Hall for trial with little prospect of conviction. Eight thousand citizens surrounded the building, clamoring for justice. Fourteen of their number—W. D. M. Howard, Samuel Brannan, A. J. Ellis, H. F. Teschemacker, W. H. Jones, B. Ray, G. A. King, A. H. Sibley, J. L. Folsom, F. W. Macondray, Ralph Dorr, Theodore Payne, Talbot H. Green, and J. B. Huie—were appointed a committee to consult with the authorities and guard the prisoners from public wrath until they should be tried. The situation may be indicated by the brief speech made by Mr. Brannan to the more conservative of the committeemen:

> I am very much surprised to hear people talk about grand juries, recorders, or mayors. I'm tired of such talk. These men are murderers, I say, as well as thieves. I know it, and I will die or see them hung by the neck. I'm opposed to any farce in this business. We had enough of that eighteen months ago, when we allowed ourselves to be the tools of those judges who sentenced convicts to be sent to the United States. We are the mayor and the recorder, the hangman and the law. The laws and the courts never yet hung a man in California, and every morning we are reading fresh accounts of murders and robberies. I want no technicalities. Such things are devised to shield the guilty.

But moderation prevailed for the moment. After another appeal to the assembled people it was decided to choose a jury from their number, as well as a sheriff, judges, a clerk, and a public prosecutor. Men of the highest standing were immediately elected for these offices: William T. Coleman, prosecuting attorney; Hall McAllister and D. O. Shattuck, counsel for the prisoners; J. R. Spence, presiding judge; H. R. Bowie and Charles L. Ross, associate judges; John E. Townes, sheriff; and W. A. Jones, clerk. While the whole town was still in an uproar the two prisoners were tried and defended, but the jury disagreed, and in spite of the shouts of "Hang them! Hang them!" from without, "The ma-

## CRIME AND FIRE

jority rules!" they were handed over to the authorities to be tried in due legal form. The result was what no doubt even those stern but still patient men may have expected: Windred, who was sentenced to fourteen years' imprisonment, found no difficulty in cutting his way out of jail and escaping; and Stuart (who turned out to be the wrong man and innocent) was sent to Marysville to stand his trial for murder.

It was then that patience ceased to be a virtue and the Vigilance Committee was organized.

They chose as headquarters rooms on the corner of Battery and Pine streets. The Monumental Fire Company was to toll the bell (instead of ringing it wildly, as for fires) as a signal for the committee to meet and try a prisoner. It was on the night of the 10th of June that the bell tolled for the first time; and its deep solemn note filled the city. Thousands of citizens who had the merest inkling of what was on foot tumbled out of their houses and gathered in the street before the lighted room to await the verdict, for they soon learned that a prisoner, John Jenkins, a "Sidney Cove," was on trial for his life.

The proceedings within were thorough but brief. At midnight the bell tolled again as a signal that the death-sentence had been passed and that the execution would take place at once. Mr. Brannan came out and addressed the crowd, telling them what had been done, that all evidence had been sifted, and asking their opinion of the verdict. The crowd expressed its unanimous approval in a shout which drowned the slow clanging of the bell. A clergyman went in to talk to the condemned man, and at two o'clock Jenkins was brought out, closely pinioned and surrounded by the members of the committee, who were

# CALIFORNIA

armed to the teeth. The waiting crowd silently fell into line behind and marched through Sansome, California, Montgomery, and Clay streets to the Plaza. The noose was adjusted and the other end thrown over a beam projecting from an adobe house. Scarcely a word was spoken, but many hands volunteered at the rope until the wretch's struggles ceased. The man was one of the most notorious of the desperados infesting the city, but had he been obscure it is doubtful if "the law" would have taken more than a perfunctory notice of this act of summary justice, being now fully aware that the majority of San Francisco's population was on the side of the Vigilantes.

The committee then emerged from its secrecy, published its roll of names in full, and, invoking an old Mexican law which forbade the immigration of any person convicted of crime in another country, ordered the Cove population to leave California at once. Some were shipped off; others, terrified by the fate of Jenkins, fled without further invitation.

Meanwhile the Committee of Vigilance had found the true James Stuart and ordered the miserable creature shivering in the Marysville jail to be set at liberty. Of all the villains of that day Stuart seems to have been dyed with the darkest and most indelible pigment. He had begun his career of crime at the age of sixteen and omitted none in the calendar. When, staring down at those rows of determined men, with their set grim faces, and at the armed body-guard against the walls, at the doors, and on the stairs, he realized that the game was up he determined to retire from the world in a blaze of glory, and told of his hundred crimes vividly and in horrid detail. After he had finished he was given two hours for repentance.

# CRIME AND FIRE

At the end of that time the big bell tolled; manacled and surrounded by drawn pistols to prevent any attempt at rescue, he was escorted to the wharf at the foot of Market Street and hanged.

At this point the governor, John McDougal, although secretly in sympathy with the committee, felt that he must make a show of upholding the law, and when it was known that two other prisoners had been taken to the rooms on Battery Street he counseled the sheriff to rescue them and take them to the official lockup. The sheriff effected the rescue by a coup; but immediately the bell tolled, and the committee hastened to their headquarters. A few hours afterward they broke into the jail, brushed aside the guards, and hurried the prisoners into a coach. A whip was freely applied to the horses, which galloped down to Battery Street, while the bell tolled the announcement that the men, Whittaker and McKenzie, were about to die. The crowd ran after the carriage, but when they reached the place of execution the two bodies, hooded and pinioned, were swinging in the air.

After this no further attempt was made to interfere with the committee, but neither were they called upon to execute further vengeance. Those of the Coves that had dared to linger on fled like rats, and for a while the city had a complete rest from crime, although seldom from excitement.

It was now a substantial-looking city, with real hotels and solid houses in place of shacks and tents; a hospital, a mercantile library, a cemetery (for a time the dead had been buried where they fell and often sickened in the streets), churches, brick and granite business buildings, and an orderly population—for a time. The better class no

# CALIFORNIA

longer gambled in public or attended bull-fights at the mission; and although the city was still unpaved and the rats ran over the citizens' feet as they floundered through the mud at night, and the prices remained so high that the San Franciscans of the '50's would have laughed to scorn the complaints of to-day, at least the proud citizens could go unarmed once more and enjoy the knowledge that their belongings were their own and that there was a reasonable prospect of dying in bed.

The population of California at the close of 1853 was estimated at 326,000, of whom 204,000 were Americans, 30,000 Germans, 28,000 French, 20,000 Hispano-Americans, other foreigners of white extraction 5,000, Chinese 17,000, Indians 30,000, Negroes 2,000. Of this number one hundred thousand were supposed to be working miners, the others forming the population of the towns and rural communities. The population of San Francisco was fifty thousand, thirty-two thousand of whom were Americans. By this time the metropolis boasted about eight thousand women, good, bad, and indifferent. Three hundred children, many of them the abandoned offspring of the criminal class, had wandered into a town which had little welcome for the unprotected. In 1851 my grandfather, Stephen Franklin, assisted by several ladies of the different churches, succeeded in founding an orphan-asylum, and gathered up such of the waifs as had survived neglect or had not gasped out their feeble lives, abandoned among the sand-hills.

There were fifteen fire-companies in this ambitious but inflammable city, which now had nearly two hundred and fifty streets and alleys, two public squares, sixteen hotels, sixty-three bakeries, five public markets, twenty bathing-

## CRIME AND FIRE

establishments, fifteen flour and saw mills, thirteen foundries and iron-works, nineteen banking-firms, eighteen public stables, ten public schools with twenty-one teachers and 1,259 scholars, besides private schools, eighteen churches with 8,000 members, six military companies with 350 members in all, two government hospitals and one private one, an almshouse, eight lodges of secret benevolent societies, a fine law library, two hundred attorneys, four public benevolent societies, twelve newspapers, a Philharmonic Society, five theaters, two race-courses, several lecture-halls, twelve large wharves, forty-two wholesale liquor houses, and five hundred and thirty-seven saloons. It was now five years since the great immigration had given a fresh impulse to the once serene little city, and it had lived at the rate of fifty. It covered three square miles, and its real estate was valued at thirty-eight million dollars. Since it had risen from the ashes of the last fire in 1851 it had begun to feel more like a veritable city, not quite like other cities perhaps, but still one of which its indomitable and sorely tried founders could well be proud. After its sweeping clean-up it breathed freely for almost three years; but although it had few delusions about the permanence of good conduct in that town of many nationalities and temptations, nothing was further from its mind than tolling the bell for another Committee of Vigilance.

But before describing those tragic and far-reaching events which led to the organization of the most formidable public tribunal in the history of modern civilization it is necessary to devote a chapter to the politics of the state from the time of the American occupation, in 1846, until the assassination of James King of Wm.

# XI

POLITICS

THE military governors of California immediately following the occupation were Sloat, Stockton, Kearney, Mason, and Riley. On April 13, 1849, Brig.-Gen. Bennett Riley, upon his arrival in California, announced that he had assumed the administration of the civil affairs of California. He found a territory seething with political problems in no wise obscured by the excitement of the gold discovery.

Congress had provided no territorial government for its new possession on the Pacific coast, although the treaty with Mexico had been ratified in May of the previous year. It was not long before the anxious and indignant Californians, their need of definite laws increasing daily, learned the reason. The two great parties in Congress had locked horns over the question of the introduction of slavery into the vast territory extending to the Rocky Mountains and known as California. The South had advocated the annexation of Texas and the Mexican War solely in the hope of increasing its own strength, Congress being equally divided on the slave question.

President Polk in his message of December 5, 1848, had pointed out that California with its abnormal conditions demanded the immediate organization of a territorial government. Its inhabitants, already numbering

## POLITICS

many hundreds of Americans, were entitled to the protection of the laws and Constitution of the United States, and yet were left without any provision according them their rights. It was true that the very limited power of the executive had been exercised to preserve and protect them from anarchy; but the only government in the country was that established by the military authority. In other words, California had a mere *de facto* government—resting on the presumed consent of the inhabitants—consisting of nine parts military authority and the rest such efforts as minor officials might make to insure peace by the enforcement of the old Mexican machinery. The Americans in California had accepted this condition on the understanding that Congress, immediately upon the consummation of the treaty with Mexico, would legislate a legal and authoritative government. New-comers and old cherished nothing but contempt for the rusty and inadequate Mexican laws, and they liked the undemocratic military rule no better. As time passed and no relief came from Washington they grew more and more indignant, holding mass-meetings all over the state, save at the gold-mines, which preferred their own laws.

All that Washington had done at the beginning of 1849 was to extend the revenue laws over the new territory, making San Francisco a port of entry, and Monterey, San Diego, and what was called later Fort Yuma, ports of delivery; authorize the President to appoint a collector of customs, and provide a complete revenue system; appoint William van Voorhies agent for the establishment of post-offices and the transmission of mails throughout the territory; and, in January, to appoint a commission under John B. Weller to run and mark the boundary line between Mexico and the United States. At the end of the Polk administration, in March, 1849, with the free and slave states equal numerically, it looked as if California might precipitate the death-struggle between the North and the South.

There were already many able men in California apart from the hardy pioneers seeking fortune at the mines; men of brains, education, political experience, executive ability, and sense of public responsibility. Some of the men— Sutter, Leese, Howard, Pacificus Ord, Walter Colton, Larkin, Hartnell, Semple, Brannan, Don Timeteo Murphy, Josiah Belden, first mayor of San José — had lived in the country for many years before the discovery of gold. A few were native Californians—Vallejo, Pablo de la Guerra (son of the redoubtable old Don José), Romualdo Pacheco, Carrillo, Covarrubias. But the ablest by far were William Gwin and David Broderick, two men who had come to the future great state to gratify their political ambitions more quickly than was possible in older communities, and share in its spectacular opportunities. Gwin was from Tennessee, a gentleman by birth, upon whom fortune continued to smile until the Civil War, a man of wide experience in politics, and, what was rare for that day, of considerable personal experience of Europe. He also had had adventures enough to harden him for the rôle of pioneer. He may be ranked as the most intellectual, brilliant, subtle, suave, and unscrupulous leader California has ever had. His one rival was Broderick, an Irish-American, a stone-mason's son, who had been a fireman and ward politician in New York. His native abilities were as great as, if not greater

## POLITICS

than, Mr. Gwin's, but he had had little education and at that time was rough in dress and manner. But there was no political trick he did not know, nor had he the least scruple in using the basest henchmen to accomplish his ends. But he was a man in whom good predominated outside of politics, as will be seen; and he possessed, and gradually developed, real greatness. Both men were Democrats, but Gwin was proslavery, Broderick violently opposed to it and determined that it should never be introduced into California. He was twenty-nine years old at this time, Gwin forty-four—so advanced an age in that era of young men that he was always mentioned as "old Gwin." He was a very handsome man, however, tall, stately, smooth-shaven, patrician. Broderick, it must be confessed, looked like a chimpanzee; his upper lip was abnormally long, and his face fringed from ear to ear, but he was quite as impressive in his way as Mr. Gwin, and had a cold blue-gray eye of extraordinary penetration and power.

Frémont also had come back to California to play a political rôle in the territory so romantically associated with his name, but his California career was practically at an end. Other men to figure in the history of the state and of San Francisco particularly were William T. Coleman, Horace Hawes, Eugene Casserly, Hall McAllister, Peter Burnett, John McDougal, Thomas B. King, James King of Wm., Joseph H. Folsom, John W. Geary, Theodore Payne, and a future chief justice of the United States, Stephen J. Field, at that time identified with Marysville.

These men were not tempted, or but briefly, by the mines. They recognized their own mental abilities as well as the future greatness of California; but they were

## CALIFORNIA

appalled by the conditions bordering on chaos, and they had asked Governor Mason to call a constitutional convention. But although Mason was the best and most sympathetic of the military governors, he was a cool and wary officer and felt no disposition toward so radical a measure. Before his administration came to an end, however, he was convinced that California in the absence of protection from Washington and with a vast and increasing number of problems, must do something for herself, and advised his successor, General Riley, to call the convention.

Riley demurred and hesitated, but when he learned that once more Congress had adjourned without organizing a territorial government for California he issued a proclamation to the effect that it was necessary to call a constitutional convention, and appointed August 1st as election day for delegates. These elections caused great excitement all over the territory, but most of the men who wished to be delegates and had organized their forces properly were sent to Monterey. It was, on the whole, a notable gathering, and among the thirty-seven delegates were many of the men already mentioned. The convention met in Colton Hall, Monterey, on September 1st, and lasted until the middle of October. There was no question from the beginning of a practically universal sentiment against the introduction of slavery into the territory; and Gwin, too wise ever to advocate a lost cause openly, strove to preserve the territorial boundaries of the cession, which embraced the present Nevada, Utah, and Arizona, and foist it upon Congress for admission into the Union as one vast state. Inevitably it would fall to pieces of its own weight, and it would then be an easy matter not only

## POLITICS

to deliver portions of it to the Southern faction, but to separate southern California from the north and capture it for slavery. The native Californians, who were already disgusted and alarmed, favored the division at once, but the whole scheme, subtle and open, was defeated. Northern men were on the watch for every move of the enemy, and the Americans of the intermediate period in California were determined upon a compact state between the Sierra Nevada Mountains and the Pacific Ocean.

The state constitution, closely following that of the state of New York, was drawn up finally, and in November submitted to the people. They adopted it promptly, and Peter H. Burnett was elected governor, John McDougal lieutenant-governor, Edward Gilbert and George W. Wright Representatives to Congress. On Saturday, December 15th, the first legislature under the constitution met at San José, and Gwin and Frémont were elected United States Senators; but Frémont drew the short term and enjoyed the coveted honor for only six months.

When the Senators and Representatives arrived in Washington the fight over the admission of California was at white-heat. Clay, curiously enough, advocated it without the slave clause, and Webster refused to vote for the prohibition, "as California was destined for freedom, and he would not take the pains to reaffirm an ordinance of nature or re-enact the will of God!" Calhoun, on the other hand, expended his dying energy in denouncing the Californians for daring to make a state without the consent of Congress, insisted that it should be remanded back to its old condition, as its admission would irretrievably destroy the equilibrium between the two national sections. Having exhausted their thunder, they put the momentous question to the vote; and in August, 1850, the bill providing for the admission of California as a state passed the Senate, all members from free states and six from slave states voting in its favor. On September 19, 1850, President Fillmore signed the bill, and California became the thirty-first state of the Union.

When the news made its slow way to the Pacific coast there was ringing of bells in San Francisco, and, in all the towns of the state, bonfires, balls, and general rejoicing. One great question was settled for all time, and the new constitution had given them the laws of an old and highly civilized state. But the laws proved to be more civilized than the inhabitants. As we have seen, the responsible citizens of San Francisco had twice been obliged to take the law into their own hands; and this was done again and again at the mines.

A community large enough for the making of money in more than living quantities would seem to be much like the human body afflicted with certain microbous diseases: the germs can be frozen out or dried out by change of climate and drastic measures, but when vigilance is relaxed they swarm back to devour the body or the body politic. If it were not for this eternal warfare between good and evil life would be dull enough, no doubt, and anathema to the reformers; but it is certainly a remarkable fact that with advancing civilization there is little or no diminution of the number and prowess of the forces of evil. As quickly as the surgeon's knife is applied to one spot and the world triumphantly informed that this particular abuse is gone for ever, the same malignant elements rooted in human nature break out in an-

FIRST ADMISSION-DAY CELEBRATION, 1850, CALIFORNIA AND MONTGOMERY STREETS

## POLITICS

other spot, are called by another name, and eat their vile way until once more they are cut from the surface and forced to burrow toward a new pasture. In other words, the good men (or the better) go to sleep after a grand display of all their latent forces, and the bad men (who have enjoyed a rest and recuperated) move silently to the fore.

In a young community like San Francisco, which had skipped the intermediate stages of growth and developed abruptly from an almost innocent and quite contented childhood to a raging, crude, and heterogeneous maturity, life was a matter of extremes. Men grew rich in a month by the inflation of prices and lost all in the reaction after a wild period of speculation; they were upright patriotic citizens, behaving themselves astonishingly well, considering the atmosphere in which they lived, or they were disreputable gamblers, pimps, and outlaws. All classes and kinds had but one thing in common—they were as extravagant as if the very sand-dunes behind the ugly uncomfortable little city were composed of grains of gold and would be renewed until the end of time. Wives and daughters had been sent for before the fifties were well advanced, and they dressed quite as brilliantly as the ladies of the lower ten thousand; many private carriages looked singularly out of place in those uneven streets fringed with garbage; there were nightly balls, and the theaters were crowded whenever artists found the way to that remote coast. In that feverish unreal life the domestic settled existence of older communities was almost unknown; business, politics, and the ever-increasing problems of the town, furnished a constant excitement for the men, who preferred to spend their

## CALIFORNIA

evenings in the private rooms of public resorts discussing ways and means. The women had to find excitement for themselves; and the consequence was many divorces. In fact, unless a woman had young children to absorb her, or abnormally high principles, or some inner capital, flirtation was practically the only distraction in that new community absolutely without the common resources of civilization. It was for that reason that when such natural social leaders as Mrs. Hall McAllister, Mrs. Gwin, and other Southern women did take hold and organize society, their laws were more stringent than anything they had left behind them. Women who would remain members of that select band must at least exercise prudence in their indiscretions; and although no one in that gossiping community was free from slander, if sufficiently prominent, at least there was a high standard, and this standard existed until almost the present time.

But these women numbered hundreds, and the women of commerce swarmed into San Francisco by the thousand and paraded the streets constantly, bolder than they have ever dared to be since—although any woman in a crinoline and a coal-scuttle bonnet must have found some difficulty in making herself look bold and unclassed —and these, besides being the decoys for the gambling-houses, saloons, and restaurants, furnished cause for many of the divorces.

And as for the underworld, it might flee the immediate wrath, but it invariably crept back—unless lynched—and was augmented by villains of a new dye. After the suppression of lawlessness in 1851 the citizens had much to occupy their attention for several years. Until 1854 money came freely, people seemed to grow richer every day. As

# POLITICS

a natural result they became intoxicated with prosperity and over-built, over-speculated, over-imported, and spent with mad extravagance. In 1854 came the inevitable reaction, which was precipitated by a dry winter and crop failures, the ruinous speculation and even dishonesty of business men and bankers, the looting of the city treasury by officials. In 1854 three hundred out of a thousand business houses failed, and in the course of the year there were filed in the courts seventy-seven petitions of insolvency, aggregating many millions of dollars. In the following year the insolvencies numbered one hundred and ninety-seven, and several banking-houses failed, crippling or ruining outright a large number of depositors and business firms.

It may be imagined that during this stormy period the excitement was greater than ever before, men were more individual and self-centered in their interests. This was the opportunity for thousands of human buzzards, and they swarmed in, fattening on prosperity and ruin alike.

By far the most devastating of these to the distracted city were the professional politicians, men of the lowest type, who had been educated in the wards of the Eastern cities, and whose sole attitude to the world was that of the looter in search of loot. Either finding it expedient to vanish from their native haunts, or scenting heavier dividends in vice, they came to the new city by every ship; and while its citizens were using all their energies, first in aggrandizement and pleasure and then to keep their unseaworthy ship above the storm waters, they quietly took political possession.

Honest men, in fact, learned to avoid the polls, gangs

of bullies being on hand to relieve the political organization from the embarrassment of honest men's votes. Conventions were a mere matter of form, the inner ring having made its decisions in secret conclave; votes were sold to the highest bidder, ballot-boxes were stuffed, the type in vogue having a "double improved back action," and in which any number of tickets could be hidden in advance: there was always danger that a few honest men might get by the bullies and cast their vote.

As this gang of clever rascals appointed all the officials it followed that the judges were as corrupt as most of the lawyers, and their social status may be inferred by the fact that they chewed and expectorated in court, sat on the bench in their shirt-sleeves, swore and shouted, and even cut their corns.

The people of the better class of San Francisco were well aware that their city was worm-eaten and threatened with decay, but, absorbed in personal matters, were unwilling to face the fact and unite in a tribunal which must mean the neglect of business for several months at least. Between 1849 and 1856 over a thousand murders had been committed, and only one legal conviction secured. The lawsuits following the failures of 1854–55 had revealed the utterly corrupt state of the law. No one was convicted, no one could obtain satisfaction; the lawyers were masters of every technicality that permitted evasion or defeat of justice; lawsuits threatened to outlast a lifetime, and an apathetic despair, which may be compared to the proverbial lull, settled upon the citizens of San Francisco, half or wholly ruined, as they watched prosperity ebbing daily; politics and law in the hands of crooks and criminals; and thieves, looters, and murderers

# POLITICS

as thick as the fleas in the sand. Even the newspapers were terrorized; and although the editors had many duels, they were not with the men they most feared.

The times were ripe for the man, and, as ever, he arrived.

## XII

### JAMES KING OF WM.

OF all the personalities that stand out so compellingly in the annals of that formative period of San Francisco James King of Wm. is the most appealing. Gifted with a brilliant mind, an upright character, an honest and generous heart, no one ever developed a more passionate scorn of corruption and love of civic decencies, no one ever was less discouraged by the remonstrances of timid men and the threats of the powerful and unscrupulous. Single-handed this dauntless little gentleman undertook to clean up San Francisco. He accomplished his end far sooner than he anticipated, but with his life, not his pen.

James King of Wm. was born in Georgetown, D. C., January 28, 1822. When he was sixteen, finding another James King in his immediate circle, he affixed his father's patronymic, and to the day of his death was rarely alluded to more briefly.

He married in 1843, worked too hard in the banking-house of Corcoran & Riggs, in Washington, broke down early in 1848, visited Peru and Chili with the view of engaging in business, but heard of the gold discovery in California and sailed at once for San Francisco. He was not strong enough for the hard physical work and exposure at the mines, however, and after a few months of indifferent

JAMES KING OF WM.

## JAMES KING OF WM.

luck went to Sacramento and obtained a position in the mercantile firm of Hensley, Reading & Co. His abilities seem to have been recognized at once, for he was made a partner in the same year. In the following year, however, he opened a banking-house in San Francisco in partnership with Jacob B. Snyder; the firm was called James King of Wm. & Co. His family now joined him, and for a time his home was one of the conspicuous centers of hospitality, refinement, and luxury, where the talk was as sparkling as the wines. But this brilliant social episode lasted less than four years. In June, 1854, his associates having involved him by speculations, he merged his firm with that of Adams & Co., and went down to disaster with that house in the panic of 1855. He surrendered to his creditors everything he possessed, and in order to explain to an excited public his connection with the outrageous frauds of Adams & Co., which he had been unaware of before the merger and powerless to arrest later, he wrote a number of pamphlets and newspaper articles. The style of these—brilliant, forcible, and direct—arrested immediate attention; and as it was known that he wished to edit a newspaper, the money was raised at once. On October 8, 1855, he issued the first number of the *Daily Evening Bulletin*, a newspaper that again and again has played its part in the history of the state.

By this time James King of Wm. was as well known to his fellow-citizens, good and bad, as a pronounced individuality ever must be in a small community. His honor, in spite of his unfortunate association with Adams & Co., was unchallenged; he never had hesitated to express his opinion openly of the civic and individual corruptions of San Francisco and to suggest remedies; hot-tempered and argumentative, he had refused to fight when challenged to a duel, but no one thought of questioning his personal courage. When he declined, however, he added that, while he was opposed on principle to dueling, and had a family to consider, he went armed and certainly should defend himself if assaulted.

Therefore when the public heard that King was about to edit a paper of his own they were far more interested than was usual in that day of many and hapless journalistic ventures. It knew that his paper would be interesting, virile, a new departure, and that it would be as fearless as himself, waging relentless war upon the forces of evil that were devastating the city. In short, lively times were anticipated, and no one was disappointed.

He began with light satiric fencing; but in the fourth issue he took off his gloves. Certain banking-firms, alive and defunct, were shown up in all their rottenness. No other paper had dared to attack them—Sam Brannan had retired from journalism and Mormonism long since, and was now engaged in becoming a millionaire—but when King had finished his exposures, written as they were by one who had grown up in the banking business, the most friendly, indifferent, and doubting were convinced. He next paid his respects to Broderick, whom he called David Cataline Broderick, accusing him of the most flagrant election frauds, of striving by corrupt means only to get himself elected United States Senator, and of complicity in the Jenny Lind Theater swindle, one of the financial disasters of the moment. He finished one of his attacks with a sentence that may have sealed his fate; for, although Broderick himself was above compassing the death of any man save in fair fight, the evil forces of the city were growing more uneasy and angry with every issue of the *Bulletin*.

"We have every confidence," wrote King, "that the people will stand by us in this contest; and if we can only escape David C. Broderick's hired bullies a little while longer we will turn this city inside out, but we will expose the corruption and malfeasance of her officiary."

But, although threatened and challenged, no attempt was made upon his life for a time, and he attacked every man and every institution given to corrupt practices, paying particular attention to the large gambling-houses (whose advertisements kept most of the newspapers going) and other traps for the weak and unwary. It is unnecessary to add that an attempt was made to muzzle him, by the offer of large and remunerative advertisements, from the most notorious of these concerns, and that he paid as little attention to them as to threats and black looks. Nor had he any hesitation in showing up the other newspapers.

Even the strongest and most upright among his friends were aghast and uneasy; in the whole history of journalism no editor had ever gone as far as this. But he was quite justified in anticipating public support. Everybody bought the *Bulletin*—those that hoped it would air the evils of the city and probe its sores until the disease had disappeared, and those that execrated it yet were afflicted with a morbid desire to read what might be written about themselves or their friends. By the end of the year its circulation was larger than that of all the other newspapers combined, and none had ever compared with it in swaying public opinion. While undeniably sensational, it was not vulgar nor blatant, and it was invariably well written and interesting. Above all, it furnished at last what many had long more or less vaguely desired— a rallying-point toward which all the decent element in the city could converge for purposes of organization.

But still nothing happened. All that he exposed was known or suspected already, and until some fresh enormity occurred it hardly would be possible for King to hasten those converging but lagging footsteps into a dead run. He knew that such an opportunity must come; and come it did, long before the public had time to tire of his exposure of well-known abuses against which the laws were powerless.

In less than six weeks after the first issue of the *Bulletin*, and while little else was discussed but the topics it furnished daily, and the people were in just the right frame of mind to burst into frenzy upon provocation, United States Marshal William H. Richardson was murdered by a notorious gambler named Charles Cora. The two men drank more than their tempers could stand in a saloon, got into an altercation, and left the place still wrangling. Richardson, it is assumed, had attacked the system of ballot-box stuffing, in which Cora was a conspicuous expert. When the two men reached the neighborhood of California and Leidersdorff streets they paused suddenly, and a bystander saw Cora grasp the collar of Richardson's coat and point a pistol at his breast. Richardson, who had his hands in his pockets, exclaimed: "You would not shoot me, would you? I am not armed." Before any one seems to have been able or disposed to go to the rescue Cora had fired and shot him dead.

This man, of uncertain nationality, was a well-known figure about town, being good-looking, young, well dressed, always to be seen on Kearney and Montgomery streets at the promenade hours, in the fashionable restaurants, and, during San Francisco's madder hours, in one or other of the great gambling-houses. He also walked the fashionable thoroughfares openly with the most famous woman of commerce in the town, Belle Cora, who had impudently assumed his name in exchange for the funds that gratified his exquisite tastes, when luck failed him at the tables. When the news flew through the city that an upright citizen and servant of the Federal government whose only weakness was the one most easily excused in mining communities had been murdered in cold blood by a creature whom all decent men regarded with abhorrence as a *maquereau*, to say nothing of his degraded life in all respects, there was immediate and intense excitement. Cries of "Lynch him!" resounded from the crowds that filled the principal streets in less than half an hour; men already inflamed by King's daily exposures were in no mood to endure philosophically the thought that this man Cora could command all the corrupt machinery of the law in his defense.

Cora had been hurried off to jail and locked up under a heavy guard; but, although the city that night held its breath as the old tocsin of the California Engine Company's No. 4 bell tolled suddenly and imperatively, and although many of the Vigilantes of 1851 promptly answered the call—the first being the fiery Sam Brannan—it was decided after several hours of debate to give the law one last opportunity to redeem itself.

On Monday the coroner's inquest pronounced that the murder had been premeditated and without a mitigating circumstance. No other verdict was possible without rousing the town to frenzy, and a few hoped for a real trial and conviction. But not James King of Wm.

That no effort will be spared to get Cora clear [he wrote in the *Bulletin*] begins now to be apparent. His friends are already at work. Forty thousand dollars, it is said, have been subscribed for the purpose. Of this some five thousand will be sufficient to cover the lawyers' fees and court charges, and the balance can be used as occasion may require. One bad man on the jury will be sufficient to prevent an agreement. Look well to the jury! . . . What we propose is this: If the jury which tries Cora is packed either *hang the sheriff* or drive him out of town. . . . If Mr. Sheriff Scannell does not remove Billy Mulligan from his present post as keeper of the county jail, and Mulligan lets his friend Cora escape, *hang Billy Mulligan*, or drive him into banishment. That's the word! . . . Oh, Heaven, it is a mortification to every lover of decency and order in and out of San Francisco, to think that the sheriff of this county is an ex-keeper of a gambling-hell; that his deputy, who acts as keeper of the county jail, is the notorious Billy Mulligan, the late "capper" at a "string game" table.

Belle Cora had retained several lawyers more eminent for brains and legal ability than bitter virtue. When they discovered that the smoldering virtue of the citizens was aroused and growing a hotter white every instant they tried to withdraw, particularly Col. E. D. Baker, who was really an estimable person, and who distinguished himself later in the Civil War. But San Francisco was a motley city where abilities of some sort were necessary to pre-eminence, and Belle Cora was not queen of the night life for nothing. She held her lawyers to their bargain—they had accepted heavy retainers—and they were obliged to make their appearance in court with their client, who was got up like a hero of melodrama. He wore a gorgeous waistcoat, light gloves, a new suit of pale material, a jaunty overcoat; his mustache was little and black, and he lolled with the gambler's air of well-bred indifference. The insolent bearing of this creature, fresh from a wanton murder, caused every one that saw him to hiss, and the crowd in the court-room was with difficulty kept in order.

Colonel Baker was one of the chief exponents of the inflamed oratory of the day, and, being trapped by a woman cleverer than himself, made up his mind to save the murderer if words could do it. His closing speech was a masterpiece, judging it by the standards of the time; and, carried away by his own eloquence, he suddenly held up Belle Cora as a model for all men to admire; picturing her as wronged, misunderstood, unfortunate, yea, but admirable. Her devotion to her lover redeemed her of frailty in the eyes of all men, particularly of himself, and he almost wept as he paid her his tribute. This speech enraged the public, but it served its purpose with the jury, which, "fixed" beforehand, could plead that it had been convinced by the great lawyer's eloquence, and that the defendant had been actuated by the highest motives in killing a marshal of the United States for objecting to the stuffing of ballot-boxes. After being out for twenty-four hours it failed to agree; in other words, the seven men that were above being "fixed," voted for murder, one for manslaughter, and four for acquittal.

The *Bulletin* rushed out an extra invoking the heavens to drape themselves in black.

> The money of the gambler and the prostitute has succeeded, and Cora has another respite. The jury cannot agree and has been discharged. Will Cora be hung by the officers of the law? No. Even on this trial one of the principal witnesses was away, having sold out his establishment for twenty-four hundred dollars and left the state. It is said that another trial cannot be had this term, and by that time where will the other witnesses be? Rejoice ye gamblers and harlots! Rejoice with an exceeding gladness! Assemble in your dens of infamy to-night, let the costly wine flow, let the welkin ring with your shouts of joy. Your triumph is great—oh, how you have

## CALIFORNIA

triumphed! Triumphed over everything that is holy and virtuous and good; and triumphed legally—yes, legally! Your money can accomplish anything in San Francisco, and now you have full permission to run riot at pleasure. Talk of safety in the law? It is a humbug. . . . Rail at the Vigilance Committee and call it an illegal tribunal? What scoundrel lost his life by their action who did not richly deserve it? Many complain of vigilance committees and say we should leave criminals to be dealt with by the law. Dealt with by the law indeed! How dealt with? Allowed to escape when ninety-nine men out of a hundred believe the prisoner to be guilty of murder? Is not this very course calculated to drive an exasperated people to madness, and, instead of a vigilance committee with all its care and anxiety to give a fair trial without the technicalities of the law, to call into action the heated blood of an outraged community; that, rising in its might, may carry everything before it, and hang the wretch without even the semblance of a trial? We want no vigilance committee if it can be avoided, but we do want to see the murderer punished for his crimes.

Day after day King poured forth his indignation in the newspaper that every man read and an ever-increasing number looked to for guidance. It speaks well for the stern school of those few years in a new and unprecedented community that the men of San Francisco restrained themselves as long as they did. They were law-abiding citizens and determined to give their law every opportunity to vindicate itself; but King knew that there was no hope in the law unless it could be shamed into vengeance upon such men as Cora and others of his ilk; into action over murders committed daily, not only in San Francisco, but throughout the lawless state. Two committed on prominent citizens under circumstances of peculiar atrocity while traveling in the country served to press his arguments home, although he needed no fresh fuel to feed his own horror and disgust.

King knew his danger, knew that his enemies, who numbered not only the entire underworld, but the corrupt in his own class, were eager to have him out of the way. They experienced the sensation of being marooned in the crater of a live volcano with upright and unscalable walls. At any moment the muttering lava tides beneath might shoot up and deprive any one of them of power and even of life. One more earthquake and their fate would be sealed. If they could reach down and choke the dauntless little stoker of that bubbling furnace all might yet be well. Life was very busy, memories were short, the other newspapers could be relied upon. Who were in the plot to eliminate James King of Wm. will never be known; possibly because the directing brains were too clever to commit themselves to anything but whispered directions in back-rooms, conveyed through an inconspicuous tool. But that it was a conspiracy deliberately planned and executed no one may doubt. And it furnished the final earthquake they sought at any price of blood or conscience to avoid.

On May 14 (1856), four months after the farce of the Cora trial, King published an article in the *Bulletin* attacking the appointment of a man named Bagley to a position in the United States custom-house. This man had been engaged not long before in a disreputable election fight with James P. Casey, one of the San Francisco supervisors. The editorial was aimed not so much at Bagley as at Casey, who was one of the most "undesirable citizens" in the town.

> It does not matter [remarked Mr. King] how bad a man Casey has been nor how much benefit it might be to the public to have him out of the way, we cannot accord to any one citizen the right to kill him nor even beat him without justifiable personal provocation. The fact that Casey has been an inmate of Sing Sing prison, in New York, is no offense against the laws of this state; nor is the fact of having

stuffed himself through the ballot-box and elected to the board of supervisors from a district where it is said he was not even a candidate, any justification why Mr. Bagley should shoot Mr. Casey, however richly the latter may deserve to have his neck stretched for his fraud on the people.

Shortly after this article appeared Casey presented himself at the *Bulletin* office, which was on Merchant between Montgomery and Sansome streets, and walking in without ceremony, demanded in a loud voice:

"What do you mean?"

King, who was writing at his desk, glanced up casually. "Mean?"

"What do you mean by saying that I was a former inmate of Sing Sing?"

"And were you not?"

"That's not the question. I don't want my past raked up. On that point I am sensitive," added Mr. Casey, naïvely.

"Have you finished?" King had not laid down his pen. "There is the door. Go. Never show your face here again."

Casey glanced through an open door. There were men in the next room. If King had been quite alone it is possible that he would have lost no time. As it was, he merely struck a belligerent attitude and exclaimed, in a loud voice, "If necessary I shall defend myself."

King rose and pointed to the door. "Go. Never show your face here again."

He did not even take the trouble to remind the hired assassin, who stalked out, that he might have selected a more plausible pretense for his indignation than the *Bulletin's* allusion to his sojourn in Sing Sing, since in the trial

## JAMES KING OF WM.

following his election fight with Bagley he had, under cross-examination, admitted the fact, and the news had been commented upon by every newspaper in town. Casey was a thoroughly bad man of violent temper, quite ready to commit a cowardly murder for a consideration, secure in the protection of an element that, in a later battle for municipal decency, came to be known as the "higher ups."

King was under no illusions, and when he left the office saw that his pistol was in his hip pocket.

San Francisco will always be a gray city, for although her winds—poetically but incorrectly known as "the trades"—make her uncommonly healthy, the fogs that roll down from the tule lands of the north and in from the sea impress their sad hue on the imagination of the builders. This may be because the Californians are an artistic people, and the law of harmony demands that the city landscape shall mate with the soft-gray tides that sweep and curl about the shelters of men, often obliterating them; or the fog-bank that marches through the Golden Gate like a mighty ship, to wreck itself upon the hills in a thousand fantastic shapes.

The streets of San Francisco are almost, and often wholly, deserted when the fogs invade the city, giving them an unspeakably dreary aspect and afflicting delicate throats. When the hour for closing comes in the business district, hundreds of men swarm down to the ferry-boats at the foot of Market Street eager to reach their homes under the sun and set with flowers; those living in the city hurry along like black ghosts, with their heads down, looking neither to the right nor the left and longing for their warm firesides.

# CALIFORNIA

At five o'clock on that evening of May 14th King left the *Bulletin* office to walk to his home on the corner of Pacific and Mason streets. He wore a slouch-hat and a cloak called "talma," which he had a habit of holding together across his chest. It is possible that he had quite forgotten Casey and the advisability of being on the alert, particularly when the fog was drifting through the city, for his hands were in their usual position and far from his pistol-pocket. He was crossing Montgomery Street diagonally between Washington and Clay, and was more than half-way across, when Casey, who had been skulking behind an express-wagon, suddenly stepped out of the fog, threw off his cloak, and pointed a large navy revolver at King's breast. Even he, it would appear, had his nerves, for he cried out excitedly:

"Are you armed? Defend yourself! Come on! Defend yourself!"

But he was probably unconscious of his words, for he fired as he spoke. His victim had no time to draw his pistol.

King staggered into the Pacific Express building on the corner. The only other person visible seems to have been Casey's friend, "Ned" McGowan, who scuttled up Washington Street; and no one behind walls noticed anything so common as a pistol-shot until King appeared, stumbling and fainting, in the office of the Pacific Express Company. Then he was tenderly cared for, messengers were despatched post-haste for surgeons, and a bed was improvised. When the surgeons arrived they found that the ball had entered the left breast and gone out of the body under the left shoulder-blade. There could be no doubt that the wound was mortal. He was in great

BACK OF A TYPICAL LETTER-SHEET SUCH AS WAS USED FOR PERSONAL LETTERS TO CORRESPONDENTS "EAST"

pain; anesthetics were administered, and his wife was sent for.

Casey had hastened to give himself up, knowing that the only safe place for him was the jail guarded by his friends and protected by "the law." He was none too soon. Although that was long before the day of the telephone, the news that King had been mortally wounded by Casey flew over the city as if there had been a town crier in every street, and in an incredibly short time there was a howling shrieking mob "down-town," composed of men as hysterical as only men can be under strong provocation, demanding that Casey be lynched on the moment. The prison officials, sure that the jail would be rushed by the black howling mass in the Plaza, sent for a carriage; and Casey, accompanied by the city marshal and the captain of police and several police officers, ran down Dunbar's alley and entered it at the corner of Washington Street. The coachman whipped his horses into a gallop, and the hack with the prisoner and his guards inside, and another friend, the chief engineer of the fire department, clinging on behind, dashed furiously into Kearney Street toward the county jail, on Broadway near Dupont Street. The crowd, shrieking "Hang him! Kill him!" ran after, but the man was safely within the stronger walls before they could catch up with the horses.

In front of the jail stood three of Casey's friends armed to the teeth, Charles Duane, Daniel Aldrich, and Edward McGowan. Thomas King, the dying man's brother, harangued the crowd of furious men, inflaming their passions further until they made an attempt to rush the jail. They were repulsed, and while they were making ready for another attack the rumor flew about that the Vigilance

# CALIFORNIA

Committee was organizing. At the same time Mayor Van Ness appeared and demanded to be heard; he made a speech, counseling patience and promising justice, and, although frequently interrupted with derision, managed to keep them quiet until three separate companies of armed citizens, willing to see Casey hung but opposed to violence, arrived and not only surrounded the jail, but stationed themselves in the corridors and on the roof. The crowd, having no leader, finally turned its back and, still cursing, went down to Montgomery Street and halted before the building where King lay. In a short time not less than ten thousand men stood there, anxious for news of the sufferer, and the police were obliged to stretch a rope in front of the Pacific Express office. Bulletins were issued every few minutes; but as the men could not contain themselves, they finally adjourned to the Plaza, where speeches could be made and some method of vengeance determined upon. But again there was no leader; and, once more hearing that the Vigilance Committee was assembling, they finally adjourned to the space in front of the county jail. About three hundred men were now on guard there.

At eleven o'clock Frederick W. Macondray and John Sime, two friends of King, and themselves citizens of the highest type, obtained admittance to the jail. When they came out they informed the crowd that it was impossible for Casey to escape or to be rescued. A half-hour later a mounted battalion under Major Rowell, consisting of the California Guards, the First Light Dragoons, and the National Lancers, reinforced the guard of citizens, and the crowd finally dispersed. Casey for the moment was safe from lynch law.

# JAMES KING OF WM.

But the next morning the same crowd, full of undiminished fury, resenting the lack of leadership and action, assembled again, drawing together like so many magnets and utterly disregarding business. Then suddenly they received a piece of news that caused them to march as one man down to Sacramento Street near Leidersdorff and stand in silence before the walls of the American, or "Know Nothing," Club. The rumors of the night before that had served to keep their passions in leash had been founded upon the futile meeting of several of the members of the Vigilance Committee of 1851. Within those walls an entirely new organization was forming, and the grim, sober, indignant citizens assembled there had found their leader.

## XIII

#### THE VIGILANCE COMMITTEE OF 1856

WILLIAM T. COLEMAN was born in Cynthiana, Kentucky, on February 29, 1824, worked on his uncle's farm and in the lumber-camps of the north, studied at night, and finally made and saved enough to carry him not only through school, but the University of St. Louis; which gave him the degree of Bachelor of Science. He joined the stampede to California, by the Overland route, and arrived in Sacramento in August, 1849. It had been his intention to go to the mines, but he found business conditions in the little town so attractive that he opened a store. It amused him in later years to tell that his principal source of revenue at this time was derived from pies made by himself from his Kentucky aunt's recipe and sold to miners—during their weekly visits to Sacramento with a bag of "dust" to get rid of—for ten dollars apiece. But as he was a young man of great force of character, courage, and persistence, and of strength of will under a modest and reserved demeanor, united to original business abilities, it was not long before he was one of the leading merchants of San Francisco. That was the day when men rose or fell with a rapidity hardly paralleled before or since.

In 1855, despite the panic and general depression, he had demonstrated his faith in the future of California by organizing a line of clipper ships between San Francisco

# VIGILANCE COMMITTEE OF 1856

and New York, believing that cereals were bound to be produced in enormous quantities in the great valleys of the state and must find a ready market in the East and Europe. Moreover, there was hardly a local issue in which Mr. Coleman did not take an active interest, and, although he never would consent to hold office, he was prominent in every movement for civic reform. To all such projects he contributed liberally, as well as to charities, and he had been a member of the first Vigilance Committee. During the five stormy years that had passed since the organization of 1851 disbanded he had risen steadily to an eminence of clean and honorable citizenship in that community whose fierce light permitted no man to be misvalued; and as his courage, fairness, and gift for leadership were equally recognized it followed as a matter of course that when a new Committee of Vigilance became inevitable he should be its president. He was only thirty-two, but few of those leading citizens, estimable or otherwise, were older.

Sam Brannan relieved his mind to the crowd outside the building in Sacramento Street while the work of organization proceeded within. Mr. Coleman counseled that the organization be impersonal, that its members should be known by their numbers only.

"It is necessary," said he, "that the organization shall be very close, very guarded. We must be very careful whom we admit."

He wrote out an oath of fealty to the organization pledging life, liberty, property, and honor, and swore in those that were present. He then directed that every member take his number and write it in a book with his name and address.

"Who will be number one?" he asked; and many cried simultaneously:

"You, Mr. Coleman."

Even then he was willing to resign his leadership if some one else was thought better qualified; but opinion was unanimous on this point, and he wrote himself down:

"No. 1."

The enrolment after this was very rapid, and so many men in addition to the old members of 1851 applied for membership that the Committee was obliged to adjourn to the Turn Verein Hall in Bush Street, and thence to a large wholesale house in Sacramento Street between Davis and Front streets; the old "water-lots" below Montgomery Street having been "filled in" and built upon for some years. Thirty-five hundred men were enrolled within two days, all sorts and conditions of men being admitted who were above suspicion. Hundreds who could not bring themselves to so radical a departure from "law and order" secretly sympathized with the Committee and sent it liberal donations; such being the noble institution of compromise invented by man! The public, barring the "Law and Order" party shortly to be formed, and the worst element, now furious and apprehensive, supported the new Vigilance Committee from the first, if only because it had complete faith in Mr. Coleman. So did the other cities, and even the mountain communities of the state, mass-meetings of indorsement being held as soon as the news reached them.

However, the Governor of California, John Neely Johnson, notified by Mayor Van Ness, came down posthaste and, arriving in the evening, went at once to the Committee rooms and remained there until two o'clock

# VIGILANCE COMMITTEE OF 1856

in the morning. Mr. Coleman advised him to take the philosophical view of the inevitable so wisely adopted by Governor McDougal in 1851. He gave him a statement in detail of the abominable wrongs of the city—the looted treasury; the filthy dilapidated streets; the impudent flaunting vice; the lack of police protection for decent citizens, the police being a part of the corrupt political machinery; the stuffing of ballot-boxes. The law, added Mr. Coleman, was a dead letter. It was merely the object of the Committee to turn San Francisco from a hell into a city fit for decent, industrious, and law-abiding men to live in; and this, Mr. Coleman gently intimated, the Committee purposed to do, governor or no governor. He so won Johnson by his eloquence without rhetoric that the chief officer of the state finally sprang to his feet and slapped him on the back, exclaiming:

"Go it, old boy. But get through as quickly as you can. Don't prolong it, because there is a terrible opposition and a terrible pressure."

But Governor Johnson was not what you would call a man of iron purpose. He underwent a change of heart before night. In truth, there was much to daunt all but the strongest, although, judging by his final words to Mr. Coleman, he already had experienced "pressure."

But men were deserting by the score from the militia companies on guard at the jail and joining the Vigilantes; and William T. Sherman, who was major-general of the second division of the California militia, and had been chosen captain of the citizens' posse about the county jail, refused to serve under Sheriff Scannell or in any capacity save that of major-general. He obtained an interview with the governor shortly after the long con-

## CALIFORNIA

ference in Mr. Coleman's office, and, having drawn an alarming picture of the state of the public mind, demonstrating that the Committee roll of membership was increasing every hour, and that the great bankers, John Parrott, William C. Ralston, and Drexel, Sather & Church, were covertly supporting it, persuaded the governor that a stand must be made for law and order, and that the only thing to do was to enter into a treaty with William T. Coleman and other members of the Committee.

Sherman was a better soldier than diplomatist. He seems to have been a signal failure whenever he attempted the office of intermediary. All Mr. Coleman would concede was that the executive should place a guard of ten men inside the jail; otherwise he proceeded with the momentous business in hand exactly as if the governor slept in Sacramento. For the present there was but one law in the city, and he was at the head of it.

Meanwhile James King of Wm., although he rallied once or twice, was slowly dying. He had been removed to a room in the Montgomery Street block, where the best of surgeons and nurses, besides the members of his family, were in constant attendance.

Charles Doane had been elected chief marshal of the Vigilance Committee's military forces. Of the fifteen hundred men he had put under arms and drilled, many had seen service in the Mexican War, others had belonged to disbanded militia companies. These helped to drill the raw recruits, and between enthusiasm and concentration of purpose this little army at the end of three days might have been composed of war veterans.

King was shot on the 14th. On Sunday, the 18th, Marshal Doane, having notified the Committee that his

# VIGILANCE COMMITTEE OF 1856

forces were ready for active and immediate service, Mr. Coleman sent word to the governor, who was at the International Hotel engaged in constant and futile conference with Sherman and others, that the Committee was about to act. At noon the companies started by three separate routes for the jail. They marched up Kearney, Dupont, and Stockton streets—King opened his eyes as he heard the slow steady tramp of many feet, and apparently understood what was about to happen—and when they converged at the jail fell into position as precisely as if they had rehearsed their parts on the spot. It was a brilliant day; the steel bayonets flashed in the May sunshine. Before the doors of the jail a cannon was pointed, and a gunner was beside it. On the hills above, on all the roofs near by, in the adjacent streets, stood dense masses of silent people. Now that men of high authority were acting, there was no impulse among lesser men to expend themselves in vain emotions.

A carriage drove up and Mr. Coleman and Miers F. Truet ascended the steps of the jail in full view of all. Sheriff Scannell, standing behind the wicket of the jail door, refused entrance. Mr. Coleman pulled out his watch and gave Scannell five minutes. The gunner beside the cannon lit the fuse. Every man in the crowd took out his watch and counted the minutes. The gunner waved his fuse. Precisely as the five minutes expired the door opened and Mr. Coleman and Mr. Truet entered.

They found Casey brandishing a knife and screaming hysterically, but upon being assured that he would have a fair trial he surrendered and went quietly out to the carriage between the president and his associate. Mr. Coleman quickly suppressed with a wave of his hand the cheer that greeted his arrival at the head of the steps, and drove off amidst an intense and ominous silence to headquarters. The carriage returned shortly after, and Cora was led out in the same manner and driven down to Sacramento Street, and then the troops reformed and marched back to protect "the fort."

From the roof of the International Hotel in Jackson Street, Governor Johnson, Mayor Van Ness, and William T. Sherman were helpless onlookers at this extraordinary spectacle; the law-and-order forces, under R. Augustin Thompson, numbered only one hundred and fifty. Sherman estimated that there were at least ten thousand people within rifle-shot of the jail. It was an impressive sight from first to last: Marshal Doane on his white horse, the invincible ranks of earnest young volunteers, the carriage driving up with the man upon whom a people had conferred the power of a Tsar, the cowed trembling figures of the murderers hurried out and away, the black mass of people covering Telegraph Hill to the top, brightened with the gay shawls and bonnets of women of every degree.

The trial of Cora began on May 20th. He was permitted to choose his own counsel and asked Miers F. Truet and T. J. L. Smedley to undertake his defense. The executive committee sat in the long upper front room before a table. There were armed guards on the stairs and on the roof and parading the square before the building.

Cora, facing those serious implacable faces, hardly could have forborne to contrast them with the packed juries of his experience; and Mr. Coleman, a man of imposing appearance and great dignity, must have seemed to him a grotesque contrast to the tobacco-chewing, shirt-

# VIGILANCE COMMITTEE OF 1856

sleeved judges of the San Francisco courts. And in a moment he trembled. Marshal Doane entered hastily and announced the death of James King of Wm., and added that the most intense excitement pervaded the city. He was directed to inform the people that the trials were in progress, but that the Committee must proceed with the utmost deliberation and that every witness would be carefully examined.

James King of Wm. died at half past one on Thursday, May 20, 1856. Every building in the city—save the gambling-houses and the saloons—was immediately draped in black; all business ceased. The bells of the churches and engine-houses tolled, and in the harbor craft of every sort displayed their flags at half-mast. No other private citizen has ever received such a tribute; the crowds that packed the streets with crêpe on every arm not only were manifesting their profound respect and grief for the man who had attempted to reform his miserable city single-handed, but a deep affection for the man himself. It was only 1856, he had lived among them but seven years, but, as has been observed, men in those days lived by lightning, and virtue that could not be hid under a bushel was regarded with awe and reverence. They knew also that if he could have lived to round out his threescore and ten he would have spent it in the public service; and personally he seems to have been one of the most lovable of men. In all the other towns of the state the people, although few had known him save as a public character, paid him a similar tribute. Stores and public buildings were draped with black, mass-meetings were held, and services in the churches.

The Committee of Vigilance sat almost continuously

## CALIFORNIA

for two days and two nights listening to the evidence for and against Casey and Cora. No two scoundrels ever received a fairer trial. They were unanimously pronounced guilty and sentenced to be hanged on Friday, the 23d, at twelve o'clock.

On Thursday King's funeral took place, and once more all the world was in the street and on the housetops, a point of vantage lost to the present generation. It was an imposing cortège that left the Unitarian Church on Stockton between Clay and Sacramento streets after the services. The Masons, Royal Arch Chapter, in full regalia, led the procession. Following, four abreast, were the officiating clergymen and surgeons; then came the hearse drawn by four white horses and attended by fourteen pall-bearers, ten coaches filled with the family and friends and the men employed on the *Bulletin;* then the Society of California Pioneers in regalia, members of the press, Sacramento Guards in uniform, San Francisco Fire Department, St. Mary's Library Association, three hundred and twenty draymen on horseback, the Stevedores Association, the German Benevolent Society, Turn Verein Association, a delegation of colored men, and forty carriages of citizens. The procession was a mile long and accompanied for a part of the distance by practically the remainder of the decent population of the city. It moved slowly out Bush Street toward Lone Mountain Cemetery, and no doubt the population would have escorted it the entire way, but suddenly a rumor spread, coming whence no one ever knew, and some ten or twelve thousand of those not in the funeral procession began to melt backward; finally, when beyond sound of the solemn music, they broke into a run.

# VIGILANCE COMMITTEE OF 1856

The executive committee had determined to execute Cora and Casey on that day while all the town was marching toward the cemetery, thus avoiding a possible disturbance on the morrow.

The condemned men were informed of their fate. Two Catholic priests were with them; and one, Father Michael Accolti, went at once for Arrabella Ryan and married her to the man whose name she had assumed long since. She was now legally Belle Cora, and perchance found some consolation in being a widow.

Wooden platforms a yard long had been run out from the second-story windows fronting on Sacramento Street, and provided with hinges at the outer edges of the window-sills. These platforms were held in a horizontal position by cords fastened at their outer ends, passing up to beams projecting directly overhead from the roof of the building. To these beams were attached ropes with nooses and slip-knots already prepared. Below in a hollow square stood the Committee troops, under Marshal Doane, with their muskets on their shoulders. There was also a detachment on the roof, in front of the great alarm-bell of "Fort Vigilance." At each end of the block a cannon was in place. No attempt was made at rescue, however, and the crowd that rapidly collected and blocked all the neighboring streets or climbed to the tops of the business buildings, were bent on seeing vengeance done.

The condemned men emerged from the windows at a little after one o'clock. They wore shapeless white garments, and their arms were pinioned. Each was accompanied by a priest, and for the moment both seemed to be firm. But almost immediately Casey broke into an excited tirade, proclaiming that he was no murderer;

attributing his present position to the faults of early education in one breath and glorifying his mother in another, he adjured each newspaper in turn not to call him a murderer. Finally he broke down completely, screaming: "Oh, my poor mother! My poor mother! How her heart will bleed at this news. It is her pain I feel now. But she will not believe me a murderer. I but resented an injury. Oh, my mother! My mother! God bless you. Gentlemen, I pardon you. God will forgive you. I know He will forgive me. O God, with the accumulated guilt of my twenty-nine years have mercy on me! Oh, my poor mother!" The priest attempted to persuade him to pray, but in vain. He continued to fill the crowd below with pity and admiration for the good mother of a bad man until his legs were strapped together, the noose adjusted, and a white cap drawn over his face and head. Cora had stood unmoved; nor did he protest when he, too, was strapped and covered. At twenty-one minutes past one the signal was given, the cords holding up the platforms were cut from above, and the two white-hooded men swung off into space.

As they had repented and been received back into the Catholic Church, the Mission Dolores could not refuse them burial in its hallowed ground. They were hurried out in the night by Belle Cora and a few friends and buried by torchlight in a corner of the cemetery that holds Luis Argüello.

# XIV

### THE VIGILANCE COMMITTEE AND DAVID S. TERRY

The Committee of Vigilance remained in continuous session for six months. They hanged two other murderers, Joseph Hetherington, an Englishman, and Philander Brace, a desperado from New York; forcibly expelled from California all on their famous "black list," packing them off by wholesale on steamers and sailing-vessels. Each was given a fair trial. It was soon understood by the most desperate as well as by the most disapproving that the Committee was implacable, and that it would not adjourn until the city was as clean as was humanly possible. All things being relative, it would be clean.

The net result of the long session was two murders as against over one hundred in the previous six months; the passing of the current joke—"a man every morning for breakfast"; a complete reform of local politics; and as peaceable and decent a state of affairs for something like twenty years as San Francisco could stand without instant dissolution.

But, although the steady processional advance of this strange tribunal's high accomplishment was like a Greek drama in its secret sinister atmosphere of blind justice and crushing inevitableness, and its achievements were phenomenal considering that mere men held the scales

## CALIFORNIA

and worked for the regeneration of one of the wickedest cities on earth, it was beset with dangers every step of the way and compelled to exert every resource of its composite brain to save its own life.

The Southerners, who for the most part formed the Law and Order party, were against the Vigilance Committee practically to a man. Their excuse was that it was every good citizen's duty to uphold the law in all circumstances, but their real reasons were so well known that in private life they did not hesitate to express them. Apart from the smoldering resentment against the Northerners for declaring California a free state at the constitutional convention, and the fact that were it not for one man, David C. Broderick (also a Democrat), the politics of the state would be entirely in their hands, there was a lively fear that those men who were making history down by the water-front in their impregnable "fort" might develop into a strong political power, able to retain a permanent control of the state. And for the present the Vigilance Committee actually was the only power in California. Not a politician dared to raise his head. The governor had issued an absurd proclamation declaring the city of San Francisco in a state of insurrection, that further paralyzed the Southern party in any attempt toward future adjustment.

The Southerners who adventured into California in and shortly after 1849, either to improve their fortunes or to find a sure and quick means of gratifying their political ambitions, were for the most part gentlemen, well educated, more or less accomplished, and all experienced in politics; in the South of that day politics was the ruling passion. Few of these men went to the mines; and the

## DAVID S. TERRY

stalwart immigrants from the North and West, farmers, mountaineers, mustered-out soldiers, who invested their gold-dust in the country that fascinated them, sent for their families and became the solid business men, mechanics, and farmers of the state, stood in awe for many years of these suave, urbane, occasionally fire-eating and always well-dressed gentlemen from the most aristocratic section of the Union. They were forced to admit that the Southerner's experience of life and politics was as superior as his manners, and if at first they did not realize the subtlety with which the stronger party so often gained its ends they were in no doubt whatever as to the effects. Before this keen, clever, but too heterogeneous mass "found itself," the Southerners, born leaders, and with politics the paramount interest in their lives, had control of both San Francisco and California.

Of these William M. Gwin was the leader. The first long-term Senator from the state, he planted a friend in every one of its federal offices, not only gratifying his sense of *noblesse oblige*, but "making himself solid" against future emergencies. "I leave for California to-morrow," he had said to Stephen A. Douglas on the eve of departure from New York. "It will become a state, and I shall be back in a year bearing my credentials as United States Senator." This prophecy he fulfilled to the letter, and during both terms of his incumbency he was an ornament to the state and of some use. But his career is too bound up with that of Broderick to be enlarged upon further in this chapter.

The Thorntons, Crittendens, Lafayette Maynards, Gwins, Bowies, Howards; the Maxwells, MacMullens, and McNutts (the "Three Macs"); the Shorbs, Hitchcocks,

# CALIFORNIA

Kelloggs, Kips, Louis McLanes, Athertons, McKinstrys, Hollidays, Kings, Gordons, Randolphs, Thibaults, Selbys, Parrotts, Redingtons, Macondrays, Otises, Maillards, Fairfaxes, Bebcocks, Poetts, Scotts, and the Hall McAllisters—either Southerners themselves or high in favor with the dominant party—are a few of the names still remembered that played so great a social rôle in the '50's and '60's, before the Civil War put many of them out of politics. It was many years, however, before the Southerners in San Francisco lost their social supremacy; they ruled as long as they had any money left, and gave a tone to that city of many epochs that is still a tradition if not a guide. Of all those Southern women that ruled society as inexorably as their husbands led in law, politics, or business, admitting and excluding as they chose, Mrs. Hall McAllister was the most brilliant, individual, and accomplished. Although her husband, so soon at the head of the California bar, was not a Southerner, she was; her position was unchallenged, not only because of her birth and gift for leadership, but because even in those days a New Yorker of family estimated himself as highly as any Southerner. Moreover, Mr. McAllister had no political aspirations.

Not all the Northerners by any means belonged to the Vigilance Committee or even helped it in secret, and in its ranks were a few who were above sectional distinctions in this far-off land. William T. Coleman himself was a Kentuckian—and a Democrat. Men from the North and the West, however, that had stood aloof at first were converted after they realized that nothing but a return of California to her old haunts under the Pacific could retard the progress of the Committee of Vigilance or interfere with its ultimate success. Admiral Farragut, stationed at Mare Island, had declined to bombard the town and exterminate the "insurrectionists," and Major-General Wool, commanding the Pacific division of the United States army, and stationed at Benicia, refused to furnish the governor with arms and ammunition. Sherman made desperate efforts to raise companies of militia to oppose the formidable and ever-growing military forces of the Vigilance Committee; but, as nearly all his old men had gone over to the enemy, and as the new recruits were for the most part contemptible in numbers and character, and as the governor could not be brought to see reason, he resigned in disgust. Governor Johnson even sent two influential men, R. Augustin Thompson and Ferris Forman, to Washington to solicit the aid of the President in restoring California to its lawful owners. The President declined to interfere, and the Vigilance Committee grew in power daily.

Both the Law and Order party and the commercial and professional men in sympathy with the Vigilance Committee contained many known as "moderate men." A number of these formed themselves into a commission to bring about some sort of adjustment between the governor and the Vigilance Committee. Judge Joseph B. Crockett, F. W. Macondray, Henry S. Foote, Martin R. Roberts, Judge James D. Thornton, James Donahue, Bailey Peyton, and John J. Williams waited upon the executive board of the Committee, and after much palaver obtained a set of resolutions whereby the Committee pledged itself to keep its forces out of the public squares and streets and offer no resistance to the admission of any writ of *habeas corpus* on consideration that the governor would withdraw his proclamation and the forces of Law and Order disband.

On June 7th the governor started for San Francisco by boat, and the Citizens' Committee, accompanied by Sherman, took the up-river boat in order to meet the executive at Benicia. They arrived first; and Sherman, waiting at the wharf, saw, to his disgust, that his chief was accompanied by Volney E. Howard, Edward Jones, Edward E. Baker, and David S. Terry, Justice of the Supreme Bench—on his way down to play his part in that long and bloody drama of the fifties.

"All of these men," said Sherman, later, "were known to be of the most ultra kind, men of violent feelings, and who were determined to bring about a collision of arms if possible."

The governor went at once to the Solano Hotel, and, counseled by his fire-eaters, at first refused to see the Citizens' Committee. All were convinced that these men were secret Vigilantes, and they alternated uncomplimentary epithets with wholesale denunciation of General Wool. But Sherman finally succeeded in assuring them of this particular committee's moderation, and that Judge Thornton, on the night of Casey's arrest, had been one of the first to seize his pistols and rush to the assistance of Sheriff Scannell, in the name of law and order. He further assured the governor that all the arms in the state not in the possession of the army and navy, were owned by the Vigilance Committee.

Finally the Committee of Citizens was permitted to come up-stairs and enter the presence; and the manners of California society in the fifties, outside of exclusive Southern circles, cannot be better illustrated than by

## DAVID S. TERRY

describing the attitude of Judge Terry, of the Supreme Bench, as the doors were thrown open, and, for the matter of that, throughout the interview. In the presence of the governor of the state he sat with his hat on and his feet on the table. He had a smooth upper lip, and a long "political beard," and, I don't doubt, was chewing tobacco.

The conference was futile. The governor had been persuaded before he left Sacramento that the Vigilance Committee was really weak and ready to "cave in." He announced his determination to enforce the law; "and if unhappily a collision should occur, and injury to life and property result, the responsibility must rest upon those that disregarded the authorities of the state." It was then that Sherman resigned.

This was virtually a declaration of war, and the Vigilance Committee proceeded to intrench itself more securely. Sewers were examined, and the lines of patrol extended and doubled. The building in Sacramento Street was surrounded by a barricade of coarse "gunny" sacks filled with sand. These breastworks, six feet thick and ten feet high, and extending out from the front corners of the building, made a large inclosure including the street. Embrasures were left for cannon, and there was an inside platform and openings for musketry fire. Cannon were also placed on the roof. Sympathizers in the neighborhood offered their stores and warehouses as depositories for arms and food, and for hospital purposes, and on the roofs of these buildings sentries were stationed. The immediate result was a great mass-meeting indorsing the Committee, and the men within "Fort Gunnybags" went on trying and banishing the bad characters of the city.

# CALIFORNIA

The state under the law was entitled to a certain quota of arms from the federal arsenal, and these Governor Johnson finally managed to extract from Major-General Wool—six cases of muskets. Two men, Reuben Maloney and John C. Phillips, went secretly to Benicia for them, stowed them into a schooner, the *Julia*, and started for San Francisco. The Vigilance Committee having been notified of this move by the captain of another schooner, a force was sent to relieve the confidential agents of their burden. The *Julia* was boarded in San Pablo Bay, and both arms and men taken into custody. At San Francisco the men were released and the muskets taken to Fort Gunnybags.

Then came a series of events which must have made the Committee wish that they had kept their hands out of one hornets' nest, at least. They determined to rearrest Maloney and Phillips, and sent Sterling A. Hopkins, of their police force, to bring them to headquarters. Hopkins suffered from an excess of zeal and no little egoism. Maloney proved to be in the office of Dr. R. P. Ashe, a captain of one of the Law and Order companies. He was surrounded by Terry, Hamilton Bowie, and James McNab. Terry, as a peace officer, forbade the arrest in his presence.

Hopkins withdrew, but instead of going to headquarters for instruction, doubled his forces and started for the office again. As he was marching down Jackson Street he met the Maloney party on their way to the armory of the San Francisco Blues on the northeast corner of Dupont Street. They were armed with guns. Hopkins and his nine men bore down upon them and attempted to seize Maloney. Terry, whose fighting-blood

## DAVID S. TERRY

always seems to have been on tap, rushed at Hopkins, brandishing his gun. The police officer caught it below the nozzle, and the two men struggled to gain sole possession, until Terry, now quite beside himself, drew his bowie-knife and plunged it into Hopkins's neck. The wounded man sank to the sidewalk streaming with blood. He was caught up and carried to the Pennsylvania Engine-house by his companions, who do not seem to have had the presence of mind to make an arrest.

The Law and Order citizens, their minds no doubt visited abruptly by a picture of those thirty men sitting in judgment behind a long table down at Fort Vigilance, ran for the armory, and, the usual crowd filling the narrow streets at once, the doors were closed and barred. A few moments later that most ominous sound known to the fifties, the alarm-bell of the Vigilance Committee, sounded its single loud deep note. Within fifteen minutes every fighting member of the Committee was armed and ready to march under the leadership of Marshal Doane on his white horse.

It was three o'clock when the tap sounded. Merchants, professional men, mechanics, the rich, the poor, dropped their work, seized their guns, and hurried to headquarters. Draymen unhitched the horses from their vehicles, mounted them, and galloped for Fort Gunnybags. At the end of another fifteen minutes not only the armory, but every building identified with the Law and Order forces was surrounded. The crowds retreated to the roofs. For blocks the streets were packed with silent rows of upright military-looking men, their muskets glittering in the sun. This was the first object-lesson the inimical party had received of the marvelous drilling, the appalling numbers, and the unanimity of spirit the Vigilance Committee was able to command with a single tap of its bell.

The horrified party inside the armory of the Blues sent out a letter to the Committee offering to surrender if assured of protection from violence. The letter was signed by Ashe, as captain of Company A, and Martin J. Reese, as first lieutenant of Company B. They received the assurance of protection provided they would surrender not only Maloney and Terry, but all the ammunition in the building. As the intrenched were disposed to dicker, two cannon were moved to a position commanding the front of the armory. They were given fifteen minutes to accept or reject the terms, and the surrender of the others in the armory was now demanded in addition to the original two. The men inside were no fools. They opened the doors without further parley, and a detachment of the Vigilance Committee forces marched in. Three hundred muskets and other weapons were carried out first, loaded on drays, and sent down to the fort. Then two carriages—"hacks," in local parlance—which always seem to have dogged those ominous musterings, drove up to the doors. The prisoners entered, police officers climbed to the box-seats and roof or hung on behind. Large bodies of infantry, which in turn was protected by cavalry, surrounded the hacks and began their march down to Fort Gunnybags. On their way they paused before other Law and Order strongholds, which gave up their arms, ammunition, and themselves without parley. Sherman must have been under a misapprehension when he informed the governor that all the arms in the city were in the possession of the Vigilance

FORT VIGILANCE, OR FORT GUNNYBAGS. WILLIAM T. COLEMAN PRESIDENT OF THE COMMITTEE OF VIGILANCE

# DAVID S. TERRY

Committee, for on that day alone they took six hundred muskets and a corresponding amount of powder and shot and other munitions of war. They also captured eleven cases of muskets and three boxes of pistols and ammunition sent down from Sacramento on the *Mariposa*. It is possible that Sherman, thoroughly disgusted and secretly believing in the righteousness of the other cause, did not care to arm the riffraff of the city, who were more likely to loot than to face the forces of the Vigilance Committee.

Terry had ruined the Law and Order cause as thoroughly as if he had been its bitterest enemy, and he was a most unwelcome guest at Fort Vigilance. As a member of the Committee remarked, "They had gone gunning for ferrets and corralled a grizzly." Terry not only was a state officer, a sufficient embarrassment in itself, but he had been prominent in California ever since his arrival, and had served his country in the Mexican War. No man was more conspicuous as a bitter partisan in politics; he had indisputable legal ability, and he was brave and reckless to a degree that might have justified him in posing as a symbol of the times. Always retaining something of the Texas ranger in his swagger and dress—to say nothing of manners—he was a picturesque figure in spite of his beard, and, like all men of violent individuality, was rabidly loved and hated.

It is possible that if Terry had made off for the interior on horseback he would not have been hunted with ardor; but, although to hang a justice of the Supreme Bench of the state was the last thing the Committee had anticipated when organizing, they were prepared to go even that length if the wound he had inflicted proved mortal.

# CALIFORNIA

Dr. Ashe, being a naval officer of the port, was almost as great an embarrassment; but, as he was innocent of attempted murder and gave his word to remain neutral and to hold himself at the disposal of the Committee, he was let out on parole. The Committee had no desire to get into trouble with the United States government. The other Law and Order prisoners were also dismissed after an uncomfortable night.

It is true that before Terry's arrest the majority of first-class men in the Law and Order party had resigned in disgust, not only because the governor, who should have adequately supported them, proved to be weak and obstinate, but they were men of brains and realized their own futility. The Vigilance party numbered thousands to their hundreds, and was supported by public opinion. They had dropped out one by one, and those that remained steadfast felt keenly the humiliation of being classed with the miserable crooks and gamblers and saloon hangers-on with whom they had been forced to fill their ranks; moreover of learning every few days that a fresh batch of these very "Law and Order soldiers" had been arrested and deported.

Of those that had remained until the day which witnessed the final overthrow of the party Gen. Volney Howard was the most conspicuous by reason of being in command of the Law and Order forces and his intimacy with Terry. He took his humiliation in no philosophical spirit, and, although a general without an army, blustered to the Vigilance Committee that he would put them down in sixty days, as he expected reinforcements from Washington. The Vigilance Committee did not even pause to smile, and he retreated to Sacramento and

# DAVID S. TERRY

poured out his indignation over Justice Terry's arrest at the hands of law-breakers until some one interrupted him with the pertinent question: What business had a justice to leave his bench in Sacramento and engage in a street row in San Francisco? There was no doubt that the entire state, with the exception of the individual remnants of the former Law and Order party, and Terry's friends, was behind the Vigilance Committee; nevertheless, men of all opinions sincerely hoped that Hopkins would live.

Terry has been blamed for not remaining quiet, dignified, passive, refusing to acknowledge the jurisdiction of the Committee or in any manner to recognize its action. If he had maintained this lofty and judicial attitude it is argued that the hostile sentiment of the city would have yielded to admiration, and there might even have been a peremptory demand from members of the Committee itself that he be discharged as outside of its jurisdiction.

But when a man has a rope round his neck, helpless in the grasp of the most powerful and awe-inspiring secret tribunal the world has seen since the days of the doges, when he is a big-bodied full-blooded Texas ranger accustomed to bluff, and to bellowing down opponents, the judicial attitude of mind is liable to suspension. He railed at the Committee, shouted over the top of his "cell," communicated with his friends outside through his wife, and never for a moment ceased to demand his liberty.

Great pressure was brought to bear upon the Committee; even Commander Boutwell, United States sloop *John Adams*, then in the harbor, demanded that Terry,

# CALIFORNIA

as a state judge, be imprisoned on board his ship. This move was intended to embroil the Committee with the United States government, an issue that Governor Johnson, under the advice of Terry, had endeavored to compass from the beginning.

But, although such powerful men as Hall McAllister, Judge Thornton, and Alexander P. Crittenden managed to delay the trial on the pretext of negotiation between Terry and the executive committee—which involved many interviews—it all came to naught. Dr. Beverly Cole had testified on the day after the arrest that Hopkins was dangerously wounded, and once more San Francisco was in a state of wild excitement. Really one wonders how those agitated brains of the fifties ever survived into the more tranquil sixties, and what time they had to attend to their flourishing businesses. San Francisco, however, despite her many trials, has always manifested an almost uncanny ability to take care of herself.

Although the trial was postponed until Friday, the testimony of Dr. Ashe was taken on the Sunday after the arrest, and that same evening Terry was indicted on the following counts. In a brief space they give not only an insight into Terry's character and career, but into the searching methods of the Committee toward any prisoner before its bar.

Resisting with violence the officers of the Vigilance Committee while in the discharge of their duties.

Committing an assault with a deadly weapon with intent to kill Sterling A. Hopkins on June 21, 1856.

Various breaches of the peace and attacks upon citizens while in the discharge of their duties, specified as follows:

1. Resistance in 1853 to a writ of *habeas corpus* on account of which one Roach escaped from the custody of the law, and the infant heirs of the Sanchez family were defrauded of their rights.

# DAVID S. TERRY

   2. An attack in 1853 on a citizen of Stockton named Evans.
   3. An attack in 1853 on a citizen in San Francisco named Purdy.
   4. An attack at a charter election on a citizen of Stockton named King.
   5. An attack in the court-house of Stockton on a citizen named Broadhouse.

Although there were now practically no arms in the city save those in the possession of the Vigilance Committee, it was feared that a sufficient number might be supplied by Boutwell to encourage the friends of Terry to rush the fort; and it is possible that this naval officer, who does not appear to have been a monster of judgment, might have done some practical meddling had he not been promptly called to order by Admiral Farragut, who had no intention of risking a rebuke from Washington. But meanwhile Fort Vigilance had extended its lines of guards in all directions, and Terry was transferred to a cell where he could not shout to possible friends on neighboring roofs.

An effort was made by the negotiators to induce Terry to resign his position on the Supreme Bench and promise to leave the state; but if his fearless spirit ever considered this road to liberty we have no knowledge of it. We do know, however, that Mrs. Terry said loudly that he never should leave the Committee fort alive save as a justice of the Supreme Court.

All the correspondence relative to the case, by the way, that issued from the Committee rooms was signed Secretary 33, a signature that caused as keen a thrill of terror in those days as the tap of the alarm-bell. The man behind was Isaac Bluxome, Jr. Finally all correspondence relative to Terry ceased and the trial began.

# CALIFORNIA

Terry was led into the long room and directed to stand before the bar of the executive committee. It was a scene that Terry knew had daunted nerves as stout as his: that long table with its sober faces, Mr. Coleman in the middle, just and implacable, no one else in the room but the prisoner, the counsel, and one witness. Seventy-five men under arms were within the building; rank upon rank without. Gunners stood beside the cannon, and a drawbridge was in readiness to be lowered from the second-story window, that Terry might be spirited away in case of attack.

The taking of testimony and the examination of witnesses occupied three weeks. Terry was defended by Miers F. Truet. Thomas J. L. Smiley appeared for the prosecution. Terry plead not guilty to all the charges, and this attitude entailed the examination of a vast number of witnesses, all of whose testimony was thoroughly sifted. Hopkins was on the road to recovery long before the trial was over, and this fact had restored all Terry's dashing confidence in himself and his destiny. On June 22d he plead his own case, reiterating what he had maintained from the beginning, that he merely had resented an insult and defended his life. This was palpably a lie, but the court was anxious to be rid of him now that he no longer was a potential murderer, and not only in his own person but as a state officer had been punished by much humiliation and loss of prestige. A vote of three-fifths was required to convict him. He was found guilty on the first charge and on one of the minor charges. Upon the second charge, that of assault with intent to kill, the committee sat up for two nights and finally pronounced him "guilty of assault." He was dis-

## DAVID S. TERRY

charged and told to leave the state; but the order was not enforced.

There is no doubt that he owed his discharge not merely to the fact that he was a white elephant—for many members of the committee refused to consider the dignified position he held on the bench—but to the utter and universal contempt which Hopkins had managed to inspire. He strutted about like a swollen turkey cock as soon as he was able to be out, and while still in bed had held daily receptions. Finally he appeared before the Vigilance Committee and offered to compromise with Terry on a money basis. The executive committee, disgusted that such a creature should have crept into their ranks, were the more inclined to be lenient with Terry, who at least was a man.

Boutwell received the justice on board the *John Adams* and fired a salute in his honor. As soon as possible Terry took the river-boat for Sacramento. There he remained quiet for a while, to emerge later in a far more important and terrible rôle.

## XV

### BRODERICK

David C. Broderick, the ablest man in California's political history and in many respects the most interesting, was also one of the most complete exponents of the Irish-American politician of the large successful type that the United States has produced. It would seem that only men of this peculiar breed can wage war against an aristocracy or oligarchy without becoming mere demagogues or deluding themselves with the fiction that they are working for the brotherhood of man, coining new names to explain themselves.

Broderick at all events cherished no delusions of that sort. He wanted the earth, and he wanted it for himself. A plebeian by birth, born in an era when the aristocracies of the republic were all-powerful, his great abilities hampered by the oligarchies he despised, he swore to conquer in spite of every intrenched and opposing force, and to achieve the highest ambitions that might be cherished by the "true-blue American." He was ambition incarnate. If he had any weaknesses or vicious tendencies he plucked them out by the roots while he was still a young man, lest they interfere with his paramount object. He neither drank nor smoked nor looked upon woman. He had warmth, and humor, but he rarely allowed these too human tendencies to appear, lest they also retard his

# BRODERICK

progress; nevertheless, they were to be divined, as well as his sense of fair play and gratitude; and in consequence his friends loved him as passionately as his enemies hated him. No man, however, was close to him—until those dark days when he knew that his political enemies had decreed that he must die, and for the first time his great soul was discouraged.

His personal magnetism and political acumen were so extraordinary that men of all ages followed him like dogs, only asking to be allowed to take orders from this born leader of men; and no one smiled when at the age of twenty-nine it was known that he had said to General Sickles, just before leaving New York for California, that he intended to return as United States Senator. He never admitted to cherishing a higher ambition still, but few doubted that if he had been permitted to outlive the Civil War he would have rounded out his career in the White House.

Broderick was born in the District of Columbia, February 4, 1820. His father was a stone-cutter, and the marble columns that support the eastern front of the Capitol were the work in part of the laborer whose son was to be the first man of humble birth to invade the aristocratic Senate chamber and force its members to listen to him. The mason moved to New York and died when David was fourteen, leaving him with a family to support. He had been apprenticed to a stone-cutter, but, being a big strong fellow and eager to take good care of his mother and brother, he joined, when he was old enough, the New York Volunteer Fire Company. He soon became its most famous member. All New York firemen are fearless, and it was not easy to win a reputa-

## CALIFORNIA

tion for reckless bravery; but he did, his reputation enhanced by the ready and effective use of his fists. Before long he was foreman of his company, and drifted naturally into politics. To increase his influence as well as the comforts of his family he opened two saloons, to which his magnetic and enigmatical personality drew all the politicians of the neighborhood.

He was a Democrat; but, although he hated the Whigs, he hated the aristocratic and powerful wing of his own party far more. The "Albany Regency" of the state, and The "Old Man's Committee" of the city, made a formidable wall for any ambitious young plebeian to scale. Nevertheless, when he was twenty-one he obtained a position in the custom-house (a mere side-issue with him, however) through the friendship of no less a personage than President Tyler. Jeremiah Lynch relates an incident which illustrates the daring and resource of this remarkable young man.

... President Tyler had received and accepted an invitation to visit New York City. A committee of officials, accompanied by eminent citizens and foreign guests, embarked on a steamer to meet the President on the Jersey shore. Although elected as a Whig, Tyler was coquetting with the Democrats, and so Tammany Hall also selected a committee, or rather two committees, to tender homage to the President.

One committee represented the ultra-aristocratic element—for Tammany was then respectable—and the other, also a Tammany selection, was made up of young men as distinct from old men; in other words, the classes against the masses. Broderick was of the second committee, which was expected to gaze, be humble and silent. However, the forty sachems—twenty and twenty—after disembarking from their steamer, walked to the President's residence, and while the mighty rich were awaiting on the lawn the President's appearance, Broderick strode to the door alone, opened it, entered, and presently returned with the President of the United States on his arm. Conducting Tyler to the astounded group, he saluted the President and then said, in the same loud tones as when directing his fire-laddies at a conflagration, "Now, then, form a circle and the President will talk to you." For a moment no one moved, so aghast were they, until one of the immaculates said like a philosopher, "Come, gentlemen, give attention to the President," and Tyler delivered a short address. After the President ceased he very naturally turned to Broderick as the leader, and the latter, quietly taking the President's arm with an injunction to all Knickerbockers and firemen to "form the line of march," led the way to the landing, where the tardy boat containing the real city committee, with its music and platoons of uniforms, had just arrived. Here he was obliged to surrender his prisoner; and, although President Tyler was so delighted with him that he gave him a lucrative position in the custom-house, he made undying enemies of the oligarchy he had humiliated.

His mother died when he was twenty-four; his brother was accidentally killed. So far as he knew he was alone in the world. But he had no leisure hours for loneliness. When politics spared him he read and studied under the guidance of educated men whom he had interested and who foresaw something of his future. He helped to carry his state for Polk, but his political course was not to be run in New York. His opponents as well as his bitter personal enemies had made up their minds that it was time to get rid of him, and when he ran for Congress not only the Whigs, but the Democratic oligarchy united against him, and he was defeated. At that age he did not know the meaning of discouragement, although he was quite astute enough to see that he could not win against so formidable a combination of forces. Just then came the news of the gold discovery in California. Nearly all his friends joined the hegira, and it was not long before he made up his mind that the new country was the place for him and his ambitions. He sailed via the Isthmus, and arrived in San Francisco on June 13, 1849.

The long unsanitary journey and the usual detention

# CALIFORNIA

in that pest-spot, the Isthmus of Panama, seriously affected his health. He was in no condition for the mines, and the ragged little city of San Francisco, with its hovels and tents, its cloth and lath bunk-houses infested with vermin, its garish gambling-houses, its unpaved streets, knee-deep in mud in winter and sand and refuse in summer, alternately in a wild state of excitement and black depression, must have looked hopeless to a young New Yorker of twenty-nine with an enfeebled body, not a penny in his pocket, and a colossal ambition. But he wasted no time in regrets or despair. Whatever jobs he could obtain to keep body and soul together he worked at faithfully, and within a month he had a lucrative business of his own.

Col. J. D. Stevenson, who had known him in New York, and appreciated his caliber, lent him a thousand dollars; in company with another New York friend named Kohler, he opened an assay office and manufactured gold slugs whose intrinsic value was four or eight dollars respectively, but readily passed as five or ten dollar pieces, so delighted were the people to get something more convenient than gold-dust as a medium of exchange. To this lucrative occupation the young men added the manufacture of jewelry, and as the women of commerce were pouring into the town the income of the firm jumped from day to day.

Broderick soon left this business to his partner, however, for, his necessities relieved, he lost all interest in money-making. After the first great fire he organized a fire company on the model of the one whose foreman he had been in New York, and his political career began almost immediately. He was elected to the first state

## BRODERICK

legislature in January, 1850, six months after his arrival, and by an overwhelming majority. He was already the best-known young politician in San Francisco, no doubt through his manipulation of that mighty influence in politics, the fire department; and he ruled certain wards despite the already growing power of the Southerners.

Gwin, when he became United States Senator, obtained the complete control of the federal appointments. Practically every office in the gift of the national Executive was filled with Southerners, more or less aristocratic, and the custom-house was currently known as the "Virginia Poorhouse." But when it came to municipal politics the Southern Democrats, astute and accomplished politicians as they were, and with the formidable strength of union, found a rival in this young Tammany man, whose rise to power and distinction was quick and spectacular even for that day.

During the second session Governor Burnett resigned and was succeeded by the lieutenant-governor, John McDougal. This left the office of president of the senate vacant, and Broderick was elected to fill it. He was now thirty-one, and already the most active and marked politician in the state of which he had been a citizen for a year and a half. As a presiding officer he won encomiums even from his enemies, of which he already had a full crop; he had acquired somewhere a thorough knowledge of parliamentary law, and he always applied his faculties to the matter in hand with that power of concentration inseparable from minds born to dominate.

Those were turbulent days in the itinerary capital of the state, as in San Francisco. The austerity and dignity of Broderick's character would have dictated an

## CALIFORNIA

unswerving attitude of lofty detachment. But the youth in him made his fists as ready as ever, and even senators appeared in the chamber bristling about the hips, although they immediately transferred both pistols and bowie-knife to the desk in front of them! Sometimes these were pushed aside by their feet or obscured by tobacco-smoke, or mayhap they fell into the spittoon; but they never were wholly forgotten. In those days politics were taken far more personally than now, and every man was ready to defend his party with his fists or the more deadly weapon, as with every resource of his brain. Broderick got into more than one fight, and had his duel. He soon proved his mettle, and, although courage and coolness were not overvalued in a community where the coward hardly existed long enough to prove the rule, still a few exhibitions of both were useful in placing a man once for all.

After the adjournment of the legislature Broderick remembered that the ambition of his life was to be a Senator of the United States. He Tammanyized San Francisco, and returned a large number of his friends and supporters to the next legislature. There his name was proposed to succeed Frémont, whose place had been vacant since March 1st of the previous year. The vote he received, although not sufficient to elect him, demonstrated his growing power.

John B. Weller was elected; and Broderick, nothing daunted, began to work for the vacancy which would occur at the expiration of Gwin's term in March, 1855.

He had three years to lay his senatorial wires, and meanwhile he was a member of the first Vigilance Committee, helped to put out the fires that ravaged the city,

# BRODERICK

and invested in water-lots the money he had made in slugs and jewelry, an investment that made him a rich man. He seems to have had little personal use for money, for he lived simply, rarely frequenting the society even of men, spending all his spare hours in study, and further improving his mind with what literature there was in the state. But he had much use for gold in his political organizations, and he not only made it as rapidly as he could, but he impressed more and more men that had it into his service. In addition to his political ambitions, recognized by all, he cherished a desire to become San Francisco's most energetic and useful citizen; and, although he had to share this honor with such men as William T. Coleman, San Francisco owed many of its improvements and public buildings to his inspiration. It was about this time that he discarded the familiar blue shirt, "pants" tucked into his boots, and silk hat worn far back; the last so distinctive of leading citizens. He sent to New York for the dignified apparel of the truly eminent and respectable, and for the rest of his life was rarely seen save in a "boiled" shirt and black frockcoat and trousers. The silk hat alone was retained.

Always reserved and dignified, he grew more so, more and more averse from talking about himself and his plans save when it was necessary to take associates or henchmen into his confidence. He must have been an imposing figure in those unsartorial days, and I would that he had looked less like a reissue of the Neanderthal race; but the preternaturally long upper lip, the tight mouth with the ruff of hair below, may have had something to do with the absence of those temptations exerted by the fair sex—in spite of his wonderful eyes, keen, penetrating, glittering like ice. I would also that, as an admirer of this remarkable and unhappy man, I could record that his political ways were above reproach, as white and open and innocuous as politics one day may be, when in their coffin; but there is little doubt that he employed base tools and that his methods were too often devious and without scruple.

On the other hand, and for the same reason—that he was a great, not a little, politician—no man questioned his word; he never broke a promise—save in the case of Latham—and he was as tender of his friends' interests as of his own, as eager to reward as Gwin himself. But the ideal half of his rapidly developing intellect was at war with the practical brain that made use of life as he found it; and while this saddened him and made him one of the loneliest men that ever lived, he realized that life was too short for one man to reform it and achieve something of his mighty ambitions at the same time.

Sheriff, district attorney, alderman, tax-collector, assessor, all were his, and the price was half their gains—nothing was said of mere salaries—to be handed over to the political organization through which Broderick ruled San Francisco. He gave the city a party system, however imperfect, but he did not interfere in local affairs. The dirty work, the ballot-box stuffing, the bullies at the polls, these he shut his eyes to. He needed an organization for his ultimate purpose, but with its details he would not pollute his mind.

He never descended to jobbery, his personal record was above reproach, and he disbursed money with a large hand, excusing his followers from contributions for bands, halls, or any of the expensive paraphernalia of

# BRODERICK

elections. He stood alone like royalty, and money was merely one of his slaves to be used for the benefit of the faithful.

It is a curious and interesting fact that Broderick from the first succeeded by sheer ability, for he had not a grace of manner, nor tact, nor policy. To his followers he was an autocrat, and he treated his enemies with open contempt.

Gwin's term was to expire March 1, 1855; Weller's two years later. To the legislature assembling in January, 1855, would fall the duty of electing Gwin's successor. But that was a mere matter of custom and precedent. Broderick had other plans.

He was sure of the legislature of 1854. He was too perfectly equipped a politician not to discount the unknown as far as was humanly possible. He determined that the present legislature should snap its fingers at precedent and elect Gwin's successor.

Some of the Broderick forces were disturbed at this bold affront to custom, for the politician heart is normally conservative; but they rallied to a man. It was Broderick or anti-Broderick. His word was law. Obey or leave.

The other forces also rallied, the followers of Gwin, of Weller, those whose personal ambitions Broderick threatened, those who opposed him on principle. His first move was to have the migratory capital definitely located in Sacramento; and so captured the votes of members of that ambitious community, and of its near-by farmers and ranchers. Then his friends and henchmen proceeded to corrupt the enemy, and there was a scandal that threatened disaster at the outset. A San Francisco banker approached an incorruptible, who caught the next boat for Sacramento to tell the story; and it took the combined brains of Hall McAllister, Stephen J. Field, and S. H. Williams to extricate the banker.

The assembly was Broderick's by a large majority, but in the house the forces were almost evenly divided. The bill was on the table for two months. Two Broderick men took an otherwise unconquerable foe out for a drive and ditched him. He was unhurt but thoughtful. There was to be no pairing. Each man was to do his own voting. There was a senator from Santa Clara named Grewell, recently a clergyman. His convictions were not iron-clad, and it was known that he had been approached; he was locked up and closely guarded. Broderick held himself haughtily aloof, but the excitement grew more intense every moment. Insults, fights, duels, sessions in which men used their firearms to gesticulate with—San Francisco had a gallant rival in Sacramento.

Grewell, who appears to have listened, at least, when offered a round sum for his vote by a Broderick agent, was kidnapped first by one side and then by the other, finally taking refuge of his free will in the Broderick headquarters. The bill came up in the assembly and passed by a vote of forty to thirty-eight. The assembly adjourned to witness the struggle in the senate. There the excitement was so intense that even Broderick was affected and found it impossible to preserve his air of cold detachment. But Grewell was produced and, voting with the Broderick forces, the result was a tie. The president of the senate cast his vote for Broderick, and on one side of the chamber the cheering made the

# BRODERICK

ramshackle building tremble on its foundations. Nobody questioned that Broderick had won, that the election of the next Senator of the United States would take place in this his session. But that night the kidnapped was kidnapped again, while his keeper slept the sleep that knows no awakening until whisky fumes have run their course. On the following day he voted for a reconsideration, which was carried by a vote of eighteen to fifteen. Then the senate voted that the subject be indefinitely postponed. Broderick had lost. Such were politics in California in the year of our Lord 1854.

## XVI

### BRODERICK AND GWIN

But Broderick was not crushed, not for a moment. It was a bitter disappointment to lose the prize that he actually had fondled in his hand; but he immediately went to work to get possession of the next legislature. His opponents, however, were equally active. They were thoroughly alarmed. So far, whatever Broderick's power in San Francisco, the state belonged to the Chivalry Democrats—"Chivs" in affection or scorn—and they were bitterly opposed to Broderick, both because he was not of their class and far more because he was a vehement antislavery man. Nor was this merely a mental attitude of Broderick's. He—and his great following—had voted down a bill against the immigration of free negroes as well as a fugitive-slave bill. Moreover, Broderick had denounced Stephen A. Douglas's indorsement of squatter sovereignty in Nebraska. But if this uncompromising attitude solidified the proslavery party against him, it attracted to his standard all that were opposed to slavery on principle and all that had begun to think for themselves. In short, he typified the antislave sentiment of the state.

The state Democratic convention assembled in Sacramento in July, 1854. Broderick as chairman of the state committee arranged the preliminaries. He hired the

# BRODERICK AND GWIN

First Baptist Church in Fourth Street and directed his followers to enter by a rear door an hour before the convention opened and occupy the front seats. The Opposition were welcome to the back of the room, where they might see or hear or attract attention as Providence willed.

But the Opposition was not asleep. It now numbered representatives of every faction opposed to Broderick, eager for the fray and determined to extinguish him. They had their spies in the enemy's camp. Knowing also that Edward McGowan had been selected by Broderick to preside at the convention, they resolved upon former Governor McDougal, and upon a list for the committee on credentials and organization.

They reached the front door of the church just as the Broderick cohorts were about to enter by the rear. Thirty men, including David S. Terry, surrounded McDougal, forced the door, and ran down the aisle toward the platform. The Broderick men, who had now swarmed in, attempted to head them off, but, although the afterward notorious James Casey and Billy Mulligan were there to use their fists, the Opposition forces managed to secure as many front seats as the Broderickites. The tension may be imagined.

Broderick walked on to the rostrum from the rear door, looking more granite than human, and called the convention to order. (The word order must have been a standing joke in the fifties.) The moment he had uttered the necessary formalities a man named O'Meara sprang to his feet and nominated McDougal for president of the convention. But simultaneously a Broderick man was on his feet (if, indeed, he had sat down) nominating McGowan. Broderick said peremptorily:

# CALIFORNIA

"I nominate the gentleman from Santa Clara. The seat of the other is contested, and I will not recognize him."

There were loud and indignant protests. Broderick ignored them and put the question on the nomination of McGowan. The other side indulged in a similar formality and carried the nomination of McDougal. Both nominees were rushed wildly to the platform by their friends. Pandemonium broke loose. Screaming, and brandishing fists and pistols, both sides struggled to get close to their men. A pistol went off. Three of the most excitable but less war-like delegates bolted through a stained-glass window. Another shrieked that he could feel blood running down inside his "pants." He was carried out fainting and quite whole.

In spite of the confusion the two candidates managed to reach the platform simultaneously. They seated themselves side by side, and while glaring at each other shouted the names of their vice-presidents. Pushing and jostling, tripped and elbow-ribbed, these dignitaries also reached the rostrum and seated themselves beside their winded superiors. Then two sets of committees were appointed, and when they had shouted themselves hoarse two sets of reports were made. Then everybody for another hour tried to make a speech, of which the only words distinguishable were "bolting" and "treachery." No doubt there were others which the polite stenographer omitted. But there were wild accusations of every sort. The men shouted, snarled, sprang on their chairs, brandished their fists, made megaphones of their hands, or tried to look oratorical.

It was quite impossible to accomplish any business. Broderick merely sat like a rock, hardly looking to the

# BRODERICK AND GWIN

right or the left, but conveying the impression that so he could sit until the end of time. The clergyman and trustees, alarmed finally at the noise, entered and asked the statesmen to leave. They were invited to go about their business. However, they refused lamps. Darkness had fallen. Some one produced two candles, lighted them, and placed one in front of each president.

At nine o'clock everybody was tired out. Both sides, which had consistently opposed adjournment, suddenly compromised. The two presidents locked arms and walked down the center aisle. The candidates for the vice-presidency followed, side by side; then the delegates, also paired, joined the stately procession. The church was restored to the trembling pastor.

Really, women, when they are sufficiently enfranchised to hold conventions, may be no better than men, but they hardly can be worse.

This uproar, part of the time in almost total darkness, had lasted five hours. Only once had Broderick been attacked personally. A man sprang to the platform and brandished a pistol in his face. "Take care!" said Broderick. "Take care! That might go off and hurt somebody." As the man's jaw fell Broderick gently captured the pistol and placed it on the table. His mere personality had conquered, as often before, and the man slunk to the back of the church.

The next day the two parties held separate conventions and made their nominations for the coming state elections. Both put up strong men, and so did the Whigs. On election day, September 6th, Broderick once more was beaten.

In San Francisco on that day a characteristic incident

took place. There were the usual bullies and fist-fights at the polls. Broderick and Colonel Peyton met when about to vote, and the "Chiv," already heated by several altercations, immediately burst into speech and informed the Tammany man what he thought of him. Finally Peyton made a significant movement toward his hip pocket. Broderick had his right hand in his overcoat pocket, and he fixed the temperamental Southerner with his cold and glittering eye.

"Move, Colonel Peyton," said he, "and you are a dead man."

Peyton knew what that meant: Broderick had a derringer in his concealed hand. His own hand remained suspended. Broderick continued in those cold incisive tones for which he was famous:

"There is no need for us to kill each other or to have any personal difficulty. Let us take a boat out on the bay or a walk under the trees and talk this matter over. If we cannot agree then I am ready to fight to the death. Come on."

Peyton nodded, and the two men walked out the Mission road. When they returned they were arm in arm. And they were friends for life. Possibly if Broderick had yielded oftener to the impulse to be conciliatory he would have won many supporters as well as admirers from the ranks of both the Whigs and the Chivs.

Among Broderick's followers were men of the highest probity, and one of them finally remonstrated with him for employing pugilists and bullies to surround the polls. "You respectable people I cannot depend upon," replied the chief. "You won't go down and face the revolvers of the other side, and I have to take such material as I can get hold of. They stuff ballot-boxes and steal the tally-lists, and I have to keep these men to aid me."

Once more Broderick was undismayed and began to lay a new set of senatorial wires. Gwin, whose term expired in March, wished to succeed himself. The legislature convened in January. Broderick knew that he could not be elected by it, during its first session at all events. But neither should Gwin. The great leader of the Chivalry Democrats had more than a majority of the Democratic members, but far from a majority of all the members put together. His only hope was to induce the Democrats to go into caucus; as the caucus nominee he would be assured of election as his own successor.

Broderick organized his forces and prevented the caucus. The entire session was frittered away. At its end neither Gwin nor any one had been elected. Broderick had persuaded a sufficient number of the legislators that he and his party represented the genuine Democracy. Gwin was far weaker than at the beginning of the term.

But there was another enemy in the field. The Whig party in the United States had been wrecked by the defeat of Gen. Winfield Scott for the Presidency in 1852. Almost simultaneously that party of short but vigorous life known first as the American and then as the "Knownothing" party (owing to its reticence) sprang into existence. Its leading principles were well enough known: opposition to foreigners and foreign immigration (meaning principally the Irish), and to the Catholic Church. They absorbed the greater number of the Whigs and many of the disgruntled Democrats, and in 1854 they had multiplied in California. In 1855 they held their first state convention in Sacramento. After the fashion

# CALIFORNIA

of political parties, they promised all good things, and nominated John Neely Johnson for governor, Hugh Murray and David S. Terry for justices of the Supreme Bench. They carried their ticket in September, and it looked as if the Broderick power was broken in California. From the following it will be seen that they used strong language, but nothing else in those days made much impression:

> Evil has followed evil, and calamity has followed calamity, until the young state which yesterday filled the world with renown to-day lies bankrupt, crime-ridden, and abject.

Not that they were so far wrong.

But Broderick did not know the meaning of defeat. During the session of 1856 he again prevented the appointment of Gwin's successor, as there was no hope during that legislature for himself. In 1857 the Democrats, united against the Whigs and the Know-nothings and the new Republican party, were once more in power. Broderick had made capital of every weak point, and recaptured the recalcitrant members of his own party, visiting them all over the state. It was the year of the presidential election — Buchanan and Breckinridge on the Democratic ticket, Frémont and Dayton on the Republican, Fillmore and Donaldson on the Know-nothing. Buchanan and Breckinridge were elected. The other parties were prostrated. Broderick ruled in California.

But he no longer purposed to be Gwin's successor in that United States Senate of his unswerving ambition. Two years of Gwin's term were gone. Weller's term would expire in March, 1857. His successor would have a full term in the Senate.

# BRODERICK AND GWIN

Nor would Broderick permit the legislature to act according to precedent and elect Gwin's successor first. He intended to enjoy this advantage himself, and then indicate his confrère at his leisure, or when the moment was ripe. He found that he lacked two of a majority, and for these he must recruit in the ranks of the contesting men—Gwin, Weller, and Milton S. Latham. He entered into a deal with Latham promising him Gwin's place if he would secure the needed number of votes. The Democrats went into caucus, decided to waive precedent, and elect Broderick for the long term. On January 9th Broderick was elected, receiving seventy-nine votes against seventeen cast for the Know-nothing candidate and fourteen for the Republican. He had achieved his ambition, and would leave California in February to take his seat in the Senate of the United States.

He was determined upon a colleague whom he could rule. Latham was not of a malleable disposition. For the first and only time in his career Broderick broke his word. He exalted the great national issue—slavery—above an election promise. Knowing Gwin's consuming ambition, he determined to use it for his own ends. Gwin cared more, he believed, for his position as a United States Senator and his social life in Washington than he did for abstract principles or even for federal patronage. Then occurred one of the most memorable, not to say melo-dramatic incidents in California history.

The caucus, after ineffectual balloting over Gwin's successor, adjourned until Monday. Sacramento snatched a few hours' sleep. Then they were on the streets again, men of all parties, excited, as usual, betting, arguing; streetcorners blocked, saloons packed with men keeping up their courage and mere physical stamina. On Sunday the excitement was at fever-heat: Monday and the convening of the legislature seemed insupportably remote.

Gwin was staying at the Orleans Hotel. At midnight he enveloped himself in a long black cloak, pulled a black slouch-hat far down over his face, and stole out of the back door of his hotel. Sacramento was poorly lighted. He found little difficulty in avoiding the groups "swapping" stories of political trickeries, wound his tortuous way through dark and narrow alleys (full of refuse and cats), and reached the rear entrance of Broderick's headquarters in the Magnolia Hotel. A henchman of the great chief was waiting for the Old Roman, and escorted him up-stairs. By this time Broderick's manners could be almost as good as Gwin's, when he chose, although never as suave. He greeted his visitor with the kindly courtesy of a monarch about to sign the death-warrant, bade him be seated, and waved his minions from the room. The two were not long coming to terms. Gwin consented to give up the patronage of the Pacific coast, and Broderick assured him that he, and not Latham, should accompany him to Washington. Gwin then wrote the document afterward to be known as the "scarlet letter," and stole back as he had come.

He was elected. Once more Sacramento and San Francisco seethed with stories of political rottenness and shameful compacts. Broderick's double triumph and the haughty "Chiv's" abasement were shouted from the housetops. But nothing could be proved at that time. Gwin, upon his return to San Francisco, gave a banquet, and many of the invited declined. On the other hand, Broderick was received with a tremendous ovation. In

## BRODERICK AND GWIN

matters of bribery and corruption you must give, not receive.

The two men went as far as New York together amicably enough. Gwin hastened to Washington to whisper into the presidential ear and rally his social forces in the Senate. Broderick remained in his old city for several days, receiving another ovation from his former political associates, who were jubilant over their old leader's rapid fulfilment of his notorious ambition.

In Washington, where he was born, he was received like a conquering hero. He was picturesque; he came to them from the most romantic state in the Union. Only six years before had he gone to it a poor boy, and in less than a year he had dominated it; he had been born on the soil of his ultimate goal. No one questioned that he was a man of extraordinary abilities, of genius. Gwin was coldly received. The particulars of his deal with the enemy were unknown, but rumors had preceded him. Broderick was the hero of the hour, and Gwin took his seat among averted faces.

But Broderick was not born to a bed of roses. His troubles at the capital of the nation began immediately. Whether or not Gwin had any intention of keeping his midnight pledges to Broderick in return for the toga, no one but Gwin himself ever knew; but it is a matter of history that he had Buchanan's ear, and that the new President took a profound dislike to the independent young Senator from California, treated him with insulting coldness, even during his first visit to the White House, and commanded him to put into writing all his requests for federal patronage. This was unprecedented, and Broderick left the Executive's presence enraged, and

## CALIFORNIA

inspired with his first doubts of Gwin's good faith. Of course, he had made the usual campaign promises, and it was doubtful if he could keep any of them. As a matter of fact, merely to save appearances, he received a few crumbs, in themselves an insult. The whole loaves, as before, went to Gwin.

Broderick became the President's bitterest enemy in Congress, although he observed the etiquette of the Senate and made no attempt to speak during his first session. He maintained a semblance of friendliness with Gwin, and told no one of the secret compact. Not yet was he wholly convinced of his colleague's treachery, nor was he in the habit of betraying confidences.

He went to California before the session was finished to look after his political interests; his enemies were active, as usual. But he was in his seat when the Thirty-fifth Congress opened in December, and the lid flew off the volcano shortly afterward.

The question agitating the country was the internal condition of Kansas and its momentous relationship to the balance of power between the North and the South. Kansas became a territory in 1854. Stephen A. Douglas, Senator from Illinois, had injected a clause into the territorial act providing that the question of slavery in the new territory should be determined by a vote of its citizens. There was an immediate rush into Kansas of emigrants from slave and free states, and the result was a condition bordering upon civil war. United States troops were called in to preserve the peace. Ultimately two legislatures were chosen. The one representing anti-slavery was dispersed by the United States marshal in January, 1857. The proslavery legislature then convened and provided for a constitutional convention, which met in September of the same year at Lecompton and framed a proslavery constitution. The antislavery party refused to vote for delegates, maintaining that the legislature which called the convention was an illegal body. Nor would they go to the polls when the constitutional question was submitted to the people. On December 25th, therefore, that famous firebrand known as the Lecompton Constitution was elected by a large majority. But there had been, meanwhile, another election and another legislature. This body submitted the Lecompton Constitution to the popular vote in January, 1858, and it was rejected by a vast majority.

But when Kansas made her application for statehood to the Congress of 1857–58 it was with the Lecompton or proslavery constitution in her hand. Buchanan, who was a Northern man with proslavery sympathies, favored the constitution which would make Kansas a slave state, and urged Congress to ratify it. The result was an immediate split in the Democratic party, Douglas at the head of one faction, Buchanan of the other. The Senate passed the bill with the Lecompton Constitution, but the House rejected it and demanded a substitute bill, which the Senate rejected. Ultimately a new bill was adopted by both Houses which provided that the Lecompton Constitution should be submitted to the people of Kansas for a third time. This was done, and once more it was overwhelmingly defeated. That settled the question as far as Kansas was concerned, but the Democratic party was now divided into two factions, calling themselves Lecomptons and anti-Lecomptons. The last drifted slowly toward the new Republican party.

# CALIFORNIA

Broderick, always opposed to slavery, gave all his support to Douglas. Gwin, naturally, came out for the President.

It was during the session of 1857-58 that Broderick distinguished himself and forced the most indifferent and hostile to admit his great abilities and recognize him as one of the inevitable forces in national affairs. He never became a polished speaker, but he possessed a pointed vocabulary and a power of invective that must have made the President writhe many times, unless, to be sure, Presidents are case-hardened long before they reach the 4th of March. Broderick controlled the minority, and dictated the filibustering tactics calculated most to annoy the Executive as well as the proslavery party. By this time he had done far more than win admiration for his gifts; he enjoyed the complete confidence of his own faction. His poise, courage, stable equilibrium, and power of quick clear thinking lifted him in Washington as in New York and California to the leadership of men. And as a notable figure in that greatest of all arenas he soon attracted the attention of the American people as a whole. His brilliant arraignments of the President, the public scalpel he applied to that unfortunate official's weak spots, delighted the enemies of the government and focused upon him the attention of men of all shades of political opinion. He became known as one of the strongest and most useful—or most dangerous—antislavery men in public life. Had he been permitted to live there is little doubt that he would have become a candidate for the presidency after Lincoln's death; and his party by that time was the only one worth considering in the country: the anti-Lecomptons were then calling themselves Republicans.

# BRODERICK AND GWIN

Mr. Jeremiah Lynch gives a number of extracts from the first of Broderick's speeches which attracted wide attention. It was also his first long speech. The body of it was devoted to a scathing attack on the President for urging another slave state upon Congress. Then he analyzed the slavery enactments of Congress from the Missouri Compromise of 1820, quoting the eminent champions on either side, down to the Lecompton agitation.

> How foolish [he concluded] for the South to hope to contend with success in such an encounter! Slavery is old, decrepit, consumptive. Freedom is young, strong, vigorous. The one is naturally stationary and loves ease. The other is migrating and enterprising. . . . They say that Cotton is King. No sir, Gold is King! [He was the first of the great moderns to put this painful fact into concrete form and fling it into the public teeth.] I represent a state where labor is honorable; where the judge has left his bench, the lawyer and doctor their offices, and the clergyman his pulpit, for the purpose of delving into the earth; where there is no station so high and no position so great that its occupant is not proud to boast that he labored with his hands. [This, it must be remembered, was flung into the face of an aristocratic oligarchy.] There is no state in the Union, no place on earth, where labor is so honored and so well rewarded; no time and no place since the Almighty doomed the sons of Adam to toil, where the curse, if it be a curse, rests so lightly as now upon the people of California.

Some haughty slave-owner in a choleric moment had applied the disagreeable term "mud-sills" to the laboring-class of the North. It may be imagined that the growl of the proletariat was deep and loud, and that the anti-slavery leaders dyed red this rag of speech and waved it aloft.

> I suppose the Senator from South Carolina [continued Broderick, alluding to the unhappy inventor of the classic] did not intend to be personal in his remarks to any of his peers on the floor. If I had thought so I would have noticed it at that time. I am, sir, with one exception the youngest in years of the Senators upon this floor. It is not long since I served an apprenticeship of five years at one of the

most laborious trades pursued by man, a trade that from its nature devotes its follower to thought, but debars him from conversation. I would not have alluded to this if it were not for the remarks of the Senator from South Carolina, and that thousands who know that I am the son of an artisan and have been a mechanic would feel disappointed in me if I did not reply to him. I am not proud of this. I am sorry it is true. I would that I could have enjoyed the pleasures of life in my boyhood days, but they were denied me. I say this with pain. I have not the admiration for the men of that class whence I sprang that might be expected; they submit too tamely to oppression, and are too prone to neglect their rights and duties as citizens. But, sir, the class of society to whose toil I was born, under our form of government, will control the destinies of the nation. [Once more it may be pointed out that this speech was made in 1858, not in 1914]. If I were inclined to forget my connection with them, or to deny that I sprang from them, this chamber would not be the place in which I could do either. While I hold a seat here I have but to look at the beautiful capitals adorning the pilasters that support the roof to be reminded of my father's talent and handiwork.

I left the scenes of my youth for the West because I was tired of the jealousies and struggles of men of my class, who could not understand why one of their fellows should seek to elevate his position above the common level. I made my new abode among strangers where labor is honored. I had left without regrets. There remained no tie of blood to bind me to any being in existence. If I fell in the struggle for reputation and fortune there was no relative on earth to mourn my fall.

Then, after a brief but pungent account of his political career in California, he once more paid his respects to the President.

I hope, sir, that in mercy to the boasted intelligence of this age the historian, when writing of these times, will ascribe this attempt of the Executive to force this constitution on an unwilling people, to the fading intellect, the petulant passion, and the trembling dotage of an old man on the verge of the grave.

During this session of Congress Broderick secured the passage of several measures important to California, energetically advocating an overland railroad; and if he could not secure the federal plums for his friends, he at least managed to extract much of their flavor.

Gwin was seldom in his seat, Broderick as seldom absent. The junior Senator introduced a bill to decrease the salaries of California officials, paid out of the treasury, stating and proving that the cost of living in the new state which had been responsible for their high salaries in the beginning was now altogether normal. The bill passed, and there was gnashing of teeth in the Virginia Poorhouse and elsewhere. Broderick's enemies became bitterer than ever, but he lost few of his friends in California in spite of his inability to keep his election promises. When the legislature of California instructed her two Senators in Washington to vote for the Lecompton constitution Broderick put himself on record without delay.

> The resolutions introduced by my colleague [he said] will have no influence upon my action here now nor in the future. I am satisfied that four-fifths of the people in California repudiate the Lecompton fraud.

When he returned to California he found that his antislavery principles, avowed in the Senate of the United States, had cost him his Southern following in the Democratic party, and that even his Northern friends were inclined to think him premature in his belief that war between the two factions was inevitable. And this was only three years before the war!

During this interval between sessions Broderick left politics alone, made money in real estate, and qualified at the bar. Nevertheless, a disturbing incident happened. He had confided to W. I. Ferguson, the intermediary who arranged the midnight interview between himself and Gwin, that compromising sheet soon to be known as the

## CALIFORNIA

"scarlet letter." Few people knew of its existence. Ferguson was what used to be known as a young man of brilliant parts. He was making a career for himself and had attracted attention by a speech in the antagonistic legislature of 1858 in favor of Douglas and Broderick, scoring the President. Soon after, while in San Francisco, a Buchanan Democrat involved him in a political dispute —no difficult matter in those days—and challenged him to a duel. Ferguson understood; he was to be killed as a warning to Broderick and because the enemy was determined to obtain possession of the letter. His antagonist was a practised duelist. He was a novice. He confided the letter to another friend of Broderick's and went out to be shot. Four balls ended his career.

The Southern element that controlled the President was opposed to an overland railroad, as it would terminate on free soil. If the road must be built, then they demanded that it lie below the parallel 36° 30′, that line being the accepted division between slavery and freedom in the Western states and territories. Moreover, it must stop at California's state line; if the Californians wished to extend it to San Francisco they could build the extra five hundred miles themselves. But far better no railroad at all.

Broderick was the first to advocate the forty-first parallel, and he was one of the most energetic advocates of building a railroad at once to connect the two oceans. When he returned to Washington for the last time he traveled overland by the new stage route. It was a journey of forty-seven days to St. Joseph, and at every city and hamlet Broderick not only learned that the demand for a railroad was practically unanimous, but that the country relied upon him to carry this great project through. He was thus enabled to speak in the Senate with first-hand knowledge. As a direct result he was dropped from the Committee on Public Lands, and his enemies were more definitely arrayed against him than before; they also had increased in numbers.

He was opposed in every newspaper, insulted at every turn, baited, derided, made to feel that he stood alone with his back to the wall. Not for nothing might a young Senator from a far Western state dare to oppose slavery, advocate free labor, denounce corrupt Indian agents, jobbery by postmasters and revenue collectors, demand a reform and retrenchment in public affairs, and propose a transcontinental railway in the teeth of feudal lords who knew the value of slow communication and painful costly travel.

In California the federal and state officials combined to drag him down. He was a dangerous man, therefore a marked man. Besides, too much success through personal effort always goes against the grain. More and more were the enemies' ranks recruited. In Washington even Douglas was afraid to stand by him openly, fearing for his own political fortunes. Probably no man of high ability has ever stood so completely alone in the United States Senate. He knew the fearful odds against him, that a combination was forming to force him out of political life, by men that had perfect faith in the continued power of the Southern faction—if not too severely threatened by such men as Broderick—but who hated him with a hatred born of fear not only personal, but of the rising Republican party, to which Broderick in all but name now belonged. It is possible that he forecast his death

# CALIFORNIA

even before there was a definite plot to kill him. Living, he would have fought on without quailing, and, as events shaped, would have seen his principles win and no doubt have achieved his highest ambitions. He brushed several attempts to challenge him contemptuously aside, but he knew that sooner or later he must fight to the death.

## XVII

### THE BRODERICK-TERRY DUEL

In 1859, after the adjournment of Congress, Gwin and Broderick hastened to California, the junior Senator to rally the state to the anti-Lecompton standard, the older and more subtle man to win it to the support of Lecomptonism and the administration.

There were tremendous Lecompton and anti-Lecompton meetings all over the state, and Broderick took the stump for the first time. Horace Greeley, visiting California during this agitation, advised the anti-Lecomptonites to join forces with the new Republican party and against proslavery Democracy. Broderick called himself a Democrat until the day of his death; but, although he did not live to see the fusion accomplished, he must stand in the history of California as the first great Republican of the state.

It was a season of uncommon political excitement, not only because men were involved. The slavery question, pro and anti, was reaching its acute stage even in California. But the sensation of the campaign was Broderick's long-reserved opinion of Gwin. He denounced him with a cold fury of invective never surpassed by himself. At Shasta he read aloud from the platform the "scarlet letter," and gave it to the press. Here it is:

# CALIFORNIA

SACRAMENTO CITY, *January 11, 1857.*

HON. D. C. BRODERICK.

DEAR SIR,—I am likely to be the victim of unparalleled treachery of those who have been placed in power by my aid and exertion.

The most potential portion of the federal patronage is in the hands of those who, by every principle that should govern men of honor, should be my supporters instead of my enemies, and it is being used for my destruction. My participation in the distribution in this patronage has been the source of numberless slanders upon me that have fostered a prejudice in the public mind against me and have created enmities that have been destructive to my happiness for years. It has entailed untold evils upon me, and while in the Senate I will not recommend a single individual to appointment to office in the state. Provided I am elected, you shall have the exclusive control of this patronage, so far as I am concerned; and in its distribution I shall only ask that it may be used with magnanimity, and not for the advantage of those who have been our mutual enemies and unwearied in their efforts to destroy us.

This determination is unalterable; and in making this declaration I do not expect you to support me for that reason, or in any way to be governed by it; but, as I have been betrayed by those who should have been my friends, I am in a measure powerless and depend upon your magnanimity.

Very respectfully, your obedient servant,

WM. M. GWIN.

In spite of verbiage and pretense there was no mistaking the real character of this letter. Moreover, it was equally obvious that Gwin had not kept his part of the shameful bargain. He took to the stump himself and denounced the letter as a "cowardly lie." But if any one doubted its authorship or that Ferguson had been killed to get possession of it, uncertainty vanished after hearing the two men speak. Gwin had little power of oratory, even of the old-fashioned sort, and he lacked the force in speaking that carries conviction; in this case he lacked the righteous indignation. Broderick, cold, implacable, rarely indulging in gestures or play of facial

# THE BRODERICK-TERRY DUEL

muscle, and with a ringing sledge-hammer logic, never failed to convince people of his sincerity, however much he might antagonize or even infuriate.

He knew that his death must have been resolved upon, and he expected a challenge from Gwin. But either the stately Southern Senator moved too slowly or it was agreed in council that the honor should be relegated to another.

David S. Terry, who so narrowly escaped leaving Fort Gunnybags by the second-story window, could be trusted to spout fire upon a moment's notice. He was a violent proslavery man and Lecompton Democrat (the Know-nothing party being defunct), and had always been among the most fervent of Broderick's political opponents. At one time the two men must have been personal friends, for when Terry was incarcerated by the Vigilance Committee Broderick supported newspapers in his defense. But that was as long ago as 1856. Three whole years had passed. For San Francisco and the fifties that was a generation.

In 1859 he was a candidate for renomination to the Supreme Bench. Before the convention he delivered himself of his present opinion of the junior Senator from California.

> They—the anti-Lecompton party—are a miserable remnant of a faction sailing under false colors, trying to obtain votes under false pretenses. They are the followers of one man, the personal chattels of a single individual whom they are ashamed of. They belong heart and soul, body and breeches, to David C. Broderick. They are yet ashamed to acknowledge their master and are calling themselves, forsooth, Douglas Democrats, when it is known that the gallant Senator from Illinois has no affiliation with them. Perhaps, Mr. President, I am mistaken in denying their right to claim Douglas as their leader, but it is the banner of the black Douglas, whose name is Frederick, not Stephen.

# CALIFORNIA

Broderick did not like this speech. Personally, I never read anything more childish, but it is truly said that no man is sane during a political campaign; which means, no doubt, that the blood—poisoned blood, at that—is in the head all the time. A few days later Broderick was breakfasting at the International Hotel in San Francisco, surrounded by a number of people. He suddenly turned to a man named Perley and said, biting out his words:

"I see that your friend Terry has been abusing me in Sacramento."

"Ah?" said Perley. "How so?"

Then Broderick, whose magnificent self-control had been strained to the breaking-point by the long campaign in the face of almost certain defeat, burst forth:

"The miserable wretch, after being kicked out of the convention, went down there and made a speech abusing me. I paid and supported three newspapers to defend him during the Vigilance Committee days, and this is all the gratitude I get from the miserable wretch. I have hitherto spoken of him as an honest man—as the only honest man on the bench of a corrupt Supreme Court, but now I find I was mistaken; I take it all back. He is just as bad as the others."

Perley said he should inform Terry of the language that so neatly summed him up, and Broderick told him to carry his news as quickly as possible. But Perley, who saw a chance here to swing his little name before the public camera, promptly challenged Broderick to a duel. No reply could be more insulting. Broderick sent him word that if he should be compelled to accept a challenge it would be from some one of his own importance and responsibility. That disposed of Perley, but Broderick's

DAVID C. BRODERICK

COL. E. D. BAKER

DAVID S. TERRY

WILLIAM M. GWIN

# THE BRODERICK-TERRY DUEL

recklessness was due not only to the certainty that his life was sought, and to the desire to have the crisis come and be done with: his health was almost shattered. The mental and physical strain of the campaign had been terrific, and, moreover, he had a heavy and persistent cold. His friends should have put him to bed; but Broderick, no doubt, like other men, was a fractious child where his health was concerned, and willing to send for a doctor only when in a state of collapse.

The following extract—apropos of Broderick's refusal to fight Perley—from a San Francisco newspaper, may be taken as significant of the general understanding that Broderick's enemies had resolved to eliminate him, and of the matter-of-fact acceptance of the methods of the day:

> For refusing to fight a duel under the circumstances the large masses of the people will honor David C. Broderick. The belief is quite general that there are certain political opponents of his who long for a chance to shoot him, either in a fair or unfair fight, and that efforts would be made sooner or later to involve him in a personal difficulty. It is wisdom on his part to avoid the traps set for him and thus defeat all the plans of those in whose path he happens just now to stand. His seat in the Senate would be quite acceptable to a number of gentlemen of this state. The people of California ought to manifest in a manner not to be mistaken their approval of the conduct of a public man who exhibits courage to refuse on any ground to accept a challenge.

Terry, knowing that Broderick would not consider a challenge during the campaign, and finding no opportunity for a fierce personal encounter in which his ready knife could do the deadly work with neatness and despatch, held his peace until after election day, September 7th. His duration of office would expire with the year. He failed of re-election, and immediately sent his resignation to the governor, left Sacramento for Oakland, and entered at once into the correspondence with Broderick that terminated in the long-expected duel. Broderick was staying at the house of a friend at Black Point, almost in a state of collapse, and undoubtedly in the first stages of pneumonia. His friends, instead of permitting him to rest until the last minute, routed him out at midnight on the 10th and drove him into the city to be presented with the cartel. Calhoun Benham and Thomas Hayes were the seconds chosen by Terry; David D. Colton and Joseph C. McKibben acted for Broderick.

Broderick's seconds, exercising their privilege, chose pistols. The principals were to stand ten paces apart, facing each other, the pistols to be held with the muzzles pointed downward until the signal was given to fire. Broderick was one of the best shots in the state, but with the long heavy dueling-pistol then in common use. His seconds might have been in league with the enemy, so little did they watch his interests. They permitted themselves to be persuaded to accept a pair of famous dueling-pistols of Belgian make and of well-known idiosyncrasies, which belonged to a friend of Terry's, Dr. Aylette, of Stockton. As a matter of fact, it transpired afterward that Terry had practised with these pistols during the interval between his provocative speech in June and the challenge in September.

Broderick was a large man with a large hand, and the Aylette pistols were very small, with a hair-trigger. It is not even certain that his seconds told him of the sort of pistol with which he would defend his life. However, it is possible that he was too much absorbed during the time that remained to him to pay any attention to the details of the meeting. He roused himself from his lethargy and

# THE BRODERICK-TERRY DUEL

put his affairs in order, seemingly convinced that he had come to the end of his days.

It would have been possible also for Broderick's seconds, on a doctor's certificate, to have postponed the duel until he had recovered his usual alertness of mind and steadiness of hand, but they did nothing of the sort. Perhaps they were merely fatalists; perhaps, like so many others, they were eager for the dramatic finale of the great political drama. The meeting was arranged for half past five on Monday morning, September 12th, but was interrupted by some legal formality and postponed until the following morning at the same time. The night before, in place of permitting Broderick to sleep comfortably in his bed, Messrs. Colton and McKibben drove him in a lumbering hack to a road-house on the old Mission road several miles from both town and the rendezvous. There they slept in one room on cots or in bunks, and on mattresses stuffed with "pulu," a Hawaiian vegetable beloved of wayside shacks and invariably infested with vermin. Nights in San Francisco, or close to the sea in any part of central California, are cold and often raw. The coverings were scanty, and between chilly and the battalions that promptly deserted the pulu, no one closed his eyes. They rose at five and were unable to obtain even a cup of coffee. Shivering in their overcoats, and depressed as only men can be before breakfast, they entered the hack and were jolted over the sand-dunes to the dueling-ground on the shores of Lake Merced. Terry and his seconds, who had slept comfortably in a farm-house near by and eaten a good breakfast, were already on the ground.

It was a dismal spot. The fog was drifting over the

bare ugly hills, the gray sea was booming in its heavy sullen fashion; but the hills were covered with people, and several other hacks stood beside the lake. The unasked witnesses to this most famous of California's duels bored people for the rest of their lives.

According to Article 7 of the dueling-code Broderick, who had brought a brace of pistols along, might have been favored by chance if his seconds had demanded that a coin be tossed to determine the choice of weapons. But they did nothing of the sort, and even when the little Belgian pistols were handed to McKibben he merely snapped a cap on the one Terry was to use and said, "All right." The armorer then inspected the two and pronounced them in perfect condition, but told Colton and McKibben that the one allotted to their principal was lighter on the trigger than the other. At the inquest he testified that the one intended for Broderick was so delicate that it would explode by a sudden jar or movement.

Broderick turned the little pistol over and over in his big hand. Then he turned to his friend Elliot More, who stood beside him until he took his position, and said contemptuously:

"My seconds are children. As likely as not they have traded away my life."

The principals were told to take off their overcoats—the seconds had talked until nearly seven o'clock. They obeyed and revealed themselves in the formal duelingcostume of the day: full black suits, the frock coat tightly buttoned, and no collars. Broderick wore a soft hat pulled low over his eyes. Both were felt over for possible suits of mail. Broderick's pistol was loaded by the

# THE BRODERICK-TERRY DUEL

armorer; Terry's by S. A. Brooks, a well-known Chivalry Democrat and relative of the powerful Crittenden and Thornton factions.

Terry and Broderick were fine specimens of men, tall, upstanding, Broderick the more massive of the two, Terry the more agile and wiry. Both were in the prime of life, but neither could be adjudged handsome by any standard. Broderick's powerful prehistoric face was the more honest, however, for Terry's mild amiable visage belied the hot temper and deadly purposes of the man.

Terry, whose favorite weapon was the knife, was noticeably nervous before the two men advanced to position; but Benham whispered, it is assumed, the encouraging information that his was the best pistol, for he immediately threw back his head and looked as if about to hum a tune. Broderick, who had been cool and collected throughout this long ordeal, in spite of his physical condition, seemed to lose some of his famous nerve, as he once more turned the little pistol over in his hand. Moreover, he had barely contained his rage at the thoroughness of Benham's exploration in search of a coat of mail. McKibben merely had tapped Terry; but Broderick, whose courage never had been called into question, was subjected to an insulting examination. Certainly the fates were obsessed in favor of Terry.

The men stood in position, ten paces apart. Broderick, upon whom apathy seemed to have descended again, and who was staring at the tiny weapon in his hand, projected his body in such a manner as to offer a fair mark. His seconds might have insisted upon his planting himself squarely, but they merely informed him that he was slightly out of line. It is doubtful if he heard them. Colton asked:

"Gentlemen, are you ready?"

Broderick adjusted the weapon between his big fingers and nodded. Terry replied promptly:

"Ready."

The duelists held their pistols vertically at their sides. Colton enunciated slowly, "One, two, three—" The men raised their pistols at the word "One." Broderick's pistol went off and hit the ground. Terry fired before Colton had time to drawl out "Two," and hit Broderick in the right breast, penetrating the lung. The hair-trigger pistol, light at that, had done what was to be expected in the unaccustomed hand, and Terry had taken an immediate advantage. Broderick raised both his arms, looked out at the heavy dull waves of the Pacific, which he had crossed with such enthusiasm ten years before, shuddered, and dropped the pistol. But he stood upright for a few seconds longer; then a powerful tremor convulsed his body, and he sank literally by inches, as if his will were protesting to the last. But when his friends reached him he lay in a heap. Terry stood with folded arms as Broderick's surgeon and seconds examined the fallen man. It was several moments before Terry was persuaded that he could not have another shot at his adversary. "I hit too far out," he said, discontentedly, demonstrating that he had shot to kill and would not be balked. But he was finally convinced that Broderick was mortally wounded, and left the field.

Broderick's surgeon lost his head, and nothing was done to relieve the dying man until Terry's surgeon volunteered his services. Then Broderick was put into the same old

# THE BRODERICK-TERRY DUEL

lumbering hack in which he had suffered tortures already, and jolted out to Black Point. His friend Colonel Baker hastened to his side as soon as the news of the duel and its fatal termination flew over the town; and Broderick, with the blood gushing again from the wound, managed to gasp out, "Baker, when I was struck I tried to stand firm, but the blow blinded me and I could not." It is no wonder that the world loves the brave and forgives them all their sins.

He lived for three days, chloroform relieving him of some hours of suffering. In his delirium he revealed plainly that he had known all along he was being hunted to death; but as often he talked of the slave power, against which he had pitted all the great resources of his mind, and for which he was to die.

"They have killed me because I was opposed to a corrupt administration," he muttered again and again. "A corrupt administration and the extension of slavery."

Some of the newspapers had the courage to express the sentiments of a community almost as outraged as at the murder of James King of Wm.

What has this man done that he should be hunted and abused? [asked one]. Wherein was his offense against the land or the nation? What law of morality or religion did he violate? What treason did he commit against his country? What widow did he wrong? What orphan did he defraud? What act of his in an official capacity ever stained his hand? What was his crime?

But Broderick knew that the legislature was composed of his enemies, and he murmured as he sank into unconsciousness: "I die. Protect my honor."

He expired on Friday morning, September 16, 1859. That Friday is said to have been the gloomiest in the history of San Francisco. There was no excitement, for

# CALIFORNIA

the duel had been anticipated for months, and Broderick's death for three days. But the bankers, the merchants, and all the shopkeepers closed their doors and draped them with crêpe or black cloth. The crowds, as the body of Broderick was carried past on its way to the Union Hotel, on the corner of Merchant and Kearney streets, looked terrified and spoke only in whispers, as if fearful that this time their city had been cursed by the powers above. Night and day there was a procession past the bier where the face of the dead man was exposed.

The funeral took place on Saturday. The casket lay on a catafalque in the middle of the Plaza; and before some thirty thousand people Colonel Baker pronounced the funeral oration, a superb flight of oratory according to the standards of the day. After this ceremony the funeral procession, accompanied by almost the entire male population of San Francisco, took its slow way out to Lone Mountain—where so many famous San Franciscans were to join Broderick, and where so much of San Francisco history seems crowded into a final chapter.

Broderick had his posthumous compensations, for not only was he venerated as a martyr in the greatest cause before the nation, but what influence he had lost during his last bitter struggle in California he regained in death. His party two years later swept back into power, their talisman the name of their lost leader, and the "Chivs" were routed for good and all. The Southerners had triumphed for the last time in California when they broke Broderick's heart and sent his body to Lone Mountain. The Civil War disposed of them as effectually as if California had returned to her old tricks and swallowed them up.

# THE BRODERICK-TERRY DUEL

As for Terry, although his trial was a farce, he expiated his sin so heavily that he demands a certain measure of sympathy. One must remember that he was a child of his times, poisoned with political bitternesses, and no more sensible of committing murder by dueling than by sending a criminal to the scaffold. He was a brave man, and willing to take his chances; and Broderick's death put an end to what ambitions he may have cherished. He never was elected to the Supreme Bench again; and although he continued to practise law in California, his position as a first-rate man had gone for ever. In the revolution of political feeling that began with Broderick's death and culminated when the next legislature expunged from its records the resolutions of censure compassed by his enemies, Terry came to be regarded more and more as a pariah, and what had promised to be one of the most brilliant careers in California was over.

During the '80's he took the case of an adventuress named Sarah Althea Hill, who claimed to have made a contract marriage with William Sharon, then one of the city's leading millionaires. The case was lost, but he married the lady himself. In the legal tangle that ensued Mrs. Terry appeared before Stephen J. Field, Associate Justice of the Supreme Court of the United States. Judge Field ruled unfavorably to Mrs. Terry, who sprang to her feet and screamed out her unfavorable opinion of the justice. He ordered her removed from the courtroom; and Terry, whose self-control had not improved with the years and the frowns of society, drew his knife and attacked the bailiffs. He was overpowered, and both he and his wife were sentenced to short terms in jail.

# CALIFORNIA

Terry emerged vowing vengeance on Judge Field. As he was not a man whose animosities burned out, but rather more fiercely for smoldering, the justice never appeared in the West again save in the company of a guard employed by the government. On the 15th of August, 1899, Judge Field and his guard, a man named Neagle, while on their way from Los Angeles to San Francisco, were obliged to leave the train for lunch at Lathrop, one of those dreary, dirty, fly-ridden eating-houses which still disgrace the West. Terry, with his wife, was on the same train, and when he entered the restaurant and saw Judge Field the blood flew to his head. He managed to control himself for a few moments, then sprang abruptly from his seat, and, approaching Judge Field from behind, slapped the esteemed justice in the face. The sequel did not consume a moment. The guard leaped to his feet and shot Terry dead. This was almost thirty years to a day from the September morning when Terry went out to Lake Merced with the deliberate intention of killing a far greater man than either himself or Judge Field. His wife lost her mind and died in an asylum for the insane.

Broderick had his grave faults, but they were the faults of the big men of history. He was a law unto himself, and in his great strength he could be crushed only by a combination of factions and enemies. It was decreed that he must die lest he emerge from defeat stronger than ever, and mount to the highest places in the land over the bodies of his foes. So he died. He was thirty-nine years old. He is still immovable on his lofty and solitary pedestal in the history of California. He remains in death as in life the greatest of her sons.

## XVIII

#### THE WAR

At the Presidential election of 1860 California surprised itself by coming out for the Union. All efforts were made to consolidate the two wings of the Democratic party; but they were irreconcilable, and the new Republican party, composed of anti-Lecomptonites, remnants of the old Whig party and loyal Unionists of any faction, stopped playing with politics and declared for the flag. Gwin's term in the United States Senate expired on March 3, 1861. He was not mentioned as a candidate when the new legislature took up the business of filling the vacancy. James A. McDougal, an anti-Lecompton Democrat, received fifty-seven votes on the last ballot; John Nugent and John B. Weller, Chivalry Democrats, thirty-nine and four. Shortly afterward there was another duel in which once more a "Chiv" was victorious and an anti-Lecomptonite killed. This roused so much and such prolonged comment that it proved to be the last of the duels in California.

Of course, there were plots and counterplots in a state that had been ruled by the proslavery faction during its brief history; and, although it was no new thing to hear that the Mexican-Californians of the South, who had been despoiled of their vast possessions by squatters, unfair rulings, and disproportionate taxation, were agitating to

# CALIFORNIA

cut California in two, this time the rumor was investigated and the unrest traced to the Chivalry Democrats, who hoped to profit by a new state so dissatisfied with the federal government. Washington was informed—rumor said by Edmund Randolph—that not only was the southern part of the state on the verge of secession, but that Brig.-Gen. Albert Sidney Johnston, of Kentucky, in command of the Pacific Department, had entered into a plot with certain federal officials in San Francisco to seize the port and hold it for the Southern Confederacy. There was no proof of this, nor has any transpired since; but all rumors are alarming in war-time, and it was thought best to replace him with a strong Union general. Before the order reached him he had been warned by way of the pony express, and resigned. He afterward distinguished himself in the Confederate army.

In spite of the fact that Edmund Randolph was a Virginian and an F. F. V. he had been openly opposed to secession and had upheld the Union at the polls and on the stump. His family was among the most prominent socially, in those days when the Southern women ruled with an iron hand, and he himself was an odd mixture of the romantic and the practical. That is to say, he was practical when the blood was out of his head, and romantic to the point of hysteria when wrought up on the stump or by any sudden acute crisis. He was a lawyer of striking ability and had been employed by the United States government in the New Almaden Quicksilver Mine case, and held his own against such men as Judah P. Benjamin and Reverdy Johnson. On the other hand, he had helped to finance the filibuster scheme of William Walker against Nicaragua—that same William Walker

# THE WAR

whom Joaquin Miller described in eloquent verse as a superb and picturesque figure in full regimentals, red sash and sombrero, standing on a hill-top and shading his eyes against the tropic sun, but whom my grandfather, who was in Nicaragua at the time, remembers in a wrinkled linen duster, battered "panama," and sandy beard.

In spite of Randolph's abilities no one was ever surprised at any of his abrupt departures from a former standard, and when he appeared before the Chivalry convention in Sacramento immediately after the news of the firing upon Sumter was received, and indulged in a wild recrudescence of all his Southern instincts, the members merely smiled; but when he died a few months later his right-about-face was ascribed to failing powers.

> Gentlemen [he cried. He is described as a distraught figure springing suddenly to his feet], my thoughts and my heart are not in this house to-night. Far to the east in the homes from which we came, tyranny and usurpation with arms in their hands, are this night, perhaps, slaughtering our fathers, our brothers, and our sisters, and outraging our homes in every conceivable way shocking to the heart of humanity and freedom. To me it seems a waste of time to talk. For God's sake tell me of battles fought and won. Tell me of usurpers overthrown; that Missouri is again a free state, no longer crushed under the armed heel of a reckless and odious despot. Tell me that the state of Maryland lives again; and oh, let us read, let us hear, at the first moment, that not one hostile foot now treads the soil of Virginia. If this be rebellion, then I am a rebel. Do you want a traitor? Then I am a traitor. For God's sake speed the ball. May the lead go quick to his heart, and may our country be free from the despot usurper that now claims the name of President of the United States.

A good many other Southerners died hard, but they died. The Rev. William A. Scott, the leading Presbyterian minister of San Francisco and a native of New Orleans, delivered impassioned sermons in the cause of secession. He created a tremendous uproar, being hung

# CALIFORNIA

in effigy in front of his own church and frequently threatened by mobs. Finally his friends took him in hand. A steamer was sailing on a certain Sunday. Passage was secured for Dr. Scott by several of his parishioners, although he was not taken into their confidence. Morning service was held as usual, and in spite of warnings from friends as well as enemies he once more denounced the government and pleaded the holy cause of a new flag and a new people. Meanwhile a mob had gathered in front of the church, and roared its threats. It was patent that this time he was not to be permitted to leave sanctuary without a dangerous mauling. But Mrs. Thomas H. Selby had her carriage waiting in the rear. Finally Dr. Scott was persuaded out of the pulpit by his anxious friends and into the carriage. The coachman whipped up his horses and raced the mob to the docks; Dr. Scott, fuming, was safely stowed away. He remained in the South until the war was over, then returned to San Francisco and resumed his pastoral duties.

My grandfather, Stephen Franklin, was a member of this church, having been a friend of Dr. Scott's in New Orleans. He came to California first in 1851, then went to Central America and returned to California several years later with his family. Although he took no part in politics, he was opposed to the Vigilance Committee on principle, being a firm believer in the written law. Formerly a cotton-planter in Louisiana himself, he voted with the Chivalry Democrats; and, a man of rigid principles, both religious and political, it was not in him to compromise either then or later with the great organization that reformed San Francisco (although devoted personally to William T. Coleman), or with the men that elevated the

# THE WAR

flag above the "beloved South." When the news flashed across the wires of the assassination of Lincoln the excitement in San Francisco exceeded anything that had convulsed it before. Word ran round the city that every house and building of any sort must drape itself in mourning or prepare for attack. No one disobeyed this unwritten order but a church, several newspaper officers, and my grandfather. He was the reverse of a violent or even a bitter man, but he did not approve of Lincoln, and that was the end of it. He would not put his house in mourning for him. The mob wrecked the church and the newspaper offices and then started for my grandfather's house. As it appeared at the head of Stockton Street, the next-door neighbors tore up a black gown, rushed in, and hung it from the upper windows. My father, Thomas L. Horn, one of the young merchants of the city, had been a member of the Vigilance Committee, and was an ardent Union man. I merely relate this bit of family history as an instance of the intensity of feeling so far from the seat of war, and as proof that I am able to be an impartial historian! I was brought up by my grandfather, and during that time and for years after I was an ardent Southerner, but I have got over it.

The following would be incredible if it were not true, and illustrates the raging patriotism of the women of the South compared to which that of the men was quite commonplace. A certain eminent judge had a family of women, pre-eminent socially, and by this time not on speaking terms with any one upholding the flag. The judge heard the news of Lincoln's assassination downtown, and, jumping into his buggy, drove furiously for home. There were no telephones in those days, but he feared his women might hear the news and disgrace him in the street. When he reached home he coaxed his wife and other female relatives up the stairs and into a room at the back of the house. There he locked the door, put the key in his pocket, and told them that Lincoln had been assassinated. His wife (who upon ordinary occasions boasted all the hauteur, repose, and suave manners of an F. F. V.) shrieked like an Indian and, picking up her skirts, executed a war-dance. (She was very short and very fat.) The other women were hysterical in their delight, screaming, laughing, and clapping. The judge was shut up with them for nearly two hours. Then he let them out only when each gave him her solemn word of honor that she would not run up and down the street shouting her satisfaction. But by this time they were exhausted and ready to behave themselves.

California contributed three distinguished men to the Union army—Sherman, Halleck, and Baker. In 1861 she sent two full regiments of cavalry, eight full regiments of infantry, besides eight companies that enlisted in the First Regiment of Washington Infantry Volunteers: sixteen thousand in all. In 1863 seven more companies of cavalry were raised, six companies constituting the First Battalion of California Mountaineers; and in the next two years two other regiments.

California was equally liberal with her gold, although she refused to submit to the imposition of greenbacks; and she became the chief supporter of the famous Sanitary Commission organized in behalf of the sick and wounded. Thomas Starr King, a Unitarian clergyman, whose fame survived him locally many years, a tomb being erected to him in the yard of his church, which

# THE WAR

stood in the heart of the city, took charge of the branch organization in San Francisco, and with his energy and eloquence raised six thousand dollars at the first meeting. That was a good deal of money for those days, particularly in war-time; but ten days later a further sum of one hundred and sixty thousand dollars in gold was subscribed and sent to headquarters in New York. In October another hundred thousand dollars were sent on, and before the end of 1862 still another hundred thousand. Being in gold coin, this contribution represented a half a million in legal-tender notes.

In 1863 California responded to another appeal and announced her intention of subscribing twenty-five thousand dollars a month as long as the war lasted. At the close of the war the report of the central commission showed that out of four million eight hundred thousand dollars contributed to the sanitary fund California had supplied nearly a million and a quarter, and Oregon and Nevada nearly a quarter of a million, the three together contributing a third of the whole amount.

The war proved to be of enormous benefit to California. The telegraph line across the continent was completed in October, 1861, putting her in direct communication with New York. In 1862 Congress granted her petition for the long-denied railroad from the Missouri River to the Pacific Ocean, the withdrawal of Southern members from both houses making this concession possible at last. And her population received an immediate stimulus. Hundreds of families, believing that the war would last for many years, emigrated to California, where they would be spared the immediate suffering, the terrible strain and anxieties of those living too close to the

# CALIFORNIA

path of war. Within a year a thousand new houses were contracted for in San Francisco; and the Russ House, the Lick House, and the Occidental Hotel, superfine hostelries for their day, went up, the last two retaining something of their old prestige until burned in 1906. Streetrailroads were built, and business of all sorts, which had been depressed before the outbreak of the war, was, from many sources, stimulated. The Republican party, of course, claimed all the credit, and, it must be admitted, ruled the state without too many iniquities for several years.

In 1867 the United States government purchased what is now know as the territory of Alaska from the Russian government, an enormous tract of land of over five hundred and eighty thousand square miles, thus shifting California almost to the center of the United States. But the most exciting event for Californians after the close of the war was the completion of the railroad in 1869. Theodore D. Judah, a native of Bridgeport, Connecticut, who had already demonstrated his ability in railroad-building locally, interested four Sacramento merchants in the scheme of an immediate railroad across the continent, now that the hostile influence in Congress was removed. It was owing to the far-sightedness of these four men—Charles Crocker, Mark Hopkins, Leland Stanford, and Collis P. Huntington—as well as to the brilliant young engineer, that California got her railroad in the sixties. They organized the Central Pacific Railroad Company, notwithstanding ridicule and opposition, incorporated it in California, raised money, obtained the consent and aid of Congress in spite of the war; and on January 8, 1863, Stanford broke the first ground in Sacramento at

# THE WAR

the corner of Front and K streets, not far from the fort where Sutter used to watch the train of emigrant wagons crawl down the slopes of the Sierra Nevada Mountains. This railroad, one of the most difficult of all engineering feats owing to the intervening chains of mountains, is a monument to the young engineer who conceived it, Theodore D. Judah, and to the four men who won as much contumely as gratitude for pushing it through and connecting the two oceans. No longer did Californians have to travel East by mail-coach, hanging first out of one side and then the other, their eyes raking the horizon for scalping Indians. No longer were they forced to take the alternative to this grizzling experience and lose a precious month at sea, and possibly their lives crossing "the Isthmus." Indeed, the greater number of California immigrants, important and insignificant, when they sent for their families, had resigned themselves never to see their native states again. But as soon as the railroad was built they became the restless travelers they have remained ever since.

# XIX

## THE TERRIBLE SEVENTIES

SPECULATION is a permanent microbe in the blood of Californians, and they are never really happy save when they have turned it loose to multiply and run riot; in other words, when they have food for excitement. After the great gold-rush, although they speculated in whatever came to hand—city *varas*, water-lots, stocks and bonds, new placers—they had no really terrific excitement financially until the seventies. Then it was so mad and so prolonged that it might have glutted even a San Franciscan.

In 1872 began the sensational history of the great silver-mines of Nevada, and witnessed the coruscations of a new galaxy of millionaires: Mackay, Fair, Flood, O'Brien, Ralston, Sutro, Sharon, Haggin[1], Tevis, D. O. Mills, "Jim" Keene, and too many others to mention here.

Of these by far the greatest personality was William C. Ralston. Born in Ohio in 1825, educated at the public schools, leaving abruptly to try his hand at ship-building, he finally started for California in 1850. At Panama, however, he was offered the position of agent of a line of steamships plying between New York and San Francisco, and accepted it. In 1853 he was sent to represent the same firm in San Francisco. Shortly afterward, his employers opened a bank, and, recognizing his great abilities, took him into partnership. The firm was called Garrison,

---

[1] James Ben Ali Haggin was a pioneer, and also a man of wealth long before this; but his family did not begin to play a leading part until the seventies.

# THE TERRIBLE SEVENTIES

Morgan, Fretz & Ralston. Later it became Fretz & Ralston, the more brilliant and adventurous member of the firm carrying it safely over the shoals of 1855. After another change Ralston in 1864 induced D. O. Mills and several other men who already were on the broad way to fortune to join in founding the Bank of California, still, in spite of all vicissitudes and changes, the great bank of the Pacific coast, and known all over the world. Mills was the first president, Ralston the cashier, but succeeding soon afterward to the presidency. William Sharon was the confidential agent in Virginia City, Nevada. All distinguished foreigners in those days brought letters of introduction to the Bank of California, and many to Mr. Ralston personally. He entertained them at his magnificent and picturesque country house at Belmont, about thirty miles from San Francisco. It was an immense white, rambling, French-looking structure, situated in a wild and windy cañon. One of the sights of those days was Ralston's four-horse *char-à-banc* crowded with guests (generally breathless) dashing along the old Mission road, himself at the wheel. It might be daylight or black midnight, it was all one to Ralston; he never slackened his pace. He generally managed to arrive with his guests, however, just after dark, when the immense house against the black background of the cañon was a blaze of light. There a banquet was always spread, the ballroom always open, and the hundred bedrooms ready. Innumerable Chinese servants in white were at the service of the guests. At the top of the staircase was a large room built like an opera-box, where it amused Ralston to sit with a few of his chosen friends and watch his company disport itself below.

# CALIFORNIA

When Anson Burlingame passed through California on his way to the Orient to conclude the treaty which bears his name, Ralston drove him down to Belmont at his usual furious rate. Shortly before dinner was announced he had him escorted to the library. This was a room rather small, handsomely finished with laurel, and, as I remembered it, never a book. There Mr. Burlingame found the large company gathered in his honor, and was asked to sit down. All the guests faced one way. A few moments passed. All knew that some sort of a surprise was in store, and felt that Ralston's originality could be relied upon. Suddenly the opposite wall gave a sort of shiver, then rose slowly like the curtain of a theater, revealing an immense banqueting-hall laden with the most splendid plate, china, and glass that had been brought to California at that period, and an almost limitless variety of flowers and fruits. As motionless as an army about to salute were the pigtailed Chinese.

The next morning the ambassador at Mr. Ralston's request picked out the site for a future town the magnate had in mind, and it was promptly named in his honor. Ralston did not live to build it, but to-day Burlingame is a fashionable little community representing many millions. One of its members, by the way, is a daughter of James King of Wm., and another a son of William T. Coleman.

For five or six years Ralston enjoyed a world-wide reputation as a host and a new-world Monte Cristo. He would take fifty or sixty guests at a time to Yosemite and the Big Trees, or entertain them at the Cliff House and other road-houses, hiring special trains and entire livery-stables. Meanwhile, the stock excitement was rising daily,

WILLIAM C. RALSTON [INSERT], WHO FREQUENTLY TOOK HIS GUESTS TO YOSEMITE AND BIG TREES, WAS THE FIRST TO DRIVE A FOUR-IN-HAND THROUGH "WAWONA"

# THE TERRIBLE SEVENTIES

There was some interest in the Virginia City silver-mines as early as 1863, when Ophir, Savage, Hale and Norcross, and Gould and Curry were opened, and they were regularly bought and sold on the Stock Exchange; but it was not until the exploitation of the Comstock Lode, with its fabulous and apparently inexhaustible riches, that California, and San Francisco in particular, suddenly broke out with the most virulent form of speculation fever; soon beyond all human power to check.

The great silver-mines of the Comstock Lode were the California, Consolidated Virginia, Crown Point, Belcher, and Raymond and Ely. Consolidated Virginia was the most popular, made a few great fortunes and bankrupted half the coast. It was controlled by four men, Mackay and Fair, practical miners, and Flood and O'Brien, who for many years had kept a saloon in San Francisco; being men of uncommon shrewdness, they extracted the salt from the oceans of mining talk always flowing over their bar.

These five mines were called the Bonanzas, and practically the whole state invested in them. Women sold their jewels, and every clerk and servant hoped to make his or her "pile." The old Stock Exchange was no longer able to accommodate the increasing number of brokers, and in January, 1872, the California Stock Exchange Board was organized. Daily and hourly, until men fell in their tracks from exhaustion, it was a scene of such frenzied excitement that the old stampeding days to the diggings were relegated to the storehouse of insignificant memories. That any one survived those years, particularly 1875, is a phenomenon that must be explained by the climate. Thousands did not. They either committed suicide or crawled away to hide themselves for the rest of their shattered lives. Only a few tremendous fortunes were made. Several millionaires, their reason burnt up with the speculation microbe, were ruined, and more of the merely well-to-do; but the greater number of people with "money behind them" managed either to come out even or save enough to begin life over; the vast number that lost all were those that had nothing to lose.

In 1872 the market value of the Nevada stocks shot up from seventeen millions to eighty-four millions of dollars, and the sales numbered many millions. Business was neglected. Even the gambling-tables languished. People invested all they had, all they could borrow, beg, pawn, or steal, in stocks. No one talked of anything else; and many women, known as Mudhens, sold stocks on the curb. Everybody assumed that one spot of earth at least had enough for all, and that this day one year he would be handling money by the bushel and proclaiming that never in this life would he do another stroke of work. Husbands must have been quite unmanageable in those days, and repellant to all but wives that were equally reckless and irresponsible.

All this went to Ralston's head, but in a totally different fashion from its devastations in the average cranium. Ralston, like Broderick, or, to soar higher, like Cecil Rhodes or Napoleon, was a law unto himself, and, as his brothers have done, discovered that sooner or later Law manages to hold its own like the wind and the waves. Nevertheless, if the crash had not come when it did Ralston's commanding genius for finance and his magnificent civic patriotism never would have been called into question; now he must be regarded as a great man

# THE TERRIBLE SEVENTIES

gone wrong. He just missed having hideous statues erected to his memory all over the state of California. What he needed was a whole mine of his own.

Between the insupportable excitement of those years and the fact that he was regarded as the uncrowned king of California he lost all sense of proportion, all power of foresight. Born one of the clearest of thinkers, and famous in the financial world for taking precisely one minute to make up his mind on questions involving millions, it would seem that his brain, being the biggest in the state, could accommodate the greatest number of microbes. His passion was San Francisco, his ambition, to make her one of the greatest cities in the Union, the rival of the proudest in the older East. With the silver floods rolling down from Nevada it seemed to him that now was the time to do it—take the tide at its flood. In rapid succession his fertile brain projected and his superhuman energy put through the Mission Woolen Mills, the Kimball Carriage Factory, the Cornell Watch Factory, the West Coast Furniture Factory, the San Francisco Sugar Refinery, the Grand Hotel, the Palace Hotel, the Dry Dock at Hunter's Point, the Reclamation Work at Sherman Island, the Irrigating Works of the San Joaquin Valley, the Rincon Hill Cut, the extension of Montgomery Street, and the California Theater. Ralston possessed one of the greatest civic imaginations the world has produced, and if he only could have found that mine he would rank with such city-makers and castle-builders as Ludwig I. and Ludwig II. of Bavaria, both of whom, by the way, nearly bankrupted their state.

One can only admire the ruthlessness of these great imaginations that elevate the beauty and prosperity of

# CALIFORNIA

their chosen territory above the commonplace needs of the "plain people," or their own safety, and wish they could discover the mines that are wasted on the sordid or the unworthy. To my mind Ralston is far more entitled to admiration and real fame than any of the thousand and one smug millionaires that live smugly, take no risks save for themselves, and leave no impress on the world. Ludwig I. found Munich a medieval stronghold and converted it into a great Renaissance city (with corners of other periods), to which all the world goes and leaves many millions of marks a year. Moreover, it is a city without a slum. The beautiful and unique castles upon which Ludwig II. spent the revenues of his state until the government, fearing bankruptcy, deposed and imprisoned him, are one of the greatest sources of revenue in Bavaria to-day. As for Ralston, practically all of the businesses he founded, as well as his other investments, survived himself, flourished, and added to the wealth and importance of his city. The Palace Hotel, finished by Mr. Sharon, became one of the famous hotels of the world.

But he did not live to see the fruition of any of his great schemes, nor the growth of the city that until the fire of 1906 owed more to him, to the tremendous impetus he gave it, than to all other San Franciscans of his era put together; for he was the first to rouse civic pride in a very selfish and self-centered community. But almost imperceptibly the mines began to show signs of exhaustion, to say nothing of unconquerable underground floods. And Ralston had been improving San Francisco with the capital of the Bank of California.

Of course, he had borrowed of other banks. It suited one of these banks, intensely jealous of the man as well

# THE TERRIBLE SEVENTIES

as of the Bank of California, to watch for the weak moment and then turn on the screws; in other words, call in its loans. On August 27, 1875, California rocked with the news—and vibrations of this earthquake were felt all over the world, for Ralston's famous institution was the agent of the Rothschilds—that the Bank of California, which had been regarded as Gibraltar's twin, had closed its doors.

Behind those doors the excitement was none the less intense for being suppressed—by men that had no time for emotions. William Sharon and others agreed to set the bank on its feet again out of their personal fortunes, but Ralston was requested to resign. The man that had made the bank one of the greatest institutions in the world, and given California a position financially she never had enjoyed before, was treated without mercy. But he must have picked up his hat and left that council chamber of the just with the hope that he never would lay eyes on one of those men again.

He was in the habit of taking a daily swim from North Beach. He drove from the bank to his usual bath-house, swam out and went down. The next excitement in San Francisco was "Ralston's suicide." That night Mr. Sharon said to my grandfather, "Best thing he could have done." But my grandfather, who was perhaps the most intimate friend Mr. Ralston had, never for a moment believed in that immediately adopted theory of suicide, a theory that gained swift credence not only because Ralston was ruined and had wrecked the bank, but because he was a man of intense pride. Some years afterward Dr. John Pitman, who was Ralston's doctor, made, at the request of one of the great Californian's

# CALIFORNIA

daughters, a written statement which should dispose once for all of the popular theory.

      Fort Wayne, Indiana, *January 5, 1903.*

 Dear Madam,—I have to-day received a letter from Mr. Charles E. Dark, of Indianapolis, telling me of your serious desire to have a statement from me regarding the death of your father, Mr. W. C. Ralston, whom it was my pleasure and honor to know.

 If I remember correctly it was August, 1875. He was President of the California Woolen Mills, California Furniture Company, and the Bank of California. He had for some time been almost pursued by Senator Sharon, whose manipulations caused the suspension of the Bank of California, which was totally unnecessary, as the bank was solvent; but Sharon played his cards causing the suspension. The day of Mr. Ralston's death was a blazing hot day, the city was a furnace of heat. I met him as he was coming out of the bank and shook hands with him. He told me he had just shifted a load of care from his shoulders by resigning the presidency of the bank, and, to use his own words, "felt like a school-boy off for his holidays." It had been a custom of his to go in swimming at North Beach, and he told me he was off for a swim, and he wanted me to go with him. I warned him that he was overheated, that the water of the Pacific was dangerously cold, and begged him to forego his bath; but he insisted. I was unable to go with him at the time, but promised if he would wait an hour I would go with him to North Beach. We then separated. I fully expected to find him waiting for me at the bath-house, but I was delayed, and the first thing I heard was the newsboys calling an extra with a statement of his suicide. The *Call* and the *Bulletin* had both been opponents of his, and were only too glad to do their dirty work. Mr. Ralston was a grand man, a noble man; he had no idea of suicide, and I so stated over my signature in the *Chronicle*. He was a courageous man, not a coward, was ready to meet all emergencies, and never discouraged. He was a friend of the poor man and the rich; he knew men, and his judgment never was at fault. His death was a great loss to the Pacific coast, and Senator Sharon and the *Call* and the *Bulletin* were guilty of the foulest lie when they accused him of suicide. His death was due to cramp produced by his heated condition and very cold water.

 Trusting these lines may be of some comfort from one who knows the facts, I am

      Yours very sincerely,

             John Pitman.

# THE TERRIBLE SEVENTIES

Mr. Ralston was only fifty; his energies—never allowed to rust—were at their supreme pitch of development; his resourceful and highly organized brain was a perfect machine, equipped for every emergency. If he had lived, no doubt he would have made another fortune and continued to devote himself to the advancement of his city. In spite of the nagging attacks of the *Call* and the *Bulletin*, which preceded his death for several weeks, it is doubtful if he ever lost the confidence or admiration of the public. And once more all San Francisco turned out for a funeral. He lies not far from Broderick in Lone Mountain.

I remember Mr. Ralston—who was the great man of my childhood—as a thick-set man with a massive face, clean-shaven above the mouth, and not too much hair below, a piercing but kind and often humorous blue eye, a tightly set mouth which could relax—rarely—into a charming and spontaneous smile—sandy hair, and a cast-iron repose. I know now that that granitic exterior surrounded a dynamo, and, no doubt, often an insupportable nervous tension. He was a great man set down into too small a field, and, like other great men that have ignored the laws made by lesser men, he paid a heavy price.

# XX

### THE CHINESE IN CALIFORNIA

WHEN California was admitted into the Union in 1850 the Chinese, welcome immigrants, turned out as patriotically as the Americans in the great parade which celebrated that historic episode, and were given an honorable position. Both Governor Burnett, the first civil governor of California, and his successor, accepted the Chinese as desirable acquisitions; and Governor McDougal, in his annual message, spoke of them as "one of the most worthy classes of our newly adopted citizens," and recommended that further immigration should be encouraged, as they were particularly fitted to work on the reclamation of the fertile tule-swamps overflowed by the rivers during the rainy season. When the Vigilance Committee of 1856 was organized the Chinese merchants of San Francisco, already a powerful and concentrated colony, contributed munificently to its funds and received a vote of thanks.

But it was far otherwise in the mines. Almost from the first there was an outcry against these frugal, thrifty, thorough, tireless Orientals. This was owing partly to an ineradicable race prejudice against color, characteristic of this land of many races, partly to an irritating sense of the economical superiority of the Asiatic, partly to the discovery that the maximum of the precious dust which

# THE CHINESE IN CALIFORNIA

had been sluiced upward throughout long vulcanic ages for the benefit of honest Americans was being sent to China—from which, it is possible, California derived her ancient populations. Whatever the motive, the Chinamen were run out of digging after digging, laws were enacted against them; before long, although here and there they were permitted to herd together at inferior placers, they began to drift into the towns, particularly San Francisco, where they proceeded to reduce the cost of living by their low charges as laundrymen, merchants, street venders, and servants. One of the most familiar sights of San Francisco for many years was the coolie with his coarse blue linen smock and wide trousers, native straw hat (that so curiously resembles his native architecture), and a pole balanced across his shoulders from which depended large baskets filled with salmon and other fish, fruits, and vegetables. These he peddled from house to house at incredibly low prices.

The children were never weary of standing in front of the Chinese wash-houses and watching the "pigtails" fill their mouths with water and eject it in a hissing stream over the underclothes and linen that their vindictive rival, the laundress, sprinkled occidentally. The Chinese quarter gave a complete illusion of the Orient, particularly at night, with its gaudy Chinese architecture and crowds and smells, its thousands of swaying lanterns, often nebulous blots of light in the fog, its ornate Joss house, its theaters of gorgeous costumes and no scenery, its underground opium-dens, its hanging balconies, over which on the occasion of a merchant's banquet drifted the hopeless monotonous wailing of the women, singing to entertain their lords. The shops were fascinating both to tourists

# CALIFORNIA

and Californians with their prodigal stock of kimonos ranging from one dollar to seventy-five dollars, their china of all prices, their jades and carved cabinets and bedspreads. Until the fire of 1906 San Francisco's Chinatown was one of the sights of the world, but to-day the shops alone have their old attraction.

The antagonism in San Francisco toward the Chinese grew slowly. In 1851 the immigration had reached about twenty-seven hundred. In 1852 there were eighteen thousand four hundred additional Chinese in California, and the uneasiness had spread from the mines and entered politics.

The celebrated phrase "The Chinese must go" is attributed to one Dennis Kearney, the "sand-lot agitator"; but Bigler, third governor of California, came out flatly with the sentiment in a special message to the legislature, April 23, 1852, giving expression to the growing belief that it was important to check Chinese immigration, particularly of coolies, who were sent out under contract to work at the mines, and would be returned to China after a fixed period by one or other of the six companies. These coolies, he advised the legislature, came to California influenced by cupidity only (here we find no mention by his excellency of the motives influencing the stupendous white immigration of 1849–50, which included clergymen, school-teachers, lawyers, editors, and other exponents of the high occidental standard, who had deserted their avocations and stampeded for the mines); he went on to say that these coolie miners received from the companies a mere wage, that not one of them intended to settle in the country, that as their standards in all things were so low (the American has always despised frugality), opposed

# THE CHINESE IN CALIFORNIA

diametrically to those of the United States, they were necessarily the most undesirable class of citizens which the country could adopt. He made no reference to the fact that in spite of the prejudice against the Chinamen at the mines it never had been found necessary to lynch one of them, whereas every white race had been represented at the end of a rope up the gulch.

However, there is no logical argument that can make the least headway against race prejudice; and if the Orientals, who, we are all willing to grant, are vastly our superiors economically, would appreciate this fact once for all, much trouble and possibly bloodshed would be averted. It is the masses that rule in this country, not the enlightened few, who, whatever their breadth of mind, are always forced to yield to the popular clamor.

Bigler, who was anything but broad-minded, attributed all the vices of all the ages to the Chinese, and in his message, at least, left them not one rag of virtue to cover their corruption. He went so far as to discourage the keeping of the contracts with the companies, and intimated that it would be an impertinence if the Chinese attempted retaliation; the conditions of California were peculiar, therefore she should enact peculiar laws; having examined the constitutional question involved, he believed that the state had the right to prevent the entry of any class of persons that it "deemed dangerous" to the interests or welfare of its citizens.

But although Bigler with this message encouraged the prejudice against the yellow race among the unruly members of the population, subjecting it to abuse and indignities, he was unable to obtain any legislation on the subject; and the answers of the Chinese merchants so far

# CALIFORNIA

exceeded his message in logic and dignity that many Californians resented the position in which their governor had placed them. On March 9, 1853, five members of the Committee on Mines and Mining Interests—James H. Gardner, T. T. Cabaniss, Benjamin B. Redding, R. G. Reading, and Patrick Cannay—presented a report which indicated that among legislators at least there was a reaction in favor of the inoffensive race that had played so important a part in developing the industries and resources of the state.

Their report asserted that there were twenty-two thousand Chinese in California, mostly from the Canton district. They had divided themselves into four departments, representing that district. Each department had a house in San Francisco presided over by two men who were elected by the department in the state. All coolies that came to the country were under the supervision of these houses, and were not allowed to leave the country until debts were settled. In sickness they were given care in hospitals in Chinatown, and in the same district all legal matters were attended to without reference to the California courts. The heads of these houses, men that stood high in the estimation of all reputable San Francisco business men, had appeared before the committee and stated that the original practice of bringing coolies to the country under contract to labor for employers had been abandoned; most of them now came as their own masters and with their own means; some had borrowed money and pledged their property; some had agreed to give the proceeds of their labor for a certain time; others had pledged their children to be owned as slaves in case of non-payment. They estimated the Chinese

# THE CHINESE IN CALIFORNIA

capital in the state, other than that employed in mining, at two millions of dollars.

There was much palaver, and then the matter was dropped for a time, although Bigler in his successive messages took occasion to scold the legislature for doing nothing to arrest Chinese immigration; and the small boy, and sometimes his father, continued to stone Chinamen in the streets or pull his pigtail when the mood was on him. Weller, the fourth governor, in response to a petition for aid from Shasta County to put down an anti-Chinese riot, sent a hundred and thirteen rifles, and the message that the spirit of mobocracy must be crushed at no matter what cost of money or blood.

Governors Latham and Downey do not seem to have taken any stand on the subject, probably because it was engulfed in the all-absorbing war; but Governor Stanford in 1862 took as positive a stand against the Chinese as the first governor had done, maintaining that Asia sent us the dregs of her population and that immigration should be discouraged by every legitimate means. Governor Low, with more independence—for the Chinese antipathy was increasing daily and had been made an issue in the recent campaign—"took strong ground against the illiberal and barbarous provisions of the law excluding Mongolian and Indian testimony from the courts of justice where a white person was a party."

Governor Haight, in his message of December, 1869, alluded to Chinese immigration in the choicest English incorporated in our democratic vocabulary: "The Chinese," said he, "are a stream of filth and prostitution pouring in from Asia, whose servile competition tends to cheapen and degrade labor." He also declared Chinese testimony to be utterly unreliable, but in the next breath announced himself in favor of "the removal of all barriers to the testimony of any race or any class as a measure not simply of justice but sound policy."

Governor Booth's remarks, which might have been written yesterday, are worth quoting:

> It may be true that the interests of capital and labor are the same [said he]; but in practice each is prompted by self-interest, and avails himself of the other's necessities; and any system that introduces a class of laborers whose wages are exceptionally low gives capital an advantage; and in so far as it has a tendency to establish a fixed line of demarcation between capital and labor and create a laboring caste, it is a social and political evil. But, however this may be and whatever the course of action the federal government, which has exclusive control of the subject of Asiatic immigration, may take in relation to it, there is but one thing to do in reference to the Chinese, and that is to afford them full and perfect protection. Mob violence is the most dangerous form by which the law can be violated, not merely in the immediate outrage committed, but in the results which often follow: communities debauched, jurors intimidated, and courts controlled by the political influence of the number that are guilty. . . .

Romualdo Pacheco, who as lieutenant-governor administered for ten months after Booth resigned to take his seat in the United States Senate, seems to have had no time to devote to the question; but Governor Irwin opposed Chinese immigration in 1875. By this time, however, the opinion of a governor on this vital subject counted for little save as it affected his chances of election. It was become the especial prerogative of the mob agitators.

Periodically labor is disgraced and crippled by agitators whose only ambition is a Utopian condition in which they can, after looting, loaf for the rest of their lives, and whose shibboleth is the brotherhood of man. The mass of laborers, unionist or otherwise, go about their business, protect themselves by well-thought-out methods, and

# THE CHINESE IN CALIFORNIA

possess brains enough to realize that all changes must evolve slowly; if radically, the result will be mob rule and, its inevitable sequence, a dictator—and a reversion to first principles after the destruction of all that steady progress has achieved. But, as in every other class, there are thousands without brains, and these are easily manipulated when conditions have arisen that present a striking opportunity to those of their number that live without work.

In the '70's, when everybody was excited and enormous fortunes were being made in the Virginia City mines—many on paper, as the events proved, for few were wary enough to sell before it was too late—agitators in San Francisco began holding meetings in empty sand-lots on the outskirts of the town and shouting that it was time for the rich to disgorge in favor of his superior in all the virtues, the day-laborer; that no man should be permitted to own more than a few acres of land. But this was a mere preliminary skirmish. They were quite willing to appropriate all the capital in the state; but as that drastic measure presented difficulties they concentrated on the unfortunate Mongolian. This was the easiest way of currying favor with the masses during that era; it was the war-cry of the politicians after votes, and the stock in trade of the agitators. And, as has been pointed out, the temperature of the '70's was high. Everybody was excited about something all the time, or if he enjoyed a brief respite he feared that he was worn out.

# XXI

## "THE CHINESE MUST GO"

DENNIS KEARNEY, a drayman, who had arrived in California in 1868 and naturalized in 1876, soon became the most conspicuous of the sand-lot agitators. He was a man of some natural ability, and, although without education, bright enough to pick up a large amount of useful knowledge. As he had that mystic quality known as personality, and made the most noise denouncing capital, monopoly, and the Chinese, he rose rapidly to the leadership of the most serious labor agitation in the history of California. There were nightly meetings in the sand-lots, lighted by torches when the moon was too young or the familiar fog drifted over Twin Peaks, at all of which an enormous amount of talking and hissing and shouting was done; but the first overt act which called out the police was in July, 1877. News had come over the wire of socialistic, labor, and railroad riots at Philadelphia, Baltimore, and Pittsburg; and Kearney & Co. had little difficulty persuading the lighter heads among the workingmen as well as the hoodlums (successors to the Hounds in intention, although less criminal in act) that these agitations "back East" were but the forerunners of a national revolution that would give the country once for all to the labor party.

On July 23d a band of choice spirits burned a Chinese

## "THE CHINESE MUST GO"

laundry and sacked several others. Then the "Sand-lotters" indulged in a grand parade, shouting that they would drive the Chinese out of San Francisco if they had to burn all Chinatown to do it. The police force of the city numbered one hundred and fifty, totally inadequate to cope with such a mob. San Francisco was for the most part built of wood. Quite apart from the burning of Chinatown, situated in the heart of the business district, if the agitators saw fit to fire houses simultaneously at different points and then were able to obstruct the fire brigade, the city would burn to the ground.

Once more William T. Coleman was the man of the hour. In response to the general demand he organized on July 24th a strong force of volunteers to be called the Committee of Safety. The municipal government, although corrupt enough, was far better than that of 1856, thanks to the Vigilance Committee, and it was not necessary to interfere with the police force, merely to supplement it.

Seventy thousand dollars were subscribed, and thousands of citizens enrolled themselves at Horticultural Hall, the Committee's headquarters, on the corner of Stockton and Post streets. Mr. Coleman was supported by the United States Government, and provided with all the arms he demanded; five war-ships came down from Mare Island and anchored in the bay. All this within forty-eight hours, and due primarily to the state and national reputation that Mr. Coleman had acquired during his administration of the Vigilance Committee of 1856.

He organized and enrolled with the simple direct methods he had employed twenty years before. But he

## CALIFORNIA

had no intention of spilling any blood if it could be avoided. The firearms were stacked to be used if all other resources failed. He ordered the purchase of six thousand hickory pick-handles, and before the night of the 5th the volunteers had been formed into companies armed with these formidable weapons and ready to reinforce the police. They became known as the Pick-handle Brigade. Only fifteen hundred went on duty that night, but there was a total force of five thousand members, who would have reached Horticultural Hall a few minutes after the tap of the alarm-bell.

Of the fifteen hundred on duty there were three hundred cavalry that patrolled the manufacturing districts and the outskirts of the city. There were also squads of police in boats along the water-front.

No one slept that night, and few but expected to see the city in flames before morning, in spite of the universal confidence in Mr. Coleman; for the rioters were known to number many thousand, most of whom no doubt were drunk. The large force of volunteers at the disposal of the Committee was still a secret. The result should have reassured San Franciscans once for all that when the strong, quick-thinking, self-reliant, and totally fearless men of that almost isolated strip on the edge of the Pacific rouse themselves, use their brains and superior powers of organization, they will put down the worst form of mob violence that could threaten their city. They may sacrifice blood and money, but they will do the work. There is always a William T. Coleman, a man of the hour.

But it was a wild night. All day there had been encounters between the police and the mob. Thousands

## "THE CHINESE MUST GO"

of people, women as well as men, stood in the streets on the long uneven ridge known as Nob Hill, where so many of the hated rich had built their big ugly houses (only the size could have excited envy in the least artistic mind) staring down upon that large flat district once known as Happy Valley; then for a time very fashionable, with substantial homes surrounded by gardens on Brannan Street, Folsom Street, and on Rincon Hill closer to the bay; now known generically as South of Market Street, and given over to factories, the dwellings of the laboring-class, cheap lodging-houses, and cheaper shops. It is bounded on the east and south by the docks.

At any moment the crowd on the hilltops expected to see one or all of the factories and dockyards burst into flames, and then a black mass of men surge forward like a tidal wave to the hills. All were prepared to break ranks and flee to the Presidio and Black Point at the first sign that the Committee's troops had been overcome by the mob.

Suddenly they did see flames. They leapt from the lumber-yards near the Pacific Mail Steamship's docks at the foot of Brannan Street, where the Chinese immigrants were landed; and the roar of the mob came faintly to the watchers on the hills. The fire-bells, which were a familiar sound in those days of wood and carelessness, rang wildly, sounding a general alarm. Almost immediately the flames were extinguished. Not a red tongue anywhere else; there had been far worse fires in that district on many other nights.

Then some one came running up with the word that the Pick-handle Brigade was administering heavy chastisement to the rioters. The angry roar below grew in volume, but only a few shots punctuated it. Finally the uproar subsided, save for an occasional drunken shout. South of Market Street went to bed utterly routed by the hickory sticks, and having let no blood to speak of. The watchers on the heights also dispersed, vowing to erect a statue to William T. Coleman, a vow which, with characteristic American ingratitude, they promptly forgot.

The mob was cowed, defeated. On the day following what had promised to be a portentous uprising of the proletariat, the working-men went sullenly to their jobs, or hung about in groups with no fight in them. This was a magnificent demonstration of what can be accomplished in a republic by the superior class of citizens over demagogues and their mistaken followers — and the lawless element of a city; a vastly different thing from the tyrannies of European states ruled by militarism. In republics agitators merely lie for their own purposes when they assert that all men's chances are not equal; cream will rise to the top until the day of doom.

The Committee of Safety disbanded for the moment, but its members had been so thoroughly disciplined, even in the short period of its existence, that they could be called together at the tap of the bell. Thanks were forwarded to Washington, and the marines and sailors asked permission to parade through the city before returning to Mare Island. Permission was given willingly, and they were an impressive and significant sight, especially for "South of Market Street."

But the times were hard. Hundreds of men were out

## "THE CHINESE MUST GO"

of work. Cowed as they were, their passions had been roused; they had had a taste of red blood, and they still were grist for the mill of the demagogue.

It was then that Dennis Kearney organized what he named the Working-man's Party of California—the W. P. C.—but what the people of San Francisco promptly nicknamed the Sand-lot Party. Every Sunday afternoon those in work and those idle from necessity or choice gathered once more in the sand-lots and listened to Kearney demand the blood of the rich, the hanging of William T. Coleman and his "hoodlum Committee of Safety," the police, the municipal officials, and certain specified capitalists whose mansions on Nob Hill (happily obliterated by the fire of 1906) they would burn to the ground. He predicted that in one year there would be twenty thousand laborers in San Francisco armed with muskets and able to defy the United States army. In another flight he predicted for San Francisco the fate of Moscow. But this was merely talk, talk, talk. Not one of his audience bought a musket or even reconnoitered Nob Hill. But the better class of these workingmen, alarmed by the continued hard times, and disgusted by the colossal fortunes made by men no better than themselves and no higher in the social scale, who now ignored their existence, doing nothing to relieve their anxieties or privations, were in a mood to do something concrete. The W. P. C. grew larger daily with the spectacular Kearney (in whom it still had confidence) as president; John D. Hay, vice-president; and H. L. Knight, secretary.

As is customary with new parties laboring under real grievances, they vowed themselves to an infinite number

# CALIFORNIA

of impossible reforms. The principles of the association were formulated as follows:

To unite all poor men and working-men and their friends into one political party for the purpose of defending themselves against the dangerous encroachments of capital on the happiness of our people and the liberties of our country; to wrest the government from the hands of the rich and place it in those of the people, where it properly belongs; to rid the country of cheap Chinese labor as soon as possible; to destroy the great money power of the rich—and by all means in our power because it tends still more to degrade labor and aggrandize capital; to destroy land monopoly in our state by a system of taxation that will make great wealth impossible in the future.... The rich have ruled us until they have ruined us. We will now take our own affairs into our own hands. The republic must and shall be preserved, and only working-men can do it. Our shoddy aristocrats want an emperor and a standing army to shoot down the people.

These sentiments and resolutions were uttered in 1877, but they have a striking family likeness to the soap-box utterances of 1914. The interval is thirty-seven years. Even yet the working-class has not learned that its agitators seek to benefit no one but themselves. If ever a leader arises among them both selfless and capable they will be a mighty force to reckon with, but so far their leaders have proved themselves to be merely the more sharp and cunning men of their class, gifted with the plausible tongue, some talent for organizing, and a commanding talent for extracting money and living at ease.

Even Dennis Kearney, poseur as he was and ignorant of history, soon discovered that he must bestir himself and do something besides vituperate if he would hold his position as leader of a large body of men that were beginning to think. Each of these men had a vote. The W. P. C. must make itself felt in the composition and then upon the performances of the next legislature.

# "THE CHINESE MUST GO"

He invented the phrase "The Chinese must go," and it became the shibboleth of the working-man's party, although the Chinese were but one of its grievances. On October 16th one leading newspaper of San Francisco published a long manifesto from Kearney demanding the expulsion of the Chinese. It was written in his characteristic style—that is to say, the style of his sort. Not one of these agitators since time began has displayed the slightest originality.

> Congress [said he] has often been manipulated by thieves, speculators, land-grabbers, bloated bond-holders, railroad magnates, and shoddy aristocrats [sic!]; a golden lobby dictating its proceedings. Our own legislature is little better. The rich rule them by bribes. The rich rule the country by fraud and cunning, and we say that fraud and cunning shall not rule us. The reign of bloated knaves is over. The people are about to take their affairs into their own hands, and they will not be stopped either by "citizen" vigilantes, state militia, or United States troops.

It has long been the wise policy of the United States and England to let agitators "talk their heads off," and the press is always willing to give them space if they are sufficiently spectacular. News is news. For the moment the sand-lotters confined their explosions to the sand-lots, the police winked, the papers gave them headlines, the citizens began to feel bored, and Mr. Coleman was not the man to sound the alarm-bell unless life and property were menaced. In consequence the W. P. C. came to the conclusion that they had intimidated the enemy and were now strong enough to take possession of the city. But some had a lively remembrance of those fifteen hundred hickory sticks, and in conference it was resolved to "go slow" at first; so they merely stoned Chinamen when no policeman was on the beat, burned laundries in the night, and continued to inveigh against the rich.

But memories are short and blood becomes hotter and hotter when inflamed with talk and potations. There was a moderate faction that advocated a constitutional convention and subsequent legislation to remedy all evils; but there were many more (augmented by the hoodlums) who finally worked themselves up to a point where only an immediate demonstration against the rich would lower their temperature. It was on October 28th that this faction was persuaded by Kearney to give the "bloodsuckers" an object-lesson of their power to take possession of San Francisco whenever they chose. Some three thousand marched up to Nob Hill, shouting that the Chinese must go, and the rich as well. They also gave to the winds their ultimate determination to demolish the big houses recently built by the railroad magnates—Crocker, Stanford, and Hopkins—as well as those of Haggin, Tevis, Colton, and others who had indulged in the heinous and un-American crime of making money.

When the mob reached the "spite fence" that Mr. Charles Crocker had built about an unpurchasable bit of land in the rear of his "palatial residence," Dennis Kearney mounted a wagon and shouted to the world at large that he had thoroughly organized his party and that he and his men would march upon these Nob Hill magnates and plunder the city just as soon as they felt like it. He would give the Central Pacific Railroad just three months to discharge its Chinamen (who, by the way, had been largely instrumental in building the road, the white man objecting to separation from his family, and preferring jobs involving less hardship), and that if

## "THE CHINESE MUST GO"

Stanford did not attend personally to this detail he must take the consequences. He denounced and threatened Crocker in similar terms, and then, in the good old fashion, proceeded to call every capitalist by name and denounce him as a thief, a murderer, a bloated aristocrat, etc.

There was, of course, an understanding between the police and the leaders of this mob, for, although the guardians of the city were out in force, they did not break up the march nor interfere with the speeches. When Kearney and his cabinet had talked themselves hoarse the crowd marched back to South of Market Street, merely emitting an occasional "The Chinese must go."

After two or three more of these demonstrations, however, the city authorities, realizing that the citizens were becoming alarmed, determined to make a display of resentment and force. Kearney, while vociferating on Barbary Coast, was arrested and jailed. As it was expected that an attempt would be made to rescue him, the militia was called out. Chinatown, which was uncomfortably close to the jail, appealed to the mayor for protection and barricaded its flimsy houses. Nothing happened, however, as is always the case when the authorities show energy and decision; and during the next three or four days several of Kearney's disciples were arrested while imitating his thunder.

This was as salutary for the city as for the W. P. C. It proved that the agitators were cowards and could be relied upon to make no war-like move unless inflamed by the eloquence of Mr. Kearney at first hand. Naturally, he could not harangue them from the inside of the jail, and they let him stay there. He and his disciples finally broke down, wept, protested that they had meant no harm, promised to call no more mass-meetings and lead no more mobs, and, in fact, to do nothing to excite further riot. So they were forgiven and told to go home and behave themselves. When Kearney emerged his own dray was waiting. He was crowned with roses, heaved on to it, and dragged to his headquarters by his still enthusiastic supporters.

Kearney had given a promise very difficult for him to keep. Much as he disliked jail and its discomforts, he loved the limelight more. So he stumped the state, pretending to talk the politics of the new party, but in reality trying to organize a vast "army." The farmer and the country laborer, however, sent him so promptly about his business that he returned a trifle wiser to San Francisco, and, as he had lost his influence with the superior men of the W. P. C., made desperate attempts to regain it. Appear on the first page of the newspapers and be discussed at the breakfast-table he must, if life were to be the prismatic orgie of his paranoiac dreams.

His influence with the superior men of the W. P. C. was gone beyond recall, but San Francisco could be relied upon to furnish a respectable following of hoodlums, vagabonds, criminals, and the hopelessly ignorant of the laboring-class; and again he led processions, this time to the City Hall to demand work, and harangued them in the sand-lots; he even had a new set of words and phrases to express his contempt of those upon whom fortune had deigned to smile. No notice was taken until he began to counsel lynching, burning the docks, and dropping bombs from balloons into the Chinese quarter.

Then the Committee of Safety reorganized. The au-

## "THE CHINESE MUST GO"

thorities, however, were now on their mettle and promptly rearrested Kearney and the worst of the soap-box offenders. Once more these wept, promised, and were discharged. The legislature passed the "Gag law," however, an amendment to the penal code, by whose provision such men as Kearney could be sent to prison for felony if they continued to incite riots. It also provided for a larger police force. Kearney, who was well aware that he had been discharged twice because there was no law to cover his offense, and send him to San Quentin, was now thoroughly disconcerted, and transferred his attentions to the elections and the proposed constitutional convention.

The working-man's party was now very strong—the W. P. C. of San Francisco was reinforced by "the Granger party" of the state. In November, 1878, it elected a senator to the new legislature, and in March, at the regular city elections, it elected another senator and an assemblyman. In Sacramento and Oakland it elected its own candidates for mayor and certain other official positions. In a convention held in January it had adopted resolutions to sever all connection with the Republican and Democratic parties. A new party was in the field, and it began to look formidable. "The Chinese must go" was its war-cry.

The best and wisest thing it did was to expel Kearney from the office of president (May 6, 1878), alleging that he was corrupt and using the organization to advance his own selfish ends. This resulted in a split, with Kearney at the head of the faction that admired his oratory. Moreover, he was a wiry little Irish fighter, and there is ever a magic in the oft-reiterated name. Kearney's

## CALIFORNIA

picture, with the familiar sweater, collarless, had been published in many an Eastern newspaper. He was still a great man.

The W. P. C., however split, was a distinct menace, and an attempt was made to fuse the Republican and Democratic parties to fight the common enemy. This proved to be impossible before 1880. An act for calling a convention to change the constitution was due to the strength of the new party. It passed the legislature April 1, 1878, and was signed by Governor Irwin.

The personnel of this constitutional convention was far more remarkable and significant than that of the one which created a state in 1849. On June 19th the election for delegates resulted in 78 non-partisans, including 32 delegates at large; 51 working-men, including 31 delegates from San Francisco; 11 Republicans; 10 Democrats; and two independents. There were lawyers, farmers, mechanics, merchants, doctors, miners, journalists, school-teachers, music-teachers, restaurant-keepers, and a cook.

The W. P. C. wing was partly communistic, partly anarchistic. The conservative wing of the convention was said to possess more men of brains, experience, and ripe judgment than any assemblage in the history of the state. The thinking people were alive to the danger to their republican institutions, which, however faulty, were far better than any yet devised by man. They were outnumbered, but if driven to extremities they meant to make the new constitution so radical that the people would not elect it. It is not for a moment to be denied that the corporations were represented among these men, but it must be remembered that they believed it to be a

## "THE CHINESE MUST GO"

death-struggle, and the "classes" no more could be expected to lay down their arms and surrender than the "masses."

There is no question that however passion may have blinded the men of the laboring-class and whipped them on to make absurd demands upon the impregnable fortress of modern civilization, they were justified in their fears for the future of their class on the Pacific coast if no restraint were put upon Oriental immigration. The Chinese underbid the white man in the shops, factories, railroad-yards, hotels, fruit-ranches, private houses; they lived on rice, sent their wages to China, were highly efficient; and they were well liked by employers not only on account of their skill and industry, but because they were polite, even-tempered, and sober. Formidable rivals, indeed, and, although the employer, particularly the asparagus-raiser and the housewife, will always regret them, it is plain justice that in a white man's country the white man should have no rival but himself.

James Bryce, in *The American Commonwealth*, has stated very succinctly the grievances presented by the W. P. C. at the convention, as well as their achievement.

### THE GRIEVANCES

The general corruption of politicians and bad conduct of state, county, and city government.
Taxation, alleged to press too heavily on the poorer class.
The tyranny of corporations, especially railroads.
The Chinese.

### THE RESULTS

1. It (the convention) restricts and limits in every possible way the powers of the state legislature, leaving it little authority except to carry out by statute the provisions of the constitution. It makes lobbying (*i. e.*, the attempt to corrupt a legislator) and the corrupt action of the legislator felony.

# CALIFORNIA

2. It forbids the state legislature or local authorities to incur debts beyond a certain limit, taxes uncultivated land equally with the cultivated, makes sums due on mortgage taxable in the district where the mortgaged property lies, authorizes an income tax, and directs a highly inquisitorial scrutiny of everybody's property for the purposes of taxation.

3. It forbids the watering of stock, declares that the state has power to prevent corporations from conducting their business so as to infringe the general well-being of the state; directs that the charges of telegraph and gas companies and of water-supplying bodies be regulated and limited by law; institutes a railroad commission with power to fix the transportation rates on all railroads, and examine the books and accounts of all transportation companies.

4. It forbids all corporations to employ any Chinese, debars them from the suffrage, forbids their employment on any public works, annuls all contracts for "coolie labor," directs the legislature to provide for the punishment of any company which shall import Chinese, to impose conditions on the residence of Chinese, and to cause their removal if they fail to observe these conditions.

5. It also declares that eight hours shall constitute a legal day's work on all public works.

To-day these provisions of the constitution of 1879 are merely a curiosity. It was elected by the people because many voters were napping (as usual), but the net result for the working-man's party was nil, with the exception of the provision for an eight-hour working-day. When the Chinese were excluded it was by the federal government, and those that remained in the state were always sure of employment; and as a temporary fusion of Democrats and Republicans in 1880 drove the W. P. C. out of existence, and as clever lawyers argued that many of the provisions of the new instrument were unconstitutional, and as, moreover, clever and more clever men went to successive legislatures, the stronger continued as ever to do as they pleased, constitution or no constitution; and, as the strong has done since the beginning of time, used their power to the full for the benefit

## "THE CHINESE MUST GO"

of their own class and laughed at the impotent anger of the weak. There is no lesson so persistently taught by history as this, and it would be well for idealists, utopians, socialists, communists, single-taxers, labor-unionists, and all the rest of them to read it, accept it, digest it, and then either make the best of conditions as they are or find a leader, cultivate their brains, let alcohol alone, avoid windy agitators like plague-bearing rats, sink petty differences, and consolidate. And the best they may do will be as naught unless they find a great leader.

This convention sat for one hundred and fifty-seven days. Of course much time was consumed in speeches on the Chinese exclusion question. There were exceptional chances for oratory. It is to be noted that a number of far-sighted and liberal-minded persons attempted to insert a plank giving the suffrage to women. But they were too far ahead of their times, and the motion was defeated. Altogether it may be inferred that the convention upheld the best traditions of California in the acrimonious liveliness of its atmosphere, the choiceness of its invective, the absurdity of many of its motions, and the dissatisfaction and disgust of everybody concerned. Of course no one got what he wanted except the proletariat, and he suffered from doubts even then.

A number of the eminent men present—W. H. L. Barnes, Eugene Casserly, Samuel M. Wilson, John F. Miller—refused to sign the instrument at all, and it is probable that such men as Judge Hager, Henry Edgerton, J. West Martin, James McM. Shafter, J. J. Winans, wrote their names only because they feared for the failure of the convention and the election of another with an even worse personnel.

# CALIFORNIA

It is not to be supposed that no good laws were passed by this angry and desperate convention. The judiciary department was remodeled, prison regulations were improved, convict labor was prohibited, as well as the granting of railroad passes (another dead letter), the University of California was recognized as a public trust, to be maintained by the state and kept free of all political and sectarian control and open to both sexes. The eight-hour law was passed, proving the forerunner of a general eight-hour law. But the attempt to "cinch" capital utterly failed.

In 1879 California voted against further immigration from China, the vote standing 154,638 to 883. Pressure had already been brought to bear upon Congress, and on March 20th the Exclusion Bill passed. President Hayes refused to sign it, as being in conflict with the Burlingame Treaty, which provided that "Chinese subjects in the United States shall enjoy entire liberty of conscience and shall be exempt from all persecution and disability." In 1880 a commission was sent to Pekin to negotiate a new treaty permitting the restriction of immigration. This treaty was ratified by the Senate in March, 1881. It gave the United States the power to "regulate, limit, or suspend" the immigration of the United States, but not to prohibit it altogether. By tinkering at this treaty, employing the amendment method, the Chinese were virtually excluded, and the conditions of re-entry for those already resident in the United States, who wished to visit China, were so severe and harassing that a large proportion made no attempt to return to California.

As for Dennis Kearney, he was disposed of by being

## "THE CHINESE MUST GO"

made a capitalist in a small way, and so adroitly that no doubt he awakened one morning to find himself no longer famous, but rich. I met him shortly before his death, and asked him how he reconciled his present conditions with his former socialistic principles, and he replied lightly:

"Oh, you know, somebody has to do the work. What's the use?"

## XXII

### LAST PHASES

ALL things being relative, San Francisco for some fifteen or twenty years after the housecleaning given it by the Vigilance Committee of 1856 was a peaceful and decent city. But, as ever, its citizens ceased to be alert to any but their personal affairs, particularly during the Comstock madness; and, logically, the body politic, unprotected by renewed vaccination, fell an easy prey to the insidious and venomous microbes of the underworld; and before the city realized that its system was even relaxed, "run down," it had broken out virulently in several places. Nor did the hostile swarms confine their activities to the police, the professional politician, the municipal organs generally; eminent citizens were infected—and they are still fumigating themselves.

Following the denunciations of the Sand-lotters, which no one attempted to refute in toto, there was a reaction in favor of the upper classes, owing to the intemperate excesses of the W. P. C. and the new constitution they were instrumental in foisting upon California. But in the course of the next fifteen years many besides the proletariat were awake and alarmed at the dangers threatening the city. The Wallace grand jury was impaneled in August, 1891. The exposures of this body, after investigations made under the greatest difficulties, so se-

## LAST PHASES

curely were the malefactors intrenched, proved a system of wholesale bribery and corruption by corporations, legislators, and supervisors.

For some years San Francisco had been dominated by "bosses," the most notorious and shameless of whom was "Blind" Boss Buckley. (The others are too contemptible for more than a passing mention.) All of them, and Buckley in particular, were experts in every form of extortion, oppression, and demoralization of their army of human tools. The investigations of the Wallace grand jury startled complacent San Francisco, and Buckley fled to return no more; but there was little improvement in conditions until another sudden awakening of the civic conscience swept Mr. James D. Phelan into the mayor's chair in 1897.

One of the crying needs of San Francisco was a new charter granting enlarged powers to the mayor, for the exercise of which he would be directly responsible. As the case stood he might be an angel of light, but his hands were tied; the legislature passed nearly all laws for San Francisco, and behind that august body of sea-green incorruptibles the "machine" could hide and shift responsibility as it listed.

Mr. Phelan at once appointed a committee of one hundred citizens to draft a charter; and, what was more to the point, he put it through. It provided for a responsible government, civil-service reform, and home rule, and declared for municipal ownership of those public utilities, light, water, transportation, so preyed upon and debauched by the municipal council, which had the power to fix the rates.

Mr. Phelan was mayor of San Francisco for five years,

and, in the estimation of any impartial student of that politics-ridden town, was the ablest and most energetic in her annals. It would be an insult to add that he was honest if he were not a San Franciscan, and the temptation to do so is irresistible, because California officials who are able, energetic, and honest are so rare that they should have at least plaster statues while alive; to be bronzed over or not, as an impartial and discriminating posterity shall advise.

Mr. Phelan stood firmly with the people against the bosses, exposed the fraudulent specifications of the lighting monopoly, and saved the people three hundred thousand dollars a year; defended the city from pillage at the hands of the supervisors, among other amounts, diverting two million dollars from reaching their itching palms by "blocking jobs"; raised the standard of the pay of laborers in the city's employ; and gave back to San Francisco in public gifts many times his salary as mayor.

Our rich men of late years have been so culpably negligent of San Francisco's interests, so long as their own have prospered, that too much emphasis cannot be laid upon Mr. Phelan's sleepless and practical concern for his city, quite apart from his munificent donations and his unostentatious help to so many in private life, and his presentation to the city of the best of its statues. His father made the fortune which he inherited and doubled, and if he had chosen to devote all his energies to business, or even if it had been his disposition to loaf, no one would have been surprised or critical. Nor, oddly enough, would he have made one-tenth of the enemies he accumulated while striving to clean up San Francisco. If he had been poor and originally obscure he would have been for-

JAMES D. PHELAN

## LAST PHASES

given, for Americans seem to understand and forgive ambition and public efforts in the impecunious; but in new communities, at least, symptoms of civic decency in a rich man are regarded with alarm as a new and mysterious germ which may prostrate the entire order. When the symptoms develop into aggression they are for stamping the traitor out of existence. All sorts of mean motives are ascribed to him, the press sneers and villifies, he falls a victim to the cartoonist, and only his friends and solid money respect him. If he survives and pursues his undeviating way this phenomenon is due to two causes only: his staying-powers and the basic common sense of the American people. As Abraham Lincoln once remarked, "You can fool, etc."

During the last two years of Mr. Phelan's incumbency there were serious labor troubles. Capital assumed a hostile attitude to large bodies of working-men striking not only for more pay, but for recognition of the union; and labor in turn becoming still more hostile, the two camps, even after the "Teamsters' Strike" was settled, remained armed and bristling. The result was the rise of Abraham Ruef and his creature, Eugene E. Schmitz.

Ruef was a little ferret-faced, black-eyed French Jew, of abilities so striking that he could have become one of the most respected and useful citizens in the history of San Francisco had he not deliberately chosen the "crooked" rôle. Sentimentalists cannot argue in Ruef's case that "he never had a chance." He was of well-to-do parents, he finished his education at the University of California, graduated into the law, and had a lucrative practice from the beginning. But although his worst personal indulgence was "candy," he was one of the most innately vicious men this country has spawned, and one of the most destructive incubated by poor San Francisco.

The stiff-necked attitude of the Employers' Organization, which denied labor's right to unionize, gave Ruef his opportunity. He skilfully engineered his friend Schmitz, an imposing, bluff, and hearty person, and a real man of the people, having been a fiddler in a local opera company, into the mayor's chair with little or no difficulty. The class line was as sharply drawn as the earthquake fault, and the proletariat and his sympathizers outnumbered the others and voted with entire independence of party lines. They wanted a labor-union man; to his bias otherwise they were indifferent. This fine figurehead at the prow, Ruef began to build up his machine.

The board of supervisors during the first two years of the Schmitz incumbency continued to be the decent men natural to Mr. Phelan's administration; for even Ruef, with his brilliant if distorted talents for organization, could not upset the work of an honest mayor as quickly as he had hoped. But he went on fomenting class-hatred to his own advantage and that of Schmitz, and simultaneously they grew rich by grafting on vice, forcing that class of establishments euphemistically known in San Francisco as "French restaurants" to pay an enormous tribute, under threat of revocation of license.

When in the elections of 1905 Schmitz was found to have lost strength with the Labor-union party, always prone to fickleness and suspicion, and to have polled a heavy vote in capitalistic districts, citizens shrugged their shoulders and "guessed" that the stories of the Ruef-Schmitz machine, holding up corporations and rich men for large sums before granting franchises, were true.

## LAST PHASES

The *Evening Bulletin*, true to its traditions, and edited by Fremont Older, of the genuine militant brand, had been thundering for some time against the police board and the administrative boards of the machine, which were making no visible use of the money raised by taxation for specific purposes. The police board could be bought by any violator of the law who came to it with the price in his hand. But the result of the elections furnished Mr. Older with new and forked lightning; the heavy vote polled for Schmitz was in the wrong quarter, and the board of supervisors were Ruef's tools, chosen from the dregs of the working-class, men with no inherited ideals to give them moral stamina, and utterly unable to resist temptation in the form of the large sum that would fall to each after Ruef and Schmitz, having "gouged" some impatient corporation, had divided the lion's share. Then once more the citizens of San Francisco "sat up," awake to the new perils that threatened their battered city.

But although the Ruef-Schmitz machine looked as formidable as an invading horde of locusts in Kansas, and grew more arrogant every day, more contemptuous of public opinion, it had its weak spots. Ruef in January, 1906, made the irretrievable blunder of putting an honest man in office. Apprehending that Schmitz was losing his hold on the Labor-union party, he permitted William A. Langdon, superintendent of schools, and possessing a large following in labor circles, to be elected district attorney. When he made the discovery that Mr. Langdon was quite honest and nobody's creature, his amazement and wrath would have been ludicrous if they had not been pathetic.

No sooner had Mr. Langdon taken the oath of office

than he began a series of raids on the various gambling institutions which paid a heavy tribute to the machine but flourished nevertheless.

Of course, San Francisco has always been a gambling city. It is in the marrow and brain-cells of her people, whether their blood ancestors were "Forty-niners" or not, and as there is no evil out of which good may not come, it is the source of their superb powers of bluff, their unquenchable optimism, and their indomitability under the most harrowing afflictions. When, after the earthquake and fire of 1906, the world was startled to learn that the people of San Francisco were planning to rebuild before the ashes were cold, David Belasco said to a reporter, "The Californians are bully gamblers!"

Therefore, when Mr. Langdon made it manifest that he purposed to put an end to the industrial manifestation of the race spirit, there was not only a terrific howl from his victims, but the well-regulated citizens themselves were amazed. Mr. Langdon, however, paid as little attention to one as to the other. He brought down the heavy hand of the law on the Emeryville Race-track (the most sordid and wholly abominable in the West), and upon the slot-machine, that lucrative partner of the saloon and the cigar-stand. In the ordinary course of events he would be crippled for funds; legal investigation and prosecution were necessary, and the coffers of the city were in the robber stronghold. But Ruef had discovered some time since that there was another dark cloud on his horizon and that in the middle of it was a star. And while the star directed a cold and hostile gleam on Mr. Ruef, it was the bright hope of the district attorney.

# LAST PHASES

Rudolph Spreckels it was who proved to be the nemesis of Ruef. This very remarkable young man had left his father's roof when a boy of nineteen, taking the part of a brother whom he believed to be a victim of parental injustice. Then he proceeded to make his own fortune; and, having that special group of brain-cells which constitute the talent for making money, he was, in the course of a few years, one of the richest men in the community. Until 1903 business and the enjoyment of life in a quiet way occupied him fully, but by Abraham Ruef—unwitting savior of his city!—his eyes were opened to the needs and perils of San Francisco.

Ruef, with the serene confidence of the congenitally corrupt that every man has his price, approached the young financier with a particularly abominable plan for enriching himself at the expense of the city, and Mr. Spreckels suddenly woke up. His enlightenment was completed by Mr. Phelan and Fremont Older. He applied himself to a thorough study of existing civic conditions, and was horrified to discover that for viciousness and general rottenness San Francisco could vie proudly with the worst cities of ancient or modern history.

He was emphatically the man for the hour. He was young, rich, energetic, honorable, implacable, ruthless, and tenacious. Mr. Phelan could help him with advice and money, but he had made too many enemies among the grafters of all classes during his five years as mayor to be an effective leader. Mr. Spreckels was greeted as a sort of knight of the Holy Grail; for in the beginning, when his sole intention was to crush the Ruef-Schmitz machine and imprison its chiefs and tools, he was acclaimed by even that capitalistic class that later accused him of every contemptible motive and trait revealed in the course of human history.

Ruef also made his investigations and discovered that Mr. Spreckels had built his fortune honestly, and was, therefore, unbribable. This, of course, was before 1906, and when the anachronistic Mr. Langdon grasped the reins carelessly tossed him by the idol of the Labor party, it became immediately apparent that if the machine would not furnish the money for the investigations and reforms Mr. Spreckels would. Moreover, Mr. Phelan, Mr. Older, and Mr. Spreckels had secured the services of Attorney Francis J. Heney, and induced President Roosevelt to give them the services of Detective Burns, then employed by the United States.

Then came the earthquake and fire of April, 1906. The reader may remember that old melodrama, "The Silver King," and the escaping convict who, watching the train on which he had escaped blazing from end to end with its imprisoned victims—he being almost the only survivor—falls on his knees and thanks God. Picture Mr. Ruef as he watched San Francisco burning. The crippled millionaires, including Mr. Phelan and Mr. Spreckels, would be occupied with their own affairs for years to come. He and Schmitz were free. So profound a student of human nature was Mr. Ruef.

An hour or two after the earthquake, when it became apparent that a large part of San Francisco would burn, the pipes of the water system being broken and thirty fires having started simultaneously, Mr. Downey Harvey, a grandson of the "War Governor," John G. Downey, and himself a citizen of wealth and influence, went down to Mayor Schmitz's office and suggested that im-

## LAST PHASES

mediate measures be taken for the protection of the city and the relief of the homeless—who were already fleeing to the Presidio and the hills beyond the city. Everybody on that terrible day was either at a pitch above the normal or hopelessly demoralized. Schmitz, being a musician, had a temperament; consequently he was in the upper register. Morally supported by the "Committee of Fifty" that he called together at Mr. Harvey's suggestion, he proved himself as admirable an administrative officer as if life had groomed him to be a symbol of all the civic virtues. In truth, he was a weak man of good intentions, but putty in the hands of a man like Ruef.

Mr. Phelan, during the first day or two, was busy in actual rescue work and in carrying dynamite in his car for the purpose of blowing up buildings—a vain attempt to prevent the spread of the fire. But he was elected chairman of the Citizens' Finance Committee, and to him as great a compliment was paid as to Mr. Coleman in 1878. Congress voted a million and a half dollars for the relief of San Francisco, but hesitated to send it via Ruef-Schmitz. When, however, President Roosevelt was informed that Mr. Phelan had been made chairman of the Citizens' Finance Committee, he sent him the money personally. The President also issued a proclamation directing the people of the United States to send their contributions to Mr. Phelan, chairman of the Citizens' Finance Committee; and the corporation growing out of this committee received all the supplies and approximately $10,000,000 in money.

Mr. Phelan as well as Mr. Spreckels and Mr. Harvey, and all the other men on the committee, neglected their private affairs for months, and the refugees were housed on the hillsides either in tents or cottages, fed, clothed, and generally taken care of. Ruef accepted the temporary domination of the committee with apparent philosophy, and himself opened an office just beyond the burned district, obviously adjusting matters for his legal clients. In reality he was looting right and left, preying upon the women of commerce, the bootblacks, the newsboys, the small shopkeepers, upon every class, in fact, to which his tentacles had reached during the years of his autocracy.

But Mr. Spreckels did not forget him nor his ultimate object for a moment. Heney, when he promised his services, was still engaged in exposing the Oregon land frauds, but he was free in June. Then he came to town, and with him Detective Burns. This was only two months after the disaster; but although Ruef was surprised, he was not particularly apprehensive; he did not believe that they could make any headway in the existing conditions.

In October sufficient evidence of extortion in the matter of the French restaurants had been accumulated to warrant District-Attorney Langdon announcing that a general investigation would begin at once. He appointed Mr. Heney assistant district attorney.

This was six months after the earthquake. Men never alluded to it any more. The women still talked nothing but earthquake and fire; but the men talked only insurance and rebuilding. They went about dressed in khaki and top-boots, exhilarated by the tremendous call upon their energies, and with all the old pioneer spirit reincarnated and intensified by the consciousness that they were about to build a great city, not merely using

# LAST PHASES

its site while "making their pile" to dissipate at a gambling-table or carry elsewhere. And this time they wanted a decent city. Schmitz, resting on his labors, had gone to Europe, and they had no intention of re-electing him.

Ruef was thoroughly frightened. But he was ever a man of resource; he suddenly played one of the boldest coups in the history of any city. Mr. Langdon was off campaigning for the governorship; T. H. Gallagher, president of the board of supervisors, was acting-mayor, and, of course, a creature of the Chief. He was ordered to remove Langdon from the district-attorneyship on the ground of neglect of duty and appoint Abraham Ruef. The city held its breath and then emitted a roar of indignation; it was quite patent that San Francisco was not as selfishly absorbed as Mr. Ruef had believed. The impudence of this plot to dictate the personnel of the proposed grand jury may be the better understood when it is remembered that the city had just been informed officially of Mr. Ruef's iniquities and that he would be subjected to prosecution. But this attempt to balk justice was summarily defeated; Judge Seawell, of the Superior Court, held that as the district attorney represented the people as a whole, the mayor had no jurisdiction over him.

After this events proceeded rapidly. On November 10th Judge Thomas F. Graham appointed a grand jury to investigate the condition of the city. It was known as the Oliver grand jury, Mr. B. F. Oliver having been elected foreman. The other members were: Maurice Block, C. G. Burnett, Jeremiah Deasy, Dewey Coffin, Frank A. Dwyer, E. J. Gallagher, James E. Gordon, Alfred Greenebaum, Morris A. Levingston, Rudolph

# CALIFORNIA

Mohr, W. P. Redington, Ansel C. Robinson, Christian P. Rode, Mendle Rothenberg, F. G. Sanborn, Charles Sonntag, Herman H. Young, Wallace G. Wise.

It will be observed that five members of the Oliver grand jury were of the same race as Ruef; in fact, practically every denomination was represented. Many of these men had close affiliations in the social and business world with "eminent citizens" they were forced later on to indict; but never did an investigating body do its work more thoroughly and impersonally.

Like Mr. Spreckels, they met with encouragement at first, their original and avowed purpose being to "get" Ruef, Schmitz, and the supervisors, without whose consent no franchise could be obtained.

It had been common talk for at least two years that every man and corporation with capital to invest or some new industry to launch was "held up" by the board of supervisors before they could proceed. Capital of every sort was grafted upon the moment it sought new outlets, and rich men in condoling with one another had ceased to comment upon the miseries of San Francisco in general. Therefore, the Oliver grand jury, as well as Mr. Heney and Detective Burns, thought that it would be an easy matter to obtain affidavits from these distinguished victims which would go far toward convicting the malefactors. At that time they had not a thought of prosecuting the "higher-ups." But, to their amazement, the rich men, individually and collectively, swore that they never had been approached, never had paid a cent of graft money. In the terminology of the hour, they refused to "come through." It looked as if the grand jury could not gather evidence enough to con-

JUDGE LAWLOR

RUDOLPH SPRECKELS

FRANCIS J. HENEY

FREMONT OLDER

## LAST PHASES

vict the machine of anything but the tribute levied on vice.

Then it was that Mr. Heney and Mr. Burns and his detectives changed their tactics. They offered immunity to the supervisors if they would give the information necessary to convict not the bribed, but the bribers. They agreed, and the grand jury was enabled to find indictments not only against Ruef and Schmitz, but against Patrick Calhoun, president of the United Railroads, and his manager, Thornwall Mullaly; the finance committee of the San Francisco Gas and Electric Company; the agent of the Parkside Realty Company; the Home Telephone; the Pacific Telephone, and the Prize-fight Trust.

It is only possible here to give a brief account of the two principal trials. To quote from the Denman report:

> The supervisors' testimony gave the grand jury the facts as to the passing of the ordinances, the payment of the money by Gallagher to various supervisors, and the payment of the money from Ruef to Gallagher. The chain of evidence, however, stopped at Gallagher's testimony that Ruef paid him the money in all but the Pacific Coast Telephone briberies, and no further evidence was discovered against the mayor in connection with the French restaurant extortions. The question then arose as to the advisability of treating with Ruef to secure the evidence as to the method by which the moneys came from the quasi-public corporations . . . it became apparent that without this man's testimony the many bribe-givers whose enrichment by the large profits of such undertakings made them equally if not more dangerous to society, would not only escape the penalty which was their due, but that even their names would not be discovered and written in the "detinue book" of the city's suspicious characters. Besides, without Ruef's assistance, the conviction of Schmitz, with the resultant change in the mayoralty, the police, and other municipal boards, seemed impossible. The district attorney had his choice in this dilemma. He could leave the mayor and his administrative boards in power, discover nothing regarding the profit-takers from briberies, and content himself with a mere change in the supervisors and a long term of imprisonment for Ruef, or he could reasonably ex-

pect the conviction of the mayor, the cleaning up of the city government, the obtaining of a complete revelation of the grafters "high up" as well as the "low down," and the possible conviction of some of them. The district attorney chose the latter alternative and bargained with Ruef. . . . A written contract was finally signed whereby Ruef agreed to tell fully and unreservedly all he knew of the briberies and to plead guilty to certain of the French restaurant extortion cases, and the district attorney agreed to use the power of his office to procure him immunity as to the other charges.

Complete immunity never was promised.

Schmitz was tried and found guilty on Ruef's testimony, and convicted on June 13, 1907. He was subsequently released on a technicality. Although Ruef had pleaded guilty to accepting bribes during his own trial, he also escaped the penalty under the decision which freed Schmitz.

Sixteen supervisors had confessed to receiving bribe-money from their president, Gallagher, who, of course, confessed that he got it from the Chief. Ruef was again indicted and made desperate efforts to escape prosecution, including a change of venue. All devices failing, he ran away. His friends, the sheriff, the coroner, and the police force failed to find him, but an elisor named by the court unearthed him. It was then that he bargained with the district attorney.

But Ruef, after promising to "come through" (in which case he would have been prosecuted for the French restaurant cases alone), fell into a panic as he reflected upon the condign punishment sure to be visited upon him did he betray his powerful associates; he resolved not to "snitch"—to quote once more from the elegant vocabulary of the moment—and attempted to pretend confession while admitting nothing.

But Heney was far more agile of mind than the now

# LAST PHASES

distracted Ruef. He caught him lying and exposed him. The immunity was canceled, and he was brought to his second trial in the bribery transactions, August 26, 1908. These trials—financed by Rudolph Spreckels—were conducted in Carpenter's Hall in Fulton Street, just beyond the burnt district, and before Judge Lawlor.

The chief witness against Ruef was the president of the board of supervisors, T. H. Gallagher. On April 29, 1908, his house in Oakland was wrecked by dynamite, but the witness whose life was sought survived and gave his testimony. The man who placed the bomb testified that he was employed by a henchman of Ruef.

This attempt at murder had been preceded by the kidnapping of Fremont Older, whose thunders in the *Bulletin* had never ceased. Naturally, statements crept into those inflammatory columns that were not wholly substantiated. One day Mr. Older accidentally printed a libel. He made amends on the following day, but he had given the enemies of the prosecution one of the chances for which they had been lying in wait. The libeled man had Mr. Older indicted in Los Angeles. Mr. Older ignored the summons, knowing well that if he went to Los Angeles he would remain there until the trials were over.

On October 27, 1907, he was lured by a false telephone message into a quiet street and forced, by several men, into an automobile, which dashed through and out of the city. The muzzle of a "gun" was pressed against Mr. Older's side; but he was wise enough not to struggle. A south-bound train was boarded at a way-station, and Mr. Older shut up in a drawing-room. One of the kidnappers was an attorney for the United Railroads, R.

# CALIFORNIA

Porter Ashe, a son of the Dr. Ashe, friend of Terry and other "Law and Order" men of 1856, who so bitterly opposed the Vigilance Committee.

The plot did not succeed. The hue and cry was raised by suspicious friends in San Francisco, and Mr. Older and his kidnappers were traced. The authorities in Santa Barbara were appealed to, and when the train arrived in the morning the party was commanded to appear in court, and Mr. Older was released. The net result of this episode was the "reform" of the spelling of the word "kidnapped," which, as may be imagined, was overworked. It is now spelt—and presumably pronounced—by the California press, kid*naped*.

In November, 1908, an attempt was made on the life of Mr. Heney. The San Francisco newspapers, with the exception of the *Bulletin* and the *Call*, by this time were indulging in furious attacks on the various members of the prosecution, and upon Heney in particular. The attacks were necessarily personal, as they would not have dared to defend Ruef, even had they been so inclined, but no doubt they were actuated by fear that Heney's hectoring methods would surprise the names of the "higher-ups" from the defiant Ruef, now in his third trial. Their diatribes, assisted by cartoons, were held responsible for the attempted murder of the assistant district attorney; but the general opinion is that the man was a hired assassin. His name was Haas. There was little doubt that attempts were being made to "fix" the jury; and, as this man had boasted that he soon would be able to live in luxury, Heney succeeded in getting him off the third jury by exposing the fact that Haas had sojourned in a State's Prison for forgery. He was altogether a miserable

Copyright by Pach Brothers.

GOV. HIRAM JOHNSON

## LAST PHASES

specimen of humanity. On the 13th of November he slipped up behind Mr. Heney in the crowded court-room and fired a pistol-bullet into his head, just before his right ear. Heney's mouth happened to be open. The ball passed between the skull and jaw and exhausted its strength in the soft lining at the back of the mouth, finally lodging in the bone of the jaw on the opposite side.

There was great excitement in Fulton Street that day. The old-time crowds were there, wrought up to the point of hysteria, and there was much speechmaking and talk of lynching. But it ended in no overt attempt to frustrate the law, and Haas meanwhile had been rushed to jail in an automobile. When searched, no other weapon was discovered, but that night he was found dead from a derringer wound in his head. Whether the derringer had been concealed in his shoe or whether it had been passed to him in his cell with orders to use it, or whether he was murdered, will probably never be known. He certainly knew too much to be permitted to stand the "third degree."

Heney was ill from the shock, although his only permanent disability was deafness in one ear. The prosecution of the Ruef case was continued by Matt I. Sullivan and Hiram Johnson, one of the ablest lawyers in San Francisco, and in full sympathy with the prosecution.

Probably Ruef himself was not more astonished, when he actually was convicted and sentenced to fourteen years in the penitentiary, than San Francisco, so long accustomed to the miscarriage of "justice," particularly when the prosecuted was a rich man. But Ruef, at least, is out of the way.

The next sensational trial was that of Patrick Cal-

## CALIFORNIA

houn, a gentleman of variegated record, handsome appearance, and fascinating personality, who had honored San Francisco with his citizenship for several years and was now president of the United Railroads. There is no space to devote to this trial, which was spun out over many weary months. He wanted an overhead trolley system, and obtained the franchise from the Ruef-Schmitz machine. His best friends never denied in private conversation that he had paid over at least two hundred thousand dollars, although he denied the charges in toto when, after indictment by the grand jury, he was brought before the bar. Witnesses disappeared, the jurymen were bribed, and copies of the reports of the government's detectives were stolen. It was impossible to convict him legally.

The bringing of Calhoun to trial was the signal for a disruption of society rivaling that caused by the Civil War. So many of the men whose families composed society were in danger of a similar indictment that they naturally herded together; and Mr. Calhoun being a social ornament, the wives were as vehement in his support as their husbands. Mrs. Spreckels, who enjoyed a brilliant position at Burlingame, the concentrated essence of California society, suddenly found herself an outsider. So did Mrs. Heney, who was a member of one of the old Southern families. Mr. Phelan also was ostracised; and the few people of wealth and fashion that stood by the prosecutors were for a time in a similar plight. One wife of a suspected millionaire and personal friend of Calhoun went so far as to demand the politics of her guests as they crossed her threshold. And among all there was a bitterness unspeakable.

# LAST PHASES

But although Calhoun could not be convicted, nor the few others that were brought to trial, the prosecution at least accomplished a moral fumigation. The first evidence of this was the election to the mayoralty, after the deposition of Schmitz, of Dr. Edward Robeson Taylor. The second was the triumphant personal campaign for governor of Hiram Johnson. The whole state had followed the trials, condemned the grafters, and made up its mind to elect the best men to office. Of course, that high pitch of enthusiasm does not last; and as Dr. Taylor refused to build up a machine of decent men, the next mayor was an objectional person named P. H. McCarthy. He disgusted the Labor party, however, and they helped to elect Mr. Rolph, the present mayor, with whom all parties are as satisfied as they ever are with any one.

The most interesting event which followed the graft prosecutions and their direct results was the passing of the Woman's Suffrage Bill in 1911. Conservative people and the liquor trust fought the campaign successfully in San Francisco; but the women, who had taken motors and visited practically every farmer and hamlet in the state, won with the country vote. What changes they will make in the moral conditions of the state remain to be seen, but there is no question that the campaign and its encouraging result have awakened the minds of the California women and developed them intellectually. They read better books, take an interest in public questions, quite ignored before, are making constant attempts to improve the condition of the poor women and children; and at the San Francisco Center of the Civic League some great or pressing question of the day is discussed by the best authorities obtainable. Its weekly

# CALIFORNIA

meetings are patronized by hundreds of women, and all men invited have long since found it quite worth their while to attend.

California, cleaned up as thoroughly as may be, is flourishing and happy, secure in the fact that with her enormous grain-supply and orchards and vineyards and cattle-ranges, her thousand healing springs, she never can go bankrupt, no matter how hard the times, and that her perennial beauties will bring many hundreds of thousands of dollars into the state annually: the tourist never deserts California, and her winter cities in the south are always crowded by the people of the Eastern states that dread the cold of their own winters, and by those from the mountain states of the Northwest, who long for sea-air and low altitudes. No matter what happens in the world beyond the Rocky Mountains or the Pacific Ocean, her orange-groves bear their yellow fruit, her skies are bluer than Italy's, her people are idle and luxurious and happy in the warm abundant south, or bustling, energetic, and keenly alive in San Francisco—which is no more California than Paris is France. She is the permanent resort of cranks, and faddists, and extremists, and professional agitators and loafers, but they are in the minority despite their noise. As a whole the state is one of the most dependable, patriotic, and honorable in the Union, and has produced great personalities, eminent and good men, and brilliant and gifted minds out of all proportion to her age. May the fools and extremists never wreck her!

PRUNE-ORCHARD

WHEAT-FIELD

Herewith a list of men and women identified with California's artistic life:

POETS—Ina Donna Coolbrith, Joaquin Miller, Bret Harte, Charles Warren Stoddard, Edwin Markham, Edward Robeson Taylor, Luis Robertson, Agnes Tobin, and George Stirling.

WRITERS OF FICTION—Bret Harte, Ambrose Bierce, William C. Morrow, Frank Norris, Jack London, Stewart Edward White, Herman Whittaker, Richard Tully, Hermann Scheffauer, Charles F. Lummis, John Vance Cheney, James Hopper, Emma Francis Dawson, Elizabeth Dejeans, Elinor Gates, Gelett Burgess, Mary Austin, John Fleming Wilson, Charles Field, Miriam Michaelson, Geraldine Bonner, Cora Miranda Older, Kate Taylor Craig, Lloyd Osborne, Esther and Lucia Chamberlain, Kathleen Norris, Wallace Irwin, Chester Bailey Fernald, and my humble self.

Horace Annesley Vachell spent several years near San Luis Obespo and wrote a number of California romances and a well-known book on California sports. Marie Van Saanen-Algi, author of *Anne of Tréboul*, is a great-granddaughter of Josiah Belden, of San José, one of the most notable of the pioneers.

PAINTERS — William Keith, Charles Rollo Peters, Alexander Harrison, Frank McComas, Jules Tavernier, Theodore Wores, Albert Bierstadt, Matilda Lotz, Clara McChesney, Julian Rix, and Frederick Yates.

ACTORS OF BOTH SEXES—Nance O'Neil, Mary Anderson, Blanche Bates, Katherine Grey, David Warfield, and Holbrook Blinn.

Lotta erected a drinking-fountain in Market Street as a token of her devotion to the city of San Francisco.

PRIME DONNE—Sibyl Sanderson, Emma Nevada, Maude Fay.

# CALIFORNIA

DANCERS—Isadora Duncan, Maude Allen.

One architect of genius we have produced, Willis Polk; one sculptor, Douglas Tilden; one composer, Edgar Kelley; and one stage-manager, David Belasco.

Newspaper writers that have made a reputation outside of California are: Ambrose Bierce, Arthur McEwen, E. W. Townsend, George Hamlin Fitch, Wallace Irwin, Will Irwin, and Ashton Stevens, dramatic critic.

Robert Louis Stevenson, Mark Twain, and Henry George are casually identified with San Francisco.

The historians and geologists have been mentioned in the preface; but the names of Benjamin Ide Wheeler, president of the University of California; David Starr Jordan, long president of Stanford University; Professor Holden; Professor Morse Stevens, so closely associated with California's intellectual life, cannot be omitted even in a brief history of the state; nor that of Luther Burbank. Chief among those that have given liberally from their private fortunes to enrich California artistically and educationally are: Mr. and Mrs. Leland Stanford, Mark Hopkins (via Edward F. Searles), Mrs. Hearst, W. R. Hearst (whose beautiful Greek Theater at Berkeley would create the perfect illusion were it not for the anachronism of the donor's name, cut deep and painted green, above the stage), Dr. H. H. Toland, Adolf Sutro, William H. Crocker, Claus Spreckels, Raphael Weill, Truxtun Beale, Rudolph Spreckels, and James D. Phelan.

To all that I may have forgotten I make humble apologies. Since California embarked upon her dædal sea she has turned out artists (using the word generically) at such a rate that it is simpler to write a history of the state than to keep track of any but those that have won a national reputation, or those that one happens to number among one's acquaintance. It is easier to recall the benefactors.

G. A.

THE END

C A L I F O R N I A
S I E R R A N E V A D A
Sacramento R.
SACRAMENTO
Oakland
N FRAN-
CISCO
San Joaquin R.
Kern R.
LOS ANGELES
Colorado

979.4
Ath

132586

Atherton.
California.

Learning Resources Center
Nazareth College of Rochester, N.Y.

DISCARDED